THE WHITE/GARNETT LETTERS

THE
WHITE/GARNETT LETTERS

Edited, with a Preface, by

DAVID GARNETT

THE VIKING PRESS
NEW YORK

To

Sylvia Townsend Warner
who in her biography of
T. H. White has given us
the real man

Preface

My friendship with T. H. White was founded on an exaggerated idea of our mutual love of out-of-door activities, particularly of fishing.

Tim assumed the airs of an expert, and I took for granted that he was. I on the other hand was a tyro who looked up to him as a master of all field sports. He boasted, until the very end of his life, of the vast number of skills that he had acquired, and of many I am no judge. But I can testify that he was a rough and ready fisherman, an indifferent shot and up till 1946 a ludicrously incompetent carpenter.

But if in the beginning I looked up to him as master of field sports, he regarded me as a scholar and a writer of genius and only slowly became partially disillusioned.

I had a great influence on his life. It was owing to me that he spent from February 1939 to September 1945 in Eire, thus avoiding any active participation in the war, and being able to identify himself with the Irish. While in Ireland he nearly became a Roman Catholic, learned some Gaelic, and wrote two books about Ireland.

On his return to England I lent him my cottage, Duke Mary's in Swaledale, where he lived penuriously and in great discomfort through the winter. Then, when he suddenly came in for £15,000 owing to *Mistress Masham's Repose* being chosen as the Book of the Month in the United States, I advised him to go and live in the Channel Islands, so as to avoid tax. He bought a house in Alderney and lived there for the rest of his life.

My first wife Ray had also a profound influence on him, though not so much in practical matters; however, she did take lodgings for him where he lived for six years.

Neither she nor I concealed anything from him. But he unfortunately concealed quite a lot, and I should have been a more helpful and sympathetic friend if he had told me, early in our friendship, what he explained to me on the last occasion that we met. It arose I think from the violent letter I had written about his criticism of my book *Aspects Of Love* in which I accused him of a monkish medieval morality and of sadism, and explained my own views about women and sexual morality. He had I think brooded on that letter for several years.

He explained to me that he was a sadist. I am so little attracted by this perversion that I had never used my imagination to realize the unhappiness which inevitably attends it. Tim explained that the sadist cannot be happy unless he has proved the love felt for him by acts of cruelty, which naturally are misinterpreted by normal human beings. It had been Tim's fate to destroy every passionate love he had inspired. He had found himself always in the dilemma of either being sincere and cruel, or false and unnatural. Whichever line he followed, he revolted the object of his love and disgusted himself.

He believed that he had inherited this perversion from a great-grandfather who was a notorious flagellant. This seems to me most improbable and that his upbringing—as described in Sylvia Townsend Warner's biography—being emotionally maltreated by his mother and ferociously flogged at school, fully accounts for it. He was an extremely tender-hearted and sensitive man and his worst acts of cruelty were not sexually inspired but due to carelessness and the cowardice of not facing the results of his mistakes. Such was his allowing a copy of *The Elephant and the Kangaroo* to fall into the hands of Mrs McDonagh who had mothered him for six years—and then, owing to moral cowardice, not going to ask her forgiveness.

But we have all made terrible mistakes of this sort and it is not for me to cast a stone at Tim.

Our friendship was deep and real, but the reader of these letters, which are only a fraction of our whole correspondence, will realize that we were frequently at cross purposes.

In the choice of what to publish, I have been guided by two principles: to omit libellous material for which I and my publisher might suffer, and to leave out letters which might be found insufferably boring. For that reason most of the letters about fishing have been omitted. For the first reason practically all our letters about his difficulties with a publisher are left out. Some are very funny. I have kept Tim's individual and erratic spelling.

I must thank Mr Julian Trevelyan for allowing me to include some lines of R. C. Trevelyan's translation from Lucretius. I wish also to thank Sylvia Townsend Warner, Michael Howard and Carol Stallings for their help and interest.

DAVID GARNETT

1936

I wrote a review of a novel, *They Winter Abroad* by James Aston, which was published on May 12th, 1932. The publishers had told me that the name of the author was Terence Hanbury White, who had chosen a pen name lest the characters in his book should recognize themselves. In my review I wrote:

> ... the novel is the description of the inhabitants of an hotel for English people in Italy and the effect which the southern springtime has upon them, awakening desires which have been dormant during the winter. Sex. Yes, indeed ... All nature stirs and quickens, the sun shines, the flowers shamelessly open their corollas to every passing, repulsive-looking insect, the birds sing and mate, lizards sun them-selves and look about for other lizards—and the poor English, creak-ing like rusty stag beetles, pour unfortunate confidences into each others' unwilling ears ... But the wit, the brilliance, the jokes! Come highbrows come, gather and fall shamelessly upon the feast.

As a result of this review, Tim made one or two unsuccessful attempts to get to know me. One was through Nigel Henderson, then a schoolboy at Stowe, who told me that one of the masters, called White, was a very wonderful person and that he wanted me to visit the school. White rode to hounds and had offered me a day's hunting if I visited Stowe. I sent back a refusal by word of mouth, explaining that I was not a hunting man, which must have led to a formal invitation from Tim to come down and lecture to the boys. I refused in an undated letter written either late in 1932, or early 1933, as it is on paper headed the *New Statesman and Nation*, 10 Great Queen Street. Later that year the paper moved its office to Great Turnstile. My refusal kept Tim quiet for three years—until just before the publication of *England Have My Bones*.

January 8th, 1936   *Stowe School, Buckingham*
Dear Mr Garnett, If you have any kindly recollections of a book called They Winter Abroad, by James Aston, will you just glance at England Have My Bones, by the same author, before you consign it to an inferior devil?   Yours sincerely, T. H. WHITE

January 10*th*, 1936   *Hilton Hall, St Ives, Huntingdonshire*

Dear White, Thank you very much for your letter. A proof copy of your book has arrived & I have read most of it & I am enchanted with it. What a queer thing it is that we should like so many things—fishing is more to me than flying—snakes I like too.

I must say I cursed you heartily at the beginning. I can only just endure reading about people who actually catch fish. This summer I camped out for 3 weeks on L. Corrib & fished almost every day & only caught one trout of 1½ lbs. I had 2 good days fishing on the Ribble after the snowstorm in May—12 one day & 8 the next. I have never tried for salmon alas. If I could catch a salmon I should die happy.

I laughed at your flying. It brought back so vividly my agonies. You ought to have spun in Bluebirds. They were heavy things that dropped like stones. At present I have a half share in a Klemm, which I want to sell, as I can't afford it. Come over before it has gone & come for a flyround in it. It is very slow & very safe & I land in fields anywhere.

I'm no longer literary editor of the New Statesman & don't serve out books but I shall try & get hold of yours. I like the ferrets. There's a lot of the love of life of Jefferies in you. And dipping sheep.

This letter is full of jealousy over the salmon. I really *hate* you because of them & so don't like to tell you how much pleasure your book has given me.   Yours ever DAVID GARNETT

January 15*th*, 1936   *The Robin Hood, Buffler's Holt,*
nr. Buckingham

Dear David Garnett, Your letter was better than a salmon. I didn't know whether I ought to have written to you. I don't yet know whether I ought to be writing this, because after all one's own affairs are rarely of interest to other people. But the length of your letter makes me bold.

I don't think I can get over to hazard myself in your Klemm, or not for some weeks, because I have sold my car. I am selling everything, and giving up everything except fishing, so as to be able to write as I think. It was terribly difficult trying to be a schoolmaster and a writer at the same time: they would'nt let me go on like James Aston (the pen name leaked out) and it was ridiculous, like cross-word puzzles, trying to fit the two things together. It meant trying to please the public without shocking its parents.

Hence two quite superficial but not unamusing novels, neither tragedies nor comedies but just stage farces, called Earth Stopped & Gone To Ground. Among the many things that I am afraid of was public opinion, and so I tried to write to please it. England Have My Bones is the same thing really: a facet only of all the things I should like to say.

Now I have grown up a bit and think (at 30) it is time to face the issue. I hope to get out of Stowe by the end of their summer term, and live in Scotland on £200 a year—which I think I can earn by writing. I want to get married too, and escape from all this piddling homosexuality and fear and unreality. That was why I wrote soliciting your good graces. Actually I had rather have no money at all than be a schoolmaster, but it would be nice to start with a little cash in hand. So I wanted E.H.M.B. to have a chance. Publishers dont ever help.

So much for that. It sounds as if I was thankful for your letter only because it might mean a puff. Not at all. I have read and possess every book you ever wrote, except the first one on how to cultivate back gardens or something—Voltaire the wrong way round!—and it means a great deal to me that you should even pretend to enjoy something of mine. I dont know any great writers, or indeed any important people at all, and so there is a terrific kick, like getting Hobbs's autograph and being knighted by him at the same time.

A pity that you have never killed a fish. When I am in Scotland will you come up and do so? It will have to be not this spring but next. Or would it interest you to kill a tunny? If I ever make any money I may be sharing a launch with Earl Haig and Hon. Simon Ramsay. (This is quite alright. I have taught the former, but never met him socially.) They are nice people and I feel that tunny are probably nice fish.

Heavens, I feel about 10 years younger just writing about fish and freedom, and finding that at last there is somebody sensible who has read one of my books. You can't imagine the public I have been writing for.

Yrs TIMOTHY WHITE

My review of *England Have My Bones* came out on March 7th, 1936, but before then I had met the author whom I had invited to come over to lunch 'with your big friend' who provided transport. I have forgotten him, but Tim himself made an immediate and unforgettable impression: first the size of the man, then the brilliant blue, rather bloodshot, unhappy eyes, and the patient voice which usually sounded as though he were very carefully explaining something to a child and which would then split with the sudden realization of an absurdity, or a shared joke. Tim was usually intensely serious when he made a remark; the comic became apparent as he gave it a second look. I took him round Hilton Green and showed him the turf maze, made by William Sparrow to commemorate the restoration of Charles II.

Tim recognized the maze as the source of Sylvia Townsend Warner's story 'The Maze', published in a collection *The Salutation* (1932), which he praised.

Sunday, [*? February* 1936]   *Stowe School, Buckingham*

Dear David Garnett, Thank you for being nice to me. I think we liked each other—like snakes. I liked your wife, and wanted to shew her so, but could'nt. It must be very galling for her when people make a dead set at you, but it is because she does'nt encourage them. I should have had to sit with her in silence, and after about half an hour just tentatively push something across for her to look at. There was no time for this. Would you tell her that it was because (I believe it was) she drew the pictures for The Grasshoppers that I drew the pictures for my next book?

I had a letter when I got back saying that the Book Society has rejected me. Well, to hell with them anyway.

Dont answer. I mean it.   Love from TIM WHITE

March 7*th,* 1936   *As from Stowe, Bucks.*

Dear David Garnett, Thank you ever so much for your charming review of England Have My Bones: much too kind, but *so* nice of you, and the turning point in my life. The trouble with that book was that, like all schoolmasters, I was only just growing up. Anyway, now I can afford to stop being one altogether. Imagine the Daily Mail choosing it as their book of the month! People congratulate me on that, but I say: Garnett's review is worth Lord Rothermere and all his staff, unto seventy times seven. It is true, even financially. You guard the public I shall have to seduce eventually, a far too affable Cerberus.

I realised last week that when I visited you I committed a gaffe which must have occasioned you some pain. I ought not so immediately to have recognised that Maze as Sylvia Warner's! It is a funny thing. For some reason it made *no* impression on me in Go She Must: I think because the story at that point becomes so poignant that one resents and mentally skips a digression. I had leisure for the Cromwell digression, and even for the one about Charles plodding up the hill, but the Maze comes in just where one can't feel about anything except the seal & poor Richard. Dont think, anyway, that I hav'nt read all your books backwards & forwards dozens of times—all except the Fox, and the Zoo, which I dont care much about. It was at about the 8th lection, last week, that I discovered the Maze.

I spend a lot of time thinking of all the presents I shall bring you when I call again. A fox cub for your wife certainly, and for you a grass snake that wont smell. Do you by any chance care for hedgehogs?

Forgive what must seem a curious choice of notepaper. I write this in the train, with the only materials available.

My paper on D. H. Lawrence was going to be printed, but the printers went on strike and the Oxford proctors banned it. They were quite right.

love from TIM WHITE
Dont answer.

March 9th [1936]   *Hilton Hall, St Ives, Huntingdonshire*
Dear White, Thanks for your letter: I am much touched by your enjoinder not to reply & rather amused by your remarks about the maze. I had, honour bright, forgotten it was mentioned in Go She Must, but I hesitated about agreeing with your praise of Sylvia's story which I didn't much like.

I haven't thanked you for the duck & the rabbit. They were both excellent & we picked the bones. I had an idea that hedgehogs killed snakes, so don't give me both! I like hedgehogs, but they have such a lot of fleas & ticks & I don't know how to wash them (they can swim of course). Have you ever heard them chirruping & singing to each [other] in the light of the moon when they make love? My father did when I was a boy but I never quite believed his story until two or three years ago when I heard a pair outside the house here & went out & saw them. Then there was a hedgehog which wrapped itself up in fruit netting, and last year a hedgehog which got drowned in our swimming pool—tumbled in poor fellow & couldn't get out.

We have hopes of having a servant soon & life of a more reposeful sort. It would be very nice if you could come over & stay a couple of nights during the Easter holidays.

My wife & you must arrange about the fox cub between you; if she accepts it well & good: I shall teach it to eat grapes like the French foxes.

I am sorry my remarks about your book were so inadequate. I was suffering from a sort of mental blanket; wrote in a great hurry, was half an inch too short, didn't see the proof, which was badly corrected & had some more chopped out to make room for a panel. I'm glad about the Daily Mail.   Yours ever DAVID GARNETT

April 29th, 1936   *Dalmally Hotel, Dalmally, Argyll*

Dear David Garnett, I am sending you by tonight's train the biggest fish I have ever killed, because you gave me the biggest success I have ever made. It weighs thirty pounds, and if you find it difficult to consume thirty pounds of salmon before it goes bad you might care to oblige me by sending on any unwanted portion, up to half, to T. R. Osborne Esq., Park Fields, Stowe, Buckinghamshire. This is purely optional, for it is *your* fish and for aught I know you may have a still more numerous progeny than I saw or a still better appetite than I suspect. Also it is a damned nuisance for you. I could have divided it myself and packed it off in two separate pieces, but I (a) didn't like to send you half a fish, (b) did'nt know whether perhaps you might not be able to manage the whole, (c) wanted you to see the fish in his (it is a he) entirety, in order that you should pay me proper homage and develop your own soul beyond trout fishing. The person whom you *may* be sending a bit on to (I shall not write to him, in case you dont) is the nicest farmer in the world, just as you are the nicest author, so the conjunction is fortunate.

The fish, in case you do send a bit on, should be divided. The guts that are extruded should then be removed and the cavity stuffed with dry nettles and a little salt. Surround the whole with nettles and wrap in paper, preferably greaseproof. You will find this either a dreadful bore or great fun.

Now you have got to hear about the fish. I have a small 13-ft salmon rod, without steel centre, which is much too weak for this river, particu-

14

larly with the wind in one's eye. Because I was lamenting this, the oldest gillie on the Orchy stepped up and lent me his own rod: the oldest rod on the same river. It is nineteen feet long, a length demoded these last fifty years: almost an antiquary's piece, a contemporary with the old man himself (who is over eighty), a cousin of the meerschaum and the barrouche. It needs a giant merely to hold it upright. It casts about 50 yards.

Your fish took a Silver Wilkinson far out in the bend of the Elbow Pool, when I was wading waist-deep in a swift current, on a long cast. I wont bore you with the story, which I could tell you step by step, beyond telling you (poor stalker after microbe trouts in piddling streams) that he took me half a mile before he died, $1\frac{1}{2}$ *hours later*, in the Pownell Pool. He leaped a dozen times and twice took me down to my last few yards of backing. When I had him at last on the bank I took out a flask of whisky and poured three drops upon his head. I drank none of it. The flask went to the old blind ghillie when we got home, who politely danced a little flourish in my honour, though it must have been well over the thousandth fish that he had seen. It may have been two hours. We had no watch. My biggest fish and my longest and hardest fight. I have cast all day with that titanic rod, beside that noonday fight, and now I am too tired to write more, except to pronounce this single malediction: God forget you if you dont turn to salmon after this, and may he punish you by his cruellest deprivation—that you should never kill a Fish.

love from your superior TIM WHITE

P.S. Have you any idea how long an hour and a half's to two hours' fighting *is?* Of course not. Boo, you sassenach!

The salmon arrived while Ray and I were in London and we were astonished to find it lying on our scullery table when we returned. It also involved us in driving off with the tail half of it to put it on a bus and sending a telegram to Mr Osborne telling him to meet it. We had not a refrigerator in those days and had to act without delay. I also made a cast in plaster of paris of the half we had kept before eating it, because I felt sure that Tim would like it as a trophy of his prowess.

A letter with plans for taking me salmon-fishing the following spring and refusing to visit Hilton in July because 'I don't feel clean here or safe to be myself ... I am mad with anxiety all during the term time here,' is omitted.

Dear David, I hope you havnt quite forgotten me, nor yet destroyed the cast of that fish. I still mean to come for it, but for some reason I dont. I can't think why. It is partly because I have relapsed into a Sir-Walter-Raleigh-ish state of mind and am skulking here in my bloody tower gnawing out the Elizabethan parts of my mind, partly because I have developed a craze for hawking and had intended to descend upon you with grey goshawk in hand, and partly because, having left Stowe, I felt the need for some financial reserve and fell to writing a novel. Anyway, for God's sake keep the fish and tell me where you intend to be until Xmas.

The reason why I wanted to startle you with a hawk was in Pocahontas.

I dont expect you will remember the circumstance, but several years ago I wrote begging you to read a paper at Stowe and offering you as a bribe a day with the Grafton hounds. I had made sure that you were a hunting man by the perfection of your description when the beautiful savage's horse put its foot in the rabbit hole. But you replied that you did not hunt. Well, I started training an eyass tiercel goshawk in July, and happened to start Pocahontas for the 6th time in August. When I got to that hawking bit I immediately put down the book and said to myself: 'This is so perfect that he cannot possibly ever have seen a hawk; and I shall ring the changes on that professor, who wrote to him about locusts,[1] by confronting him with the living article as soon as it is ready.'

So I kept holding off the visit, which I was looking forward to, and of course I lost the gos the day before I meant to come. Do you remember writing that Lathom galloped off 'with an expression of torment on his face'? Perhaps you have trained a hawk, and I am teaching my grandmother to suck eggs. With anybody but you, one would be certain of it. But, in case not, I just have to tell you that this sentence is the austringer's epitome. My new passage goshawk should arrive in a week or two, and a month after that I want to come and show you *my* face. I look about 60; but a noble, satanic 60. It is a result of associating with hawks.

I guess that you have read Latham's Falcons Lure & Cure, but dare

[1 Professor Uvarov had written to me after reading *The Grasshoppers Come*, asking me if I had made notes on locust swarms in Outer Mongolia. I replied that all my knowledge of locusts came from his book *Locusts and Grasshoppers* in the London Library.—D.G.]

not hope that you possess it. If you do I will get you to lend it me, handing over to you my own copy of Bert's Treatise as a hostage.

The novel which I have just finished strikes me as being bloody and very unwise to publish at this stage. It is satirical and about education. I might publish it under James Aston. At the moment I hate it. Generally I admire my books very much, so hating it may not be a bad sign. I started by liking England H.M. Bones, which now gives me the cold shivers, so let's hope this will be the other way about.

Now we come to what this letter is really about. I want to make a play out of Sir Walter Raleigh, beginning in the tower with Northumberland. I dont want to *fiddle*, but I do think that I ought to read at least one thorough book about Raleigh. My (the penultimate) edition of Enc. Brit. mentions no authorities later than de Selincourt—Great Ralegh 1908. Will you tell me what *one* book I am to read if, as far as the history is concerned, I want only enough good facts for a play? The fellow's character I understand already: it is my own.

One day I shall get you to come here for a week-end. I dont know how to set about this at present, have not even the audacity to ask. But as a preliminary I shall just tell you where I live. It is a gamekeeper's cottage in the middle of a wood seven miles from each of the three tiny towns Buckingham, Brackley, Towcester. I have painted every stick and stone in it, including varnishing the ceilings, by myself, and furnished the whole for about £100. Outside, it is a semi-detached five-roomed cottage. Inside, the pile carpets (£66 out of the £100) are an inch thick, the whole so sumptuously snug that even a badger would have no reason to complain. I sit each evening, alone, with my hand on my dog's head, before the fire, in a winged brocade armchair (Sir Walter Raleigh-Latham) and leisurely consume one bottle of madeira.

It is a modern sort of Thebiad (is that the word?) and something will come of it in the end. I am the same age as my Saviour was, anyway.

Your bed has a feather mattress and the bedroom is lit by 10 candles. It is entirely surrounded by early victorian gilt mirrors and everything is either blue or gold. It has only been slept in by a baroness, so far, who then stated that she felt like a royal concubine.

There is plenty of the madeira left.   love from TIMOTHY WHITE

November 19th, 1936　　　　*The Cottage Hospital, Buckingham*

Dear David, Sometimes I think that god and those people are making a dead set at me. It is enough to give one persecution mania. The lastest is that they have just been hacking out my appendix, and a most unrewarding feeling it is.

It has knocked my hawking edgeways as well as everything else. Also it has given me a pain.

Curiously enough I reviewed Francis Chichester's last book in the Spectator last week and said that he was the only fairly good writer in the list. (I also said that you were the only person who had carried the history of Eng. Lit. into the air.)

Was your falconer called Gilbert Blaine or Knight or Lascelles?

Sorry. My pen is running out and I dont like to ring for a nurse.

Rember about Sir W. Raleigh.[1]　　　　Love from TIM WHITE

[1 See p. 17.—D.G.]

1937

Early in 1937 Tim and I planned to go fishing together in Wales. This led to several hectic letters from Tim who tried to discover cheap or free water from his friend John Moore. However, at the last moment my friend Wogan Philipps (now Lord Milford) lent me a stretch of water on the Wye belonging to his father.

The following is a typical example of one of Tim's fishing letters.

McMail was the keeper at Llyswen.

FOR ALL PRACTICAL PURPOSES, TEAR THIS UP WITHOUT READING IT.

February 15*th*, 1937   *The Cottage, Stowe Ridings, Buckingham*

Dear David, I only write because if I dont I shall lose my reason. There is no point in writing, for I shall ring you up tomorrow. I have tied 3 dozen flies, made a new fishing case, tested both lines, greased one of them, oiled reels, polished the minnows, had a row with Ogden Smiths, and now there is nothing else to do but write.

I have entirely recovered from the 'flu, or rather changed the nature of the fever. I dont sleep at all now, nor eat, but only pace up and down looking at the fishing case.

My God, what a genius you are! If you knew what shifts a Soapey Sponge like me is put to in order to get the smell even of a private water! But I suppose you just mention a wish to some secret worshipper (who is actually just as excited because D.G. is fishing on his water, as D.G. is excited to be fishing) and there we are. Never mind, I intend to be famous myself one day; and then, by God, my fans shall rue it if they have water.

Do you remember all that balls I wrote to you about pike taking Orenos sideways? An assistant in Hardy's once told me that story and I, like a sheep, believed him. Since writing it out for you, however, I have thought it over, and none of it signifies anything. What does signify is that the pike *bolts* the lure immediately, while the salmon merely closes his mouth on it and swims off to his lie, to swallow it (?)—(or just crush it sadistically) there at leisure. If the bait is positively bristling with hooks he will *feel them* too soon, and, re-opening his mouth at once, reject the whole before there has been a chance of making a connection. Hence the *single* hook (less quickly munched upon as dangerous) must always be best for the salmon. Owing to the *inelastic* breadth of the Oreno (unlike the elastic fly) the *single* hook has to be sacrified to the treble, but more than one treble immediately becomes little more than a danger-signal to the salmon and a lever for prising one hold out against the other—unconsciously, of course.

Let me see whether I can explain what I mean by 'inelastic', if I draw a picture

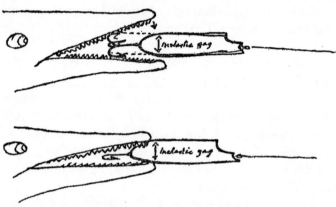

You see that the second pike has bitten on the oreno, but missed its hook because it was a single one. He would not have missed the single hook in a *fly*, because that would have squashed. I drew him as a pike because I liked his teeth, but he might just as well have been a salmon.

PART TWO

I rang Ray up today, and she claimed that not only would it be safe for me to go with you, but John Moore also. I shall ask you about this when I telephone tomorrow (before you get this letter) but now I may as well tell you something which I may have been shy of telling you over the telephone. It is this. John Moore is ... barely sane (hence his failure to do very much for us) and he *may actually be so daft as not to* WANT *to fish*. I have already written to him, to find out, and all we can do in this case (provided that Ray is right in saying that we all 3 might go) is to await his answer. But if you do want him to come, and he does want to come, what about us three conducting a RESEARCH? I thought (merely a passing thought) that it might be interesting, in the cause of this the most noble of all the sciences, if one of us were to stick entirely to the greased line, one to the sunk fly, and one to the minnow. We should take two thermometers with us (I have them) and write up the conditions of each day. I have tackle for all three methods, and dont care a fig which is allotted to me. I will lend the superfluous tackle.

The Wye would probably be the most amiable river in the British Isles for such an experiment. It is *said* to be a spinning river (so the minnow man would be happy), all rivers are expected to be sunk fly waters in early spring (so the sunk fly man would be happy) and greased line enthusiasts claim to be successful everywhere, provided that the air is warmer than the water (so the greased line man would be happy.) This, at present only food for thought and something to write about in order to keep me sane, might be talked over as we drive west.*

PART THREE

I shall tomorrow ask you over the telephone (1) about transport and route to Builth, (2) whether it would not be best (rather than firmly putting it off for a fortnight) to leave the whole thing to McMail. Personally I think that I shall only be telephoning for the same reason as I am writing this letter—merely from fever.

PART FOUR

The whole point of this letter. DONT ANY MORE PAY ANY ATTEN-TION TO ANYTHING I WRITE, TELEGRAPH, OR SAY ON THE TELEPHONE—even on Tuesday 16th, past by the time you get this letter. I have lost all sense of proportion and shall do everything I can to persuade you to go west at once. I have no moral feelings or judgement any more. If I had my way we should be at Builth tomorrow. It is up to you to think for us and keep us straight.   love from TIM

P.S. If you keep me hanging about for a fortnight I shall be dead.

P.P.S. You bloody genius (I have been drinking neat whisky for the 'flu ever since I started writing this letter) it is *I* who shall catch the fish for the Cromwell Road Museum. God came to my christening and cursed me in every direction except that of fish. But he forgot them, bless him. Fish! Do you remember them? I was making water in a wood today, when I looked down and found I was peeing on a snowdrop.

* In actual practice I should be much surprised if you did not *choose* the sunk fly, John the minnow, and I the greased line.

We drove, in Tim's car, via Gloucester, and arrived at Llyswen too late to start fishing, on the evening of the 18th of February. Next morning we had a leisurely breakfast in the pub, where we were the only guests, and while we waited for McMail we had what seemed later a strange conversation.

A carrion crow came and perched on the garden fence outside the window and cawed persistently. I told Tim how one had hung about the Cearne garden when my father was nearly dying of typhoid. Tim then repeated to me the ballad of *The Twa Corbies* and I told him that my own views about death were the exact opposite of the ballad-maker's. I should rejoice to be sure that after my death, my hound, hawk and leman should forget me and lead happy lives. In my opinion the tragedy of death was that it was impossible to forget the dead and that they poisoned the lives of the living who had loved them. That was the last thing one wanted to do to those one loved.

Tim was surprised by my attitude but after we had talked a little, he understood it, and may even have agreed. Presently McMail came and we went down to the river, put up our rods and began to fish. McMail went away. About an hour later I saw him coming back with a strange expression on his face. He handed me a telegram from Ray saying that my father had died suddenly that morning. It had happened shortly before our discussion about death. We left McMail to take down the rods and Tim drove me at once to a railway station. He stayed on at Llyswen until some time after our invitation had expired, unable to tear himself away from the neighbourhood, but he caught nothing.

[*March* 1937]

My very dear Bunny, I went to Hilton on monday and stored your fishing stock in a corner of the garage. When you take it out, will you (a) look and see how much of your spinning line I have lost: if much (I can't remember what it looked like before) I should feel more comfortable if you would let me buy you another, and I believe it was much, (b) pull out your gaff to full length? Before I packed it I did this, and found that it was growing rusty. I wiped off all the rust and *buttered* it, because it was the only unguent I could lay hands upon. It now strikes me that there is salt in butter, which may not be good for steel. So dont leave it without a look, and perhaps a bath in water with a little oil afterwards.

I came to stay with a friend of mine who is a bath superintendant in Bedford after that. On the way I stopped for bread and cheese at the smallest of your local pubs. The publican's wife, who had just recovered from 'flu, invited me into the parlour to eat my meal by the fire. There, with all the windows shut, I found the publican, who was prone upon a sofa, suffering from (1) T.B. (he was once at Papworth), (2) Influenza, (3) an ulcer in the middle of his back. His daughter, who was bearing him company, has epileptic fits and had just broken her arm while having a fit in the earth closet. She had influenza too. We talked about death for some time while I gobbled my food in a perfect palsy, and then I drove away to Bedford in a snow storm, and got 'flu myself—or a feverish chill, or something—and I have been here ever since with a high temperature, not much of a guest for the bath superintendant.

I have kept my promise by reading Lady Into Fox again, and I still detest it. Since it was in the same book I did the Man in the Zoo also, and thought it better than I had: indeed I almost liked it. Today, getting up for the first time, I went to get a book from Boots' Library. They are terrible places. After wandering in a dizzy torment for 30 minutes I came upon Beaney-Eye, so I rescued him thankfully and have just finished him. I have only read him once before. What a triumph! You have done him so wonderfully that I can *recognise the family likeness.* You know how one can sometimes say: Oh, those two must be father and son. Well, now that I know you, it is perfectly uncanny how I feel the same about Mr. Butler & you. I feel the same shock too, that one does when one sees the same features in a father and son standing together.

I am going to chance it that it will make you happy rather than the reverse if I mention things about your father now. I do not think that the corbie was entirely a co-incidence. The presence of the crow was a coincidence, but not that we talked so long about it. You said at some length exactly what your father would have said. I cannot explain this properly and do not mean quite what the words seem to mean, but I think that fathers do actually persist in their children. There was a link at that moment, like the link which brings carrier pigeons home or works the wireless. For one thing we are all actually parts of our parents. I dont think anybody ever dies while he has got children. This is'nt anything about 'living in one's children's memories' or any of that stosh, but something much nearer the concrete assertion that your father came to you then and took refuge, got inside. Yet I dont quite want to say that.

It is something between that and the obvious fact that you are yourself very largely Mr. Butler.

I had better leave it alone.

The bloody old Major Hoare, I am exceedingly sorry to say, caught two fish (23 lb., 26 lb.) after I left. I hope they poison him.

Joan Price has got boils and is treating them with Xtian Science.

I have sent the lovely Indian colonel a copy of one of my own books— a very goodish book, called Farewell Victoria—and had a letter from Mrs. Michael Hoare saying that she loved The Grasshoppers. So she must have sense as well as blue eyes with black hair.

Brownie says that she is going to have puppies, but I wont believe her. On being asked whether I am to send her love to David Garnett, she makes a demonstration.   love from TIM

Early in June I invited Tim to stay with Ray and me at our cottage Duke Mary's on the edge of the moors, looking down at Low Row in Swaledale. He accepted but was not able to come because Brownie, who had been on hunger strike owing to her jealousy of Tim's goshawk, got a combination of pleurisy and distemper and nearly died.

June 10th, 1937   *Stowe Ridings, Buckingham*

Dear David, I have been sleeping out for weeks anyway, so I shall bring the camp bed in case you dont object and the weather holds up. Brownie (who is on hunger strike at the moment, as a protest against the hawk) will not chase sheep and can be made to keep to heel. But I will bring a chain as a sort of outward and visible sign for the keepers. I must warn you that I am at present quite impossible to be lived with, and beg you to be as kind as possible. For eight weeks I have been chained for 14 hours a day to the hawk, who is mentally a kind of Ludwig of Bavaria, and now when he gets liverish I get liverish too. If you frighten him you will frighten me. When he glares I glare. And since everything frightens him (including inanimate objects) and he glares all the time, we are not a very sociable pair. Also we hate each other like poison.

His is the form of mania which attributes all mischances to forces out-side himself. (You know the kind of person who kicks a table because he has stubbed his toe on it or breaks a golf club because he has missed the

24

ball with it.) And I have caught this from him, so that if anything goes wrong when I am in your company I shall blame you.

Will you be patient then?

On the other hand it is perfectly possible that Cully will be in a good mood, in which case you will find me radiant. We *can* be the best company in England.

We are in sore need of gentleness.

Dont trouble to meet us.   love from

Monday   *Stowe Ridings, Buckingham*

Dear Bunny, So far as I can see it is quite impossible that I should get to Yorkshire this week. My sweet Brownie has distemper as well as pleurisy and even if she does live will be quite unfit to travel for some time. I have not left her day or night for two days now—quite the little hospital nurse —damn all these 'quites'—and it is the bloodiest disease. Why can't they let us die clean, and all the same way? I dont see why there should be such a lot of ways of dying, so slow and putrid. I am not at all good as a nurse, as I am alternately furious with them and with Brownie herself. I can't help her, of course, only give her Brand's essence and sit with her and cry. The hawk has had to go to buggery. And I did so want to come to Yorkshire. I was going to impress you in a very impressive way with the hawk.   love from TIM

She is going to live, of course.

June 18th, 1937   *Stowe Ridings, Buckingham*

Dear Bunny, Dogs have died e'er now, and worms have eaten them, but not for love. Brownie turned the corner last night. I had to hide the hawk for 24 hours and to stay by her constantly since last sunday, but she will live now. As for your cruel charges, if she were intelligent enough to know that I loved the hawk she should also have been intelligent enough to know that I feared and hated it. She must realise that I have to earn her living as well as mine, and the only way I can earn it at present is by writing a book about hawks ...

Brownie is now having a high time insisting on being fed from a spoon, when it is perfectly unnecessary. On wednesday night she lost her reason and ran away in the dark, so that I spent all night wandering through the woods with a candle and whistling. Apparently the bug gets into the brain. It was awful. She lives on Brandy & Brand's Essence, except that I have a horrid lust to eat it myself. Goodbye, you Job's comforter. love from TIM

November ?15th, 1937 *Stowe Ridings, Buckingham*

Dear David, I had as a matter of fact already been invited away for next week end (20th) but I shall go to see the woman tomorrow and explain that one is not, after all, invited to stay with David Garnett every day. If she proves shirty (which she wont) I will have to send you a wire saying I can't come after all, but, if not, I will arrive on Saturday 20th about tea time.

Juan Marks has been writing to me again about being a sort of sports editor for Night & Day, and I have submitted a plan to him by which I contribute a sort of weekly series called These Typical Days—or something like that. It would mean writing typical days hunting, hawking, shooting etc. but what I want particularly to do this winter is to *shoot a goose* (I could make it pay for itself by writing a typical day's flighting). You once told me that you knew Peter Scott.[1] Do you know him well enough to *beg* the name of a place to shoot geese in, off him, for me, under every pledge of secrecy? If necessary I would meet him at Norwich or somewhere and let him take me the rest of the way blindfold.

May I bring Brownie on saturday, but not the hawk?

love from TIM

Tell him (few can have reached such a pitch of devotion) that I have collected *all* his cigarette cards in Players' 50s.

December ?15th, 1937 *Crown Hotel, Wells, Norfolk*

Dear David, If you were a rich, famous author like me, you would be able to afford to drop everything and come here. I dont suppose you could dash over the same day, if I were to ring you up one morning? Just for a night? I am going to stay here all winter. It is lovely. We call

[1 I was name-dropping. I had met him twice when he was an undergraduate at Cambridge, and he took me duck-shooting one evening.—D.G.]

the East wind's bluff by getting as close to him as possible, and it is quite warm. Driving from Wales right across England, I found this was the only mild place. We are under the wind's guard and the sea saves us. Attack best method of defence. You get up every morning at 5 o'clock, drink tea with whisky in it, stagger out blear-eyed to an enormous, crisp, snowy beach (the frozen Norfolk sand feels like what eating a well-iced Fullers cake tastes like) and see in the marigold dawn the high skeins gaggling in with cries of warning and perturbation, like a pack of peekinese. That is when you stand in the dunes, and the marram hisses. Or you lie in a vast stretch of mud—what dreary lives the wildfowl lead nobody can imagine: it is worse, worse than poor old Ibsen and his Wild Duck, Russian if anything—in a sand grave full of water, out of sight of sea or land, and it hails. Only the wind and the sea roar. Or it snows. Sometimes we stand huddled together, quite out of the Earth, like Shetland ponies. The others turn their backs to the wind. I face it, partly because my ears stick out and partly because I dont like the elements in my arse, through the split of my coat. Then we come back for such a fine breakfast, and a warm bath if you like (it is long enough for me to lie flat) and 2 glasses of stout at mid-day. At 3.30 or so we are out again, after lunch, and are lying on our backs in some sea-weed or is it zostera marina, in this strange world that is neither land nor sea—No man lives there, neither Englishman nor German of the ocean—waiting for widgeon (which are silly and come back over the guns) or, as I did today, shooting with clean misses at shelduck, which are quite big enough to be geese, and are inedible. It is a perfect sport. Geese are as rare and valuable as salmon. The best wildfowler (professional guide) on this coast has never killed more than 74 in a year. That was ten years ago. I have not had a shot at one in a week. Nothing could be more humane. It is real sport, because of its incredible difficulty, and this is by far the best place to do it in at present, because there are no geese here anyway. These rich and famous people like Peter Scott, with their private marshes and condescending resolutions not to shoot more than a dozen geese at a flight, have no idea of the triumph we feel at achieving a single thump. I know I shall be drunk for a week if ever I get a left-and-right. They are'nt sportsmen, only gentlemen. It was the same with that Wye and Sir Lawrence Philipps. If we had killed a fish there in February we should have got more out of it, for less suffering to the rest of creation, than Sir L. in the whole of the rest of the season. Silly old pig, squatting in a boat rowed by somebody else, as if he were stuffed. (By the way, Sir L. had the worst year on record last year and started a fund for buying off the net-fishers at the mouth of the river with a donation of £1000. Anybody who reads, I mean unless they were quite illiterate, could have told him that it would be so and that his net-fisher scheme is ludicrous. It was a seventh year, as I think I told you at the time, and in any case the net-fishers did no damage at all. They also had one of their worst years. But I will tell you about all this when I see you.) [Forgive all these 'telling-you's. You know more than I do about everything, but I enjoy pretending that you dont.] So, really, if you were a true sportsman, you would come now, when it is a thousand to one against your killing a goose, but I am going to condescend to you, and ring you up later on, when the geese have come and there is a sensible chance. But you wont really burst with joy if you get one then, not as you would if you had stuck it out here for a blank week. I wish I could tell you what a difference it has made to me. I dont look ten years older than my age any more, but almost younger—never dry, extraordinarily abstemious, hair impossible to brush, yesterday's chin, no tie. You have to go with a professional guide, of which there are three or four. They all hate each other like poison, and compete against each other, and are real people. Mine, who is the best, longest-experienced and loveliest of all, is consumptive. He lies incessantly, shoots very badly, talks because he does not realise what a genius he is, and is quite impossible. His name is Sam Bone. I have served a week's apprenticeship with him, and shall soon launch out on my own. I am quick on the uptake, though I say it as should'nt. During this week he has fired 20 cartridges, with only one teal to shew for it. He missed a double at geese today, slap over him and 30 yards up. He spent an hour explaining this. He is the man who killed the 74. It is quite impossible for me to give you any idea of all these feelings in one letter.

Yesterday I was invited to a Norfolk hare shoot, and assisted at the butchery of some pheasants, pigeons and rabbits and 201 hares. No joy at all. Like being a butcher with a humane killer. Just business. Not a single hare got through the line.

The Pink Foot which I send you as a Xmas present was not shot by me nor Sam. It is the only goose killed at Wells this week. I bought it.

Love from TIM

P.S. That girl was no good at all.

1938

Tim invited me to go goose-shooting with him at Wells-next-the-Sea where I had once seen a flamingo far out on the sands at low tide when I was staying there with Gerald Brenan, but I was unable to do so. During the summer I was busy finishing the editing of *The Letters of T. E. Lawrence*, and for that reason I was unable to take a holiday. Meanwhile *The Sword in the Stone* had been chosen in America as Book of the Month and Tim's finances had been transformed.

January 24th, 1938   *Crown Hotel, Wells, Norfolk*
Dear David, I may probably be leaving here at the end of this week, so if you still think well of goose-shooting you ought to come before then. But on the whole, I wouldn't come, unless you are mad on it. It is impossible to say that any given day would be a good day, since all depends on the wind, and it would mean either that you came the night before, and chanced a wind next morning, or got up at 4 o'clock in the morning in order to drive over here by six. I think you are probably too sane to need to do this. But if you feel like it, try ringing me up any morning at nine o'clock or evening after eight.

I had quite a piercing joy this morning, sitting with several thousand widgeon and some gulls beside Lord Leicester's lake. It is a bird sanctuary. Usually I dont notice anything, but the sun shone so beautifully that I suddenly began to observe for myself. I found

(1) that widgeon do not drop their legs before landing on water. They land exactly like a flying boat, with their legs straight out behind them and heads up, at this angle: They hold off stick more like an aeroplane than any-   thing I ever saw.

(2) Gulls land with less commotion than any other water bird. This they do because they have the sense to keep their wings stretched out until some moments after landing. In fact, they hang on the wind like a glider until they are actually in the water. They fly in the water as well as in the air.

They *sail* out of the water really (or into it) by offering their big wing spread to the lift of the wind, and can land or take off without a ripple.

They just open their wings as below and by altering the surface and angle of incidence allow themselves to be either lifted out or dropped in, by the wind. Of course, there was a wind. But they are so infinitely less clumsy than the duck family—it seems to me that the high-speed widgeon has just the same dangerous landing-speed as Perceval's high-speed racing

aeroplanes—and so beautiful in the air. At one time it *snowed* gulls, all the white flakes twisting and turning against the sunny winter blue, just like the globes with water in them and a tin lady holding an umbrella that you turn upside down.

(3) The greater black-backed gull floats down by the head: his ballast is all forward.

love from TIM

August 18th, 1938   *The Angel, Heytesbury, Wiltshire?*

Dear David, I am afraid I have probably been both silly and inconsiderate, but I was so sick of repining as an unrecognised genius in that cottage that, as soon as they all gave me all this money, I rushed off without leaving any address, to spend it. So I dont know whether you have been writing to me or not.

Now I have fallen on my feet at Heytesbury. Siegfried Sassoon (I came here quite by chance, forgetting his address) is most charming and important and beautiful, and the greatest living falconer is next door, with even more beautiful peregrines and goshawks, and the inn is as clean as a whistle, and my two hawks are flying in record style. I have been invited to spend a night with Sir S. Cockerill (also a darling) in Kew on Thursday 25th. Do you think it would be alright if I assumed that you would not be finished with Lawrence before the 26th? Alternatively to this, do you think it would amuse you to come down to this Inn (it really is a gem) BEFORE the 26th? Because then you could (a) bask in Siegfried Sassoon,

(b) see not only the best merlins flown in England, but also a superb peregrine which is just about to be entered by the lovely man who lives next door, and (c) possibly get hold (doubtful) of some of the priceless dry-fly fishing which exists in this neighbourhood. S. Sassoon might help you in this, but I forgot to ask him. He says he loves you very much.

I think the best plan is for me to tell you that (a) I am prepared to alter all or any of my plans to suit you and Lawrence, but (b) if you dont tell me to do any other definite thing I shall stay on in Heytesbury till 25th, then spend a night in London, then either go back home or do whatever you say. But I can't help feeling you wont again get a chance of bagging S. Sassoon and Major Allen (the falconer) in one village. Do try to come here, if it is only for a night. It would brighten you up on Lawrence, if not finished. Ralph Hodgson (the man who wrote about the Bull) is also staying with Sassoon, and the latter said the most affecting thing to me about him. (Hodgson is *very* nice, often good fun, but inclined to be too loquacious.) He has been staying with the Sassoons for at least a week, and upsetting his host by insisting on talking. Sassoon said: 'Ralph is a darling, *and I would do anything for him because of his poems*, but etc. And it would be a great blessing for me if you would take him off my hands just for this afternoon, as I dont want to talk any more.' The part which I thought was affecting was the underlined part, as it was said with absolute sincerity, and I thought it was a good thing that people should do things altruistically for one another on such a noble account. Siegfried then went off to weed the lawn.

So you see, I am moving in *real* circles. Tomorrow Sir L. Wooley (if that is not a cricketer—I intend it to be the name of an anthropologist) is to join our galaxy at luncheon. I am at the Inn, although they pressed me to stay at the Hall or whatever it is: but in these matters I am of Dr. Johnson's opinion—see his private remarks to Boswell, when discussing whether they should or should not stay with the Earl of somewhere, and decided that the best was to wait till he asked them twice.

Mrs. Sassoon (and of course he) seems to remember your last visit with relish.

I find it is *very* nice to meet humane people.   love from TIM

Posted on a Tuesday.
August the somethingth, 1938   *Stowe Ridings, Buckingham*

Dear David, I have just got home to find your heart-leap of a letter, and I had another one at Heytesbury before I came away. I am probably here till next wednesday—this is written on a friday—and then I am going to make my way slowly northwards. If nothing goes wrong on the way (or particularly right—such as a shaft through the heart or anything like that) I shall seek out you and your brood eventually in Yorkshire. Now that I am a millionaire I shall be able to stay in the nearest really expensive hotel and come over occasionally to you with a few crates of champagne. So just wait till you see an enormous grey car hoving in your purlieus with a cigar sticking out of the window, and you will know it is me. But if you dont see it you will know that I am busy copulating somewhere (but in the kindest way) and then you will know not to expect us. In any case dont let's decide anything, for all the best Quests work out themselves. If we do manage to get together on a fishing one, I have no doubt we shall catch a dolphin. The main thing is that I know where you are, and the rest God will decide. Ralph Hodgson turned out to be an oaf, S. Sassoon a charmer but a millimetre too self-centred, and Sydney Cockerell pure gold. You come between Sassoon and Cockerell. He has the advantage of you by having no sense at all, a talent which I'm afraid you can't lay claim to.

By the way, I am *painting* the illustrations in presentation copies for you, Sassoon's son, Masefield, Potts and myself. So dont mark your copy. You will have to swap it for the one I bring.   love from TIM

September 2nd, 1938   *Stowe Ridings, Buckingham*

Dear David, I read your generous and memorable review[1] this morning. Thank you for it a thousand times. You were quite right about the Anthropophagi: I had always felt uncomfortable about them, and the American book club made me substitute 3 complete chapters about griffins, wyverns etc. for them, before they would take the book. But you are wrong about Galapes. On the contrary, I *have* been subjected to dictators and rubber truncheons more than most people (I was beaten about once a week at Cheltenham College) and in that chapter I am being more grown-up about dictators than you are. You see, I have been able

[1 Of *The Sword in the Stone.*—D.G.]

to laugh at them. You will find that if we ever get a fascist revolution in England it will be me that is hanged, for that one chapter, long before Kingsley Martin is, for all his whining. It is the stuff about their tummies that hurts them, and ridicule: not denunciation.

I got your last letter also this morning, saying that I was not to come to Butts Intake. I am *very* sorry for Ray, because I like moors more than anything else also. Whatever is the matter? Tell her to take barley sugar, cloves and butter: the butter is the vehicle, the cloves warm the stomach and the sugar is an aperient for hawks. It is an infallible specific for all hawks, and should do for her, as she is fond of moors. I have loosed my one remaining merlin (the best one died in heart-breaking circumstances) to go back to the moors. Give it my love, if you see it. It is a Jack, and should be addressed as 'he'.

I am going to Norfolk tomorrow and may be coming on to Yorkshire from there, not to visit you, but to fish in a secret river. If I happen to be near Richmond before the 6th, I will call, but I wont make a point of it.

love from TIM

The premature worries about what to do during a war were due to the Munich crisis.

September 22nd, 1938   *Stowe Ridings, Buckingham*
Dear David, I have written to Siegfried Sassoon and the headmaster of Stowe (my poor list of influential people) to ask them if they can get me any sensible job in this wretched war, if it starts. You are the third and last notable, and you have got to take it. This is the ultimatum: I propose to enlist as a private soldier in one month after the outbreak of hostilities, unless one of you three gets me an *efficient* job before that. What are you going to do yourself? I would do anything under you, or Siegfried, or anything intelligent thought of by Roxburgh, but otherwise I prefer to be killed penny plain. I could skunk out of this actually in two ways (1) because I have enough money to run away to America, for the first time in my life, and (2) because I spent 6 months in the Brompton Hospital once, and have probably got lungs like a collander. But for some reason I can't manage to do these. I am left with the fairly rational outlook that either I must be a war person who uses his brains—damn, it is'nt everybody who has got a first with distinction at Cambridge and the Book of

Month Club choice in America—or else I am going off with humble people to be blown up as a genuine piece of cannon fodder, Private White. It seems so much as if all the arts of peace were done for now that one might as well go with them, but my last hope is that there may be some constructive department even in war, and that somebody could get me into it. love from TIM

[*September* 1938]
Monday morning   *Hilton Hall, St Ives, Huntingdonshire*
Dear Tim, Just got your letter as I am starting off. This is a hurried scrawl: reasoned statement to follow later.
1) The most important work in this war is propaganda—& on whether its good or bad the length depends, & the violence. If we can split the Germans into Nazis & non Nazis (old Christians etc) we shall soon win.
I have written to Ld. Lloyd & Lady Astor to try & press my propaganda views on them. It is a writer's job & as we have truth on our side shall have a wonderful opportunity if only we (English) keep our hands clean & prevent the newspapers screaming against 'the Huns'.
What we want is to appeal to the historic Germany to remember its traditions: storks on the roof—texts on the wall, Bruno Walter conducting German music on the wireless—chosen bits of Mein Kampf set against Dr Niemöller etc.
Propaganda is equally important in U.S.A.; Argentine; & the Empire.
If I can get such a job I shall; if I can get you in I shall. So don't enlist. Its mad.
Cannon fodder isn't wanted. Its useless & if used will lose the war quickly.
Surely Passchendaele taught even soldiers something.
Love from DAVID

September 27th, 1938   *Stowe Ridings*
Dear David, Thank you for your letter. It struck fire from my mind. Anything you tell me to do, I will do. If you are going to America, will you take me with you, if not, will you send me? The reason why I want

34

to go is that I think the fact of being their prospective Book of the Month will make me useful as a propaganda lion. I have been thinking hundreds and hundreds of plans, but the proper thing would be to see you, instead of writing. I shall spend most of today ringing up various places to try and trace you. Then, if I fail, I will write at length.   love from TIM

Tim came for a week-end to Hilton Hall before going on to try and shoot geese again at Wells-next-the-Sea. From there he moved to Holbeach St Marks after less than a week. Between Christmas and New Year I joined him for a night and sallied out before dawn with Tim and Brownie to wait for the geese to fly in from where they roost on sandbanks ...

They were pink-foot geese and they came in thousands, but as there was not a head wind, they passed high over us, well out of shot, before spiralling down to earth a mile or more away in an immense arable field where they ate the rotten potatoes turned up by the plough.

During this visit I must have told Tim about my cousin Dicky Garnett's plan to take The White Mills water on the Irish Dee below Ardee, Co. Meath. I suggested that Tim should join Ray and myself at Ardee after Dicky's departure.

December 13th, 1938   c/o *Leslie Barker*,
    What about David's flamingo now? ——>   *Ostrich House*,
                                                Wells-next-sea, Norfolk

Dear Ray, I think I have managed to divert my fowling piece from Hilton, for I rang up the gunmakers when I arrived here and gave this address. There are hardly any geese here at the moment at all, but it is excessively glorious. We took one gulp of the air and immediately swelled to 3 times our natural size. Brownie looks like a Borzoi and smells of sea-weed. She has done her hair very handsomely with some mud and stuff (sort of burrs) and lies quite quietly in her basket—we have been on the shore all day—without having to sniff the furniture any more. Her little nose is full of scents. The great goose murderer here has helped a lot with the examination paper.[1] He has filled in:

A   13 : Quist = Wood pigeon
C   4 : Longline = Trot
C   7 : Alderman = Carp
       Sweet William = Grayling } probably
C   8 : Guffin = some sort of complicated baiting for pollack
D   4 : Substitute for fruit = crab with candle on back
D   7 : Breast of Caper = greenish black
       Legs of Shoveller = pinkish yellow
D   8 : Teal doesnt dive
       Gadwall doesnt dive
D   10 : Col. Hawkes killed the bats & moth.

He also knew quite a number of those we had already filled in.

I am only going to stay here until next monday, just to paddle about in the creeks without bothering about geese, and then I am going to find lodgings near my bombing range in Lincolnshire. Holbeach is about 10 miles from the sea and I want to find a snug little hovel between the two, as near the sea as possible. It is all utterly flat and featureless: all the better for the north wind and the fire indoors. Thanks to David's care over the week end, I only drank 2 pints of beer yesterday. All my old friends here are still alive and happy. They all said: 'We were only saying yesterday, leave him alone and he'll turn up.' I feel quite proud of having done what they said. It is lovely to be alive—sometimes. Thank you for being kind to me.   Best love from TIM

Instead of a noose   We have a place near here   My piece has
A pink foot goose   called LAPWATER HALL   arrived, and
About my neck is hung.   (but there, you are a mere   splendidly
                            boor and no poet), also   makes fire.
                            one of the 'i' villages—
                            Tervi St. John.

December 19th, 1938   *The New Inn, Holbeach St Marks*
Dear David, I am so very very happy here, and so busy from before dawn till after dusk that I am not writing letters. Any spare time seems

[1] I rather think that this may have been in *The Field*. It cannot have been *The Times* Christmas questionnaire because of the date.—D.G.

36

to be so precious for having a sumptuous doze in, and then you wake up like a cockerel. The frost is terrific. I took a complete ice bucket out of a bucket when I came back from this morning's flight. I can't stand upright in any of the rooms here, and such a gale blows subterraneously in the shit house that it perfectly dessicates the fundament. I have not been drunk, or anywhere near it, since that week end at Hilton, and my belly is shrinking away. I dont have to shave or brush my hair, and when I saw myself in the mirror at lunch today, the fellow loomed at me like a buccaneer. Splendid! I could almost write Hoots! like that fellow in your cellarage. I live with the family and eat in the kitchen, and there is a feather bed and from five to ten thousand geese in the Wash. The Lawrence letters came into my possession last Thursday, and I read them dosing (can't spell it: snoozing, I mean) but can't get through. Very pleased about this, as I hope to make them last. He was a noble fellow, and nearly always absolutely truthful and sensible about himself and his works. His critical standards were genuine. He was the only critic of the Seven Pillars who saw it clearly as it was (bad). I dont think he was in the least bit eccentric, and I dont think he posed in his letters. Indeed I find them peculiarly constant to his correct idea of himself. The picture I get is of a sincere man surrounded by insincerity, romanticism, humbug and misunderstanding (in his correspondents). So there.

How are you, you Bunny? Keep off the drink, man, and writing, which is worse than drink. If you were half a man you would hang your pen on a weeping willow tree, and drive hither post-haste, with all your wives and descendants, so that I could drown you all in the Wash. I dont know the marsh a bit, and only have the tides in my head, but I go alone. Will you arrange the funeral when I am washed ashore? Stick some goose feathers up my arse and I will fly to my heavenly mansion. There, there. Enough.   love from TIM

[date omitted]   [address omitted][1]
Dear [name omitted]
    [ninety-nine lines omitted]

                                           Best love from
                                            [signature omitted]
Happy [Xmas omitted].

[[1] I had accidentally left out a page of one of my letters to Tim.—D.G.]

37

Xmas Day
December 25th, 1938

                    The New Inn, Holbeach St Marks, Lincolnshire

Dear David, Your telegram was a great pleasure and I should have loved to come, but the roads here were quite impassible. As it then seemed, it would have taken half a day to get through, and the weather here promised to be just suitable for geese. Tell your family (the ornithological section) that I have shot widgeon, golden-eye, mallard, red-breasted merganzer (female) and two unidentified species (vague, dirty-coloured creatures, like a cross between male and female Tufted, but without the tuft) and that I have seen plenty of pink feet (5,000), brent and sheld-duck (shot one of them, I'm ashamed to say, but I wanted to look at it close) also a big consort of whooper swans—beautiful. I also saw a Barnacle (branta bernicla—can't spell him in English). I have just had a letter from Naomi Mitcheson, who says in a P.S. 'It is sometimes interesting to know why people buy books: I sent for it at once on David Garnett's review in the Statesman.'

Brownie and I send you our love. She says we are as tough as nuts and eat steel screws and her master is growing a beard. We are so well and happy that we hardly read at all—are not yet through the Lawrence letters, which we nod over in the evenings at a page a time. How I am admiring that man! But he never understood you—not fully. He was quite right about Lady into Fox, of course, but he hasn't the faintest idea of the magnificence of No Love—absolutely off the rails about it—and he did not speak adoringly enough of the Grasshoppers for my taste. I did not like the extract from your letter to him. I will not have my gods prostrating themselves.   love from TIM

1939

On January 7th I wrote Tim a letter telling him how to get to Ireland with Brownie and his car via Fishguard and Rosslare, what it would cost and what documents would be necessary. I also gave him full information about wild geese in Ireland, taken from a natural history of that country dated 1851.

He did not bring the car, an S.S. Jaguar that he had recently purchased, as I think he was genuinely afraid that it might provoke the I.R.A. to attack him, so none of my information was of any use to him.

January 20th, 1939   *Ostrich House, Wells-next-Sea, Norfolk*

Dear David, I have in my possession some folios of instructions about geese and motors and licences and everything else in Ireland. And I would be prepared to make a dash for the place on Feb. 1st, except for these wretched dynamiters. I see in todays paper that they have tried to blow up young Chamberlain, and my grey motor strikes the Irish half of me as just the kind of motor which ought to be blown up. I dont want to have it served like this. What does Ray think? Would it be better to wait until you go over, and forget about the geese this year? I half fancy this course, as I am getting pretty fed up with the Anatidae in any case. Besides, I should much prefer to be blown up in your company. It would add a cachet. When are you going? I could simply come over a few days after, and join you on the Dee by train. They tell me the Dee opens on Feb. 1st, but I do hope we shall have a chance with the fly. Minnows are such dull things, just a sort of dip in the bran tub. My news is small but opulent. Walt Disney is signing a contract for the S. in the S. and some people called Paramount British want me to go to Hollywood as technical adviser on an Arthur film. If only I can get out of this doomed country before the crash, I shall be happy. Two years of worry on this subject have convinced me that I had better run for my life, and have a certain right to do so. I may just as well do this as shoot myself on the outbreak of hostilities. I dont like war, I dont want war, and I didnt start it. I think I could just bear my life as a coward, but I couldnt bear it as a hero. It seems best to do what is natural, in these as in all other circumstances.

No doubt I shall be able to dull the sufferings of conscience with a protective coating of some sort. However, you dont want to hear about all this, and I am only hurting myself writing it.

The geese have eluded me in a way which can only be called marked. The wild fowling guide here is a friend of mine, and lets me come out with him free. I have been out with him, morning and evening, for the past 10 days—except on 3 occasions. i.e. I have been with his party 17 times out of 20. On the 17 occasions nobody in the party has had a goose. On the 3 when I stopped at home, they killed five. I am shunned in the streets by all fowlers (who are, indeed, contemplating buying a whale to throw me to) and dare not shew my face in daylight. Children spit as I pass. The guide crosses his thumbs when he speaks to me. I have begun to hate myself, and shall have a complex soon, if something is not done about it. In fact I am a miserable fellow, and dont know what to do about anything. love from TIM

On arrival at The White Mill, my cousin and I discovered that our stretch of river had been netted the previous day by the local poachers and that there were salmon scales and the marks of hob-nailed boots on the bank. In consequence there would be no salmon there until a spate enabled them to cross the bar at the mouth of the river and run up. We therefore did some pike-fishing in the upper reaches of the river, catching quite a number. One day, after Dicky's departure I saw an elderly gentleman fishing our water at The White Mill and told him politely that I was afraid he was wasting his time. When he realized the position he generously promised me a fish if I would go to his water on the Blackwater just above Navan. I did so and half an hour later grassed a salmon of nineteen and a half pounds. Ray and I then drove into Dublin, gave the fish to a fishmonger to keep in his refrigerator, and met Tim and Brownie at Westland Row railway station. We then drove back to our hotel at Ardee. As there was still no rain, we were glad to hear of free fishing in the river Boyne above Trim. We drove there and half an hour later I grassed another salmon of fourteen pounds. There was a snow shower while I played the fish. The following morning, after a night of rain, I caught a seven-pounder at The White Mill.

Tim had fallen in love with Ireland and was so much overcome at the sight of my Boyne salmon that he asked Ray to find him lodgings near

the river. While we went on fishing in the snow showers she went to the
nearest farmhouse and took rooms for him. Tim lived there off and on
for six and a half years, and his landlord and landlady, Mr and Mrs
McDonagh, and Tim himself, are the chief characters in his book *The
Elephant and The Kangaroo*. One result of our visit to Ireland was that
he henceforward regularly called me by my nickname, Bunny, which he
had already used in two earlier letters.

April 5th, 1939   *Doolistown, Trim, Co. Meath*
Dear Ray, Thank you for the photographs. Mary Quin's face reminds
me of John Cornford's, except that he was ugly. I dont like the ones of
Bunny with his fish a bit: I think the fish spoils them, does'nt he? (Ha!
Ha!) I am not a bit depressed here really, as I am writing away at my
new book like a house on fire. Also the people are quite the most charming. Mrs. McDonagh and I have exchanged charms. I gave her a Benze-
drine Inhaler and she gave me (since the pork-pie gospel) a beautiful
rosary. Now I have to say the rosary with them every evening before
going to bed. Luckily I once learned how to do this (in Latin, however)
and as I go to mass rigidly am accepted as a devout catholic. The evening
rosary is great fun, as we gallop it in seven minutes. It goes like
this:
Mrs. McD: Hail Mary, Fuller Grease, Lard swith Thee, But Art Thou
          Manx Trim, and Blist the Fruit of THY woom, Jaysus.
Mr and Paddy McD simultaneously: Hum, Hum, Hum, Hum.
Mrs. McD: What did you say, Paddy? Wake up.
Paddy: Eh?
Mrs. McD: Hail Mary etc.
Us: Hum, Hum, Hum, Hum.
    As soon as we have finished it 'Amen!' we cry triumphantly, and both
turn upon me, panting for breath. 'Now, Mr. White, how long was it
that time?' I consult my watch solemnly and pronounce 'Seven and a half
minutes, but Paddy left out two Hail Marys in the fourth decade.' 'There,
Paddy!' And I am escorted off to bed with a candle, while everybody says
to everybody: 'Goodnight now, and a good night's rest to ye.'
    When I come to see you in England, I must bring my diary with me,
as it is full of reality. I try to write down the things quickly, and some of
them turn out to be gems. For instance, there is a local religious schism

called The White Mice. But I will leave all this till I can read it to you. I have no fish yet, and rarely try for them.

We are just at the peak of Lent now, and hardly a day passes without some excitement. Yesterday was Spy Wednesday (I wonder who was the spy?) which is a Black Fast. I spend nearly all the time when not writing in fasting, saying novenas, searching for horse-shoes, touching wood and picking up bits of lead. Did you know lead was as good as horse-shoes?

The farm hand here is called Paddy Quin, and he lends me his bicycle. So I gave him 5/– for Dulistown Races and told him to put it on Mr. Floods horse, which won at 10 to 1.

Sundays are days of pilgrimage when all Mrs. McD's innumerable relations are allowed to come out from Trim to look at me. My reputation for piety, learning and knowledge of race horses is such that even the priests (who are of course the rulers of the district) send me friendly messages.

I have a wood fire in my bedroom every night.   love from TIM

After Hitler's invasion of Austria Herbert Herlitschka and his wife, whom I had got to know because he translated my books into German, had had to leave their home, so I invited them to stay with us during part of the summer of 1939. This explains the references to refugees.

[*After April* 10th, 1939]   *Doolistown, Trim, Co. Meath*
Dear Bunny, Thank you for your long letter. It was heroic of you to write it, surrounded by refugees and rumours of war. Sometimes I think it is not worth worrying about Hitler and that everybody—including you and me—is gradually going insane. A most splendid old professor of some sort, speaking last week in the Irish wireless programme about the history of Connaught, said: 'But, in spite of all this, you wont find me on the banks of the Shannon prepared to defend it against all comers. Connaught is only a NAME.' I have half a mind to stay here for the rest of my life, and not worry about shedding my blood for your friend's silver candlesticks ...

I stop now, for I am off to fish yet again. If Jesus Christ had been half so patient as I am, we should all have been in heaven long ago. A propos of this, I have discovered why Mrs. McDonagh makes such a fuss of me.

She believes me to be St. Joseph (the beard, you see) whose statue she has in her bedroom & whom I closely resemble.

This letter has been going on for weeks. I keep hoping to have a fish to report, and so hold it back. But now it really shall go off.

I read Crossley's book[1] twice, from cover to cover, and wrote him a letter.

Please give the enclosed letter to Ray. She complains in her letter that one result of all your Jewish refugees is that everybody is always making untrue generalisations. Not if I know Ray! The more I think about her, the more I am astounded at her strictness in veracity. I have never met anybody so fiercely bent on truth—or indeed anybody else who never spoke without considering. Is it a strain on her, or does it just go naturally with her eagle eye? None of my hawks have ever seen as well as Ray does. Do you remember the two female hands with frilled cuffs which are door knockers here? They are charming—cast iron—and of course one notices them. Ray only saw them once, but she drew them on her envelope to me. She drew them both as left hands. 'Ah' I said to myself. 'How well she has remembered them! Even the frills. But of course she is wrong about their both being left hands. Naturally one is left and one is right. Still, it was clever of her to do the frills.' But when I went out to the front door they were both left hands.

Mrs. McD. is charmed with the envelope, and has begged it to keep.

If it would be good for Ray, tell her how much I love and admire this faculty of hers. But I was terrified to write her a letter, for fear that it would'nt be true. She must just be kind to it.

I am bursting to read you my Irish diary. I have quickly put in it all the things which seemed to taste of Ireland—including those 3 old ladies in the mansion. Do you remember?

Mrs. McDonagh said to her spouse angrily one evening, in the course of argument: 'What you are saying is nonsical. Why would'nt he be locked up, and he bejingled in his brains?'

So we're off to Albania now (I hear on the wireless while writing this). Well, well. We ain't got much money, but we do see life. Really, I'm sick of the whole business.

Love to your ghetto.

Brownie sends her love.   TIM

[1 *The Floating Line for Salmon and Sea Trout* by Anthony Crossley (Methuen, 1939).—D.G.]

One of the best things about Mrs. McD. is that she has fallen in love with Brownie. This is one of the main reasons why I am staying in Ireland. Brownie is so comfortable and happy, and gets fatter.

A magpie flies like a frying pan.

May 29th, 1939   *Doolistown, Trim, Co. Meath*

Dear Ray, I wonder how you are, and what you are doing? Would Bunny like me to send his gaff and would you like me to send that canvas case of yours by post? The fact is that you did a queer experiment in bringing me to Ireland: I seem to have disintegrated or something. I came over to England this month to fetch my car and wind up my affairs, sailing on a wednesday morning and back within four days. Do you think I shall stay here forever? I have read two enormous histories of Ireland—one of them Father D'Alton in 8 volumes—and begun to learn Irish. Now that I have my car I spend about 2 days a week pacing the hill of Tara, the rest of the time lying on the banks of the Boyne and talking politics. I think I will be in it soon: but in what? The hand already strays towards the dynamite and the harp. I will write you a letter from the scaffold. I am going off on a two weeks' tour next Thursday, please God, along the south and west, then back here to train a peregrine if I am lucky enough to get one. I hope to hire a grouse moor in the autumn—you can get about 10,000 acres for £10 from the Land Commission. I want to fly the peregrine at the grouse, not shoot them. I have also bought a superb Iceland jer-falcon, and, if she lives through the summer moult, which is unlikely, I shall want to try her at geese. This may mean coming back to the East Coast of England in the winter, as I expect to find that our west coast geese here are all grey-lags (too big for a hawk) while the Irish east coast is unsuitable as regards country. We have had the most superb weather here ever since I can remember. It never seems to rain, and the rain is much wanted. But I can't help liking the sun, even if the fishing and everything else is spoilt. I am very happy with the Irish now, and they speak well of me. I have been to mass every sunday since you left, also to a Mission we had here—a frightful trial. We say the rosary every night. I have 2 authentic relics of St. Theresa, one medal blessed by Pius XI, one gospel which has touched the Holy Crib, 2 blessed Virgins of Knock, one sacred heart, a pair of scapulars blessed by the Passionists, and a

44

rosary blessed by the parish priest. The car has two medals of S. Christopher, and Brownie has a medal of S. Bernard on her collar, who is kind to animals. She had another one of the Little Flower, but she lost it. I gave Mrs. McDonagh a statue of the Infant of Prague, which she adores. He is about 2 ft. high and looks like this:

I am afraid I have drawn him rather badly, as he is more stumpy. The cope spreads out more. I have finished my book called The Witch in the Wood and left it to be typed in England. It may not be any good. I went over to Dunsany Castle last week, but Dunsany was in England. I shall go again. It is an ugly Victorian gothic structure in a very beautiful park. When are you two coming over again? You will have to avoid me if you dont want to be bossed about: I behave as if I had bought the island. I have bought Finnegan's Wake. What do you think of it? Personally I find that life's too short. I cannot learn Irish and read Joyce both at the same time. When I was over in England I had the diluted pleasure of sitting up till 5 a.m. with Compton McKenzie. He said (1) that there were only 2 names remembered in Greece, Lord Byron & Compton McKenzie, (2) that at one time he could have raised the whole of the six counties against England, but refrained in order to avoid bloodshed. How true are either of these? At present he is busy sending telegrams to the Duke of Windsor. By the way, will you tell Bunny that now I will not be able to help him with his propaganda in the next war? I have at last decided with O'Connell that bloodshed is wrong in any country in any circumstances, and also I am too busy to attend to such matters. My job is to labour smally at increasing civilisation, not to join in destroying it. So I am going to claim the immunity of the Irish bard, confirmed in A.D. 500 or so at the convention of Drum Cuit. I am sorry about this, but I am also right about it. How are your Jews? Can you Anglo-Normans summon the energy to write to us Gaels? But I am forgetting you are a Gael yourself. ıs mıse vo ċaṛa vılıs. (Impostor!)   Best love from TIM

The reference to Ray being a Gael is almost true. Her mother was pure Irish on both sides and her father's mother was a Spring-Rice. Tim claimed to be Irish because he said his father was born in Ireland, but he

45

also claimed that he was related to Samuel White (Siamese White) who came from Bristol, and that his family arms were those of White of Fyfield in Berkshire. (See page 249.)

June 5th, 1939   *Great Southern Hotel, Mallaranny*

Dear Bunny, So far as I can make out, I am taking a fishing and shooting lodge on the Owenduff during August for £100 a month. It is a place absolutely beyond words—neither human being nor habitation nor tree nor cultivated field within sight: a great bowl of flat bogland 5 miles across, surrounded by fine mountains. You will find it on any big map of Sligo & Mayo. It is called Sheehan[1] Lodge. It is a 'flood' stream i.e. has no particular salmon season, but after every flood you can catch them for 8 hours. If God is good to us with the weather (note the 'us') we might kill 60 fish. At the same time the sea trout are very good in August, and there are a few grouse which I hope to pursue with peregrines. The lodge is a good sized house—I should think it must have from six to eight bed-rooms, and there is a resident Keeper with a sister who looks after it. The present occupant (Count John MacCormack) has an extra maid and a cook from Dublin, but I am sure these are not necessary. Now my suggestion is that you and all your brood should come over and share it with me. You would get the fishing free (and the grouse) and I should hope that Ray would do the catering for all of us—i.e. arrange about the food and pay for it. I would pay the Keeper and his sister. Your sons could not find in any part of the world any place so suitable for sons. It is Childe Rowland's dark tower. If there be any virtue, think on these things. My address is still

> Doolistown
> Trim
> Co. Meath.

The deal for the Sheehan Lodge is not yet completed.   love from TIM

Do not forget that I have been spying this country for 4 months. It is no River Dee that I am offering you, and anyway you wont have to pay for it.

[1 Tim got the name wrong. Actually Sheskin.—D.G.]

46

Dear Ray, You must forgive this shower of letters: I feel like a collision of meteors in september or something. I got back this morning to find your letter about thinking you were $\left.\begin{array}{l}\text{dieing}\\\text{dying}\\\text{dyeing}\end{array}\right\}$ for 2 days. It is not clear in the letter whether you still think anything of this sort. When I was 19 years of age I was told by 3 doctors that I had 6 months to live (T.B.) and —not to exaggerate—well, here I am. At that time I believed those doctors for more than six months and I was always getting letters like this one I am writing to you, which only served to infuriate me. My visitors in hospital either commiserated with me (when I thought they wr ghouls) or told me that when they were 19 years of age they were told by 3 doctors that they had 6 months to live (in which case I considered them frivolous imbeciles). So it is difficult to write to you in any particular way. I just thought I would tell you this true story about myself. I have never believed a doctor since. So far the materialist. As for the other side of life, I gave your love to Mrs. McDonagh (she was thrilled) and told her that you were not well, or had not been well. Then it was bed time and we said our rosary, but after it, before we unknelt, Mrs. McDonagh said: 'Wait a bit, Mr. White, before you get up: do you mind if we say 5 Hail-Marys with an intention for Mrs. Garnett?' We said these, and then I said: 'As a matter of fact, I said all mine for her, before you mentioned it.' So Mrs. McD. said: 'We will say a novena of them for her, ending on the feast of the sacred heart.' This means that we will be saying the whole rosary for you for the next nine nights. Do you consider this an unwarrantable intrusion on your privacy? You ought not to, for the McD's really believe that they are helping and whatever I may believe in I suppose it is no harm to have kind thoughts. So you see I am sending you a bit of my mumbo-jumbo with a vengeance. Yes, you are quite right about Will. It would be cruel madness to force him into anything at 17. He realises this, of course, himself, and when advancing various theories about architecture and mathematics is really playing for time. I know you will give him this without forcing him to play for it. Turn all those Jews out and invest the money in *time* for William to think. About the bombardment of post-cards and letters which I have been sending to you and Bunny this week: neglect them. The exquisitely beautiful Sheehan Lodge which I wanted for August has fallen through for the moment. I am writing again, offering twice the money, but without much hopes. If you *can* manage to answer this, tell me your views on spending August with me (as per my last letter to Bunny) *should I be able to find another place as good as Sheehan.* I am working very hard at finding one, both by letters and inspection, and it would help me to know quickly whether there was any chance of fixing things together, in the way that I suggested to Bunny. My suggestion (in case you hav'nt seen the Bunny letter) was that I should pay the rent and wages, while you should pay for the food and bring your family with you. The rent of Sheehan was £100 a month, plus Keeper, plus 2 maids—but it was magnificent fishing and good grouse and looked like the p.c. I sent you. N.B. we might have caught 60 salmon & innumerable sea trout, and I would have had my hawks with me. It is infuriating to read your letter, as I cannot tell whether you are still ill or not and what of. The friend who quarrelled with you and made you tremble with rage by saying that you spread gloom may have thought it would be good for you to tremble with rage. And it seems to have been. About my trip in the west: nothing could have been more glorious. The temperature was reported in Galway at 110° and we never saw a drop of rain. I am off the drink and was bathing naked in mountain lochs and generally rampaging about. I am a mountainy man by nature (I think my father must have come from there) for I began to cry when I first saw them. I have some exceedingly funny photographs of myself, if only they come out, standing in the Atlantic in a bathing dress with the beard and the comic hat. They should beat your photographs to a frazzle. Thank you for sending them. Now Ray, Mrs. McDonagh has been upstairs to fetch the two enclosed for you. She thought you might like them. Do not be cross with us. Do you know how many people admire you? I have a gospel just like this: the pork pie one: and it has done me not a bit of good. Or has it? It has melted my bitter heart a little. Brownie has already eaten S. Bernard, as you advised. You might eat the pork pie. If you do, do tell me what is in it. I dare not open mine.

Best love from TIM

Friday, June 23rd, 1939   *Crossmolina*

Dear Ray, I have today written to the owner, asking for Sheskin Lodge in September. Is there any hope of getting Bunny to make up his mind rather soon, as if you dont come I should like to get other company? If

Bunny must work, he can probably work better at Sheskin than anywhere else, as it is 15 miles from everywhere, and nobody will be indoors
all day. It seems to me that the whole thing turns on whether your sons
have holidays in september or not. If so, I think it would be madness not
to come, for their sakes. The Lodge is the most extraordinary building in
Mayo, the result of a liason between a 19th century bungalow and a
conservatory. Only it is the runt of the litter. It is furnished in impoverished
1880 style, all the plaster comes off the walls, no ornament. It has 3 double
bedrooms and 2 single ones at a pinch and a sort of bathroom activated
by calor gas. There is a large living room, full of peeling leather chairs
(very comfortable) and a sort of miniature winter garden of glass. It is
single storied. The whole is surrounded by a huge wilderness of rhodo-
dendrons and pines, in which some 3 gardeners work ceaselessly without
any effect whatever. I do not mean that they produce a small effect—i.e.
mow a few feet of lawn—but that they do not produce *any*. In the house 2
maids work with the same result. I do not remember a lovelier place.
Round the rhodedendrons there extends a vast bog, ten miles across, with
a rim of mountains all round it. The highest is 2500 (about). The nearest
neighbour is 3 miles (Irish) away, along a road which would break the
heart of a tank. Shopping is done in Crossmolina (15 miles) or Bangor
Erris (8). It is only the last 3 miles of road which is bad. The fishing
depends entirely on rain. The worst September I could hear of, they got 6
salmon: the best September was between 30 and 50. Last year, which was
a very bad grouse year, they got 27 brace that month. It seems to me that
if you come we cannot fail to enjoy ourselves. When the rain comes, the
fishing is good. When the sun comes, I can fly my hawks. There is an
exquisite loch to bathe in. I suppose they dye it once a week with Recketts
blue, for it is a piercing ultramarine, and they have arranged a lot of little
white waves all over it, to give contrast. The sea is only a few miles to the
north, over the mountain. I have invited one other person, J. G. Mavro-
gordato, the secretary of the British Falconers Club. He is a charming
man, two feet high, and an excellent falconer, though inclined to bigotry.
He is bringing his hawks, and you will have to feed him as well as me, as a
penalty for not making up your minds sooner. Do come. Bunny can get
up at 4 a.m. to fish, and be left alone all the rest of the time. Nobody will
want to talk in the evenings, as we shall all be too tired. If you bring a
car (I have fetched mine, and Mavro *may* have one to bring) there is no
reason why we should be tied together. The place is Paradise. The cost

49

to yourselves of feeding me and Mavro (largely on the fish and grouse, I hope) surely cannot be an extravagance, and I only suggested anyway so that you { should feel free / should not feel dependant. } If you are still off colour, it may help to have 2 maids. I meant to write you a long letter about { dying / dieing / dyeing } (I did not give a lead over the spelling simply because I cannot spell it myself: we two are, I fear, no more than the blind leading the blind) but this one will have to do instead, as it is much more important. (Think that out.) I will write the death letter later, when I hear for sure that my bid for Sheskin is accepted. So you have 2 or 3 days to make up your minds, and then will come a last lecture from me, after which I think the subject (d..ing) had better be dropped. Coming from you it is absurd anyway, and I wont have it.   love from TIM

Sheskin! Sheskin! Sheskin!

June 28th, 1939   *Doolistown, Trim, Co. Meath*

Dear Bunny, I wrote this letter for Ray last week, then kept it to see what would happen. I now learn that I have got Sheskin definitely, so you must make up your minds soon. If you decide to come only for a fortnight, let me know, wont you, so that I can invite somebody else for the other fortnight? What is all this pedantry about making your son learn French? You are a draconic father. As for saying that Irish is not a substitute, I never heard such nonsense. What is this son of yours anyway, a commercial traveller? Tilly-fally. You and/or your family or any part of it or various parts of it at different times will be welcome at Sheskin for any part or all of September collectively, dispartitely or in relays, so now make up some sort of a mind between you and dont keep aggravating me any more. I am in training already, have been on the water-waggon for 10 days and have 2 peregrines arriving tomorrow.   love from TIM

July 6th, 1939   *Doolistown, Trim, Co. Meath, Eire*

Dear Bunny, Well, this is splendid news. I am so glad you have got over all that common sense of yours and come back to your right wits. And as for war, there wont be one—Hitler is too cunning. If there had been going to be one, it would have been last week. I wish I could wean you from paying attention to the subject anyway. You are living an unnatural life with all those Jews about you. Why dont you wash your hands of the whole affair? The human race is fundamentally beastly wherever it is, and it is your job to make it less so. You are best at doing this by writing books—not propaganda, just books. Anybody can keep tame Jews and even Ld. Lloyd can do propaganda. You are probably quite mediocre at these, and that is why your life is 'more than complicated'. It is your unconscious mind begging to be allowed to go on with its real job. No doubt Shakespeare did a lot of good work sheltering Catholics or non-jurors or something, but it was a much better thing that he should have written Macbeth.

Practical: No, I can't get Sheskin or Shehan in August. I have begged hard for both, but September is the earliest. If Ray *likes* Sheskin, I should like her to stay the whole month: but I dont want her to stay only to help me. After all I shall have 2 handmaids! We can leave this till she sees the place. A frightful judgement has fallen upon me, and I have lost 2 peregrines, but not the jer-falcon. Mavro is bringing 3 tiercels, so this wont affect your enjoyment, though my beard has turned white in a night. I *may* be able to get another falcon for myself, and if so it is possible that I shall go to Crossmolina in August. Could your family's canoe trip connect with Lough Conn, I wonder? I am going to write to somebody or other for a license to import firearms, and then I wonder, if I sent the license to Hilton, whether Ray or you could call at my cottage on your way and bring my shotgun from it? It might be useful for shooting us grouse. Dear Bunny, the most frightful fate is pursuing me all the time: being in Ireland is turning my poor head and I have been on the waterwaggon for nearly three weeks, but this is not the worst of it, for I believe I am going to be the Master of a pack of hounds next winter. They are only harriers fortunately, but this is nearly as bad as fox-hounds, and I shall go dashing round in a comic hat blowing a bugle, to the derision of the nation. Indeed, you have much to answer for. Then, when I have spent all my money, I am going to frequent race meetings trying to collect tips in my velvet hat and telling stories in Irish to the terrified peasants of the west. So you can see how maddening it is when you try to do your common sense on me. I can honestly say that I feel *none* the better for being on the water waggon. How is Ray? How are you? Cheer up. Pray for

poor TOIRÐEALBAČ Ò ZEALAZÀIN

[*mid-August* 1939]   *Hilton Hall, Hilton, Huntingdon*

Dearest Tim, I will go & fetch your gun in a few days & shall not buy one. I shall bring a trout rod and a salmon fly rod.

Ray & the boys went off bound for Kerry on Wednesday morning. I am staying for a few days in Sussex with friends & then going off for a tour. I am very happy. Sheskin still seems rather remote & heavenly. I expect to shoot a lot of snipe which writers have always been good at. The reason is that the man who aims to one side of the snipe usually gets it—or at any rate has an even chance. The man who aims at it always misses it.

I saw another grass snake yesterday & picked lots of mushrooms.

Please don't lose your hawks until we arrive. I shall cross to Dublin on the night of Wednesday Aug 30. If you could meet me there in the morning of Aug 31st we could go to Sheskin together. Would that be all right? Tell me if you want me to bring you any English luxuries. Love to Brown & the Falcons   Yours ever DAVID GARNETT

Is there any point in bringing my salmon spinning-rod? I shall not unless you tell me to.

Did you see poor Anthony Crossley was drowned or suffocated in a plane crash on the way to Sweden, no doubt to fish.

August 23rd, 1939   *Doolistown, Trim, Co. Meath*

Dear Bunny, If any of the facts in this letter are *wrong*, then you ought to answer it. Otherwise we can assume that we understand each other.

I shall go in to Dublin on Wednesday Aug. 30th and shall put up for the night at the Wicklow Hotel. On the morning of Thursday Aug. 31st I shall meet the *second* boat train at Westland Road. I do not know what time this train arrives, and shall not know until I ring up the station on the night of the 30th, so all we can arrange is that you are not to catch the first boat train. Tell them on the boat to let you sleep on until the last available train, and I will meet that.

Then we come back to the Wicklow for breakfast.

As soon as the shops open, we go to get cartridges. Unfortunately my permit to own cartridges in Ireland is written on the pink form in your possession, so, although I have ordered some, I cannot collect them until you turn up with the permit. We get these at your namesake's* so if *you* want any extra fishing tackle you can get it then.

Now we drive to Trim to have lunch and collect the 2 peregrines. There is just one thing about this. *For the love of God bring as little luggage as you can.* I have to carry: Ourselves, Brownie, 2 falcons, 6 pigeons. The falcons take up exactly the same amount of room as two human passengers. They exactly fill the 2 back seats.

After lunch we drive over to Crossmolina, where we stay the night. On 1st Sept. we move in to Sheskin.

Can you take it? OR would you like to have a day in Dublin to recuperate from the first part of your journey? If I hear no more, I shall assume that you can take it, and proceed according to above schedule.

love from TIM

No, dont bring spinning rod./ /Yes, I did see about Crossley./ /Dont be too hopeful about snipe.

P.S. When you get hold of my gun case, look inside it. If there are any cartridges inside, throw them away. You wont be allowed to import them.

I duly arrived at Westland Row and was met by Tim with his S.S. Jaguar car in which a wooden perch had been fixed across the back seats on which there were two hooded peregrine falcons. Brownie sat on my lap and by leaning a little forward I was just out of reach of the peregrines should they have darted blindly forward. However they did not. According to my recollection, which I am told is wrong, we reached Sheskin Lodge that evening and the peregrines were fastened to stumps driven in to the lawn. According to Tim's diary we spent the night at a hotel and settled in at Sheskin next morning.

Ray had had the fear of cancer of the breast hanging over her for ten years. There had been an operation and several treatments with radium needles. The muscles of her right arm were becoming very weak, and her physically feeble state was the reason for my anxiety while waiting for her arrival at Sheskin Lodge.

Ray and my sons did not arrive until late the day following, driving from Dingle where they had been camping out with Arthur and Noel Olivier Richards and their family. I was anxious both about Ray and because we were on the brink of war with Germany in which case I should be called to the Air Ministry.

<hr>

* Garnett's sports shop in Dublin.

Actually I only stayed a few days at Sheskin Lodge. However, I thoroughly enjoyed being there and during my visit I went out with Tim and a falcon on the grouse moor, drove with Ray to Crossmolina to buy a portable wireless, tried in vain to fish with Tim in the Owenmore river, but we were driven away by midges, and went out fishing for sea-trout in the estuary during which William caught two nice fish.

Then a telegram came from the Air Ministry and I took a train from Ballina to Dublin, leaving Ray and the boys to follow ten days later.

The following passages from Tim's journals show that the Garnetts' visit had proved trying.

Bunny was all the day fussing about telegrams, the wireless and the non-arrival of Ray and his children. His reaction to the fact that the world now seems certainly doomed to a war of extinction within a few hours, was to moan, fuss, bother and rave: mine to curl up and go to sleep. O I only wanted to keep quiet and be alone and behave as if I were already dead.

Ray did not turn up till after nine o'clock at night, so I had Bunny on my hands all the time. His attitude was that he must do things, or else go mad, so I took him for two or three hours walking on the moor and read to him and made him talk about things. The thing which worked best was when I asked him to come and cheer me up, instead of making me cheer him up (implied not said) which resulted in him doing this most sweetly. We got through the day somehow and went to bed at 10.30.

There is no entry in the journal until September 21st, after Ray and the boys had left. It is headed:

Convalescent writing
... The child of today, who has never been treated as a nuisance, is a terrible nuisance. They expect everything because they have always been given everything—except the stick. Manners and social insincerity are an invaluable labour-saving device. Telling the truth and being broad-minded are not. The truth and the breadth of mind are commodities too rare and valuable for social currency. I cannot spare them from my books to waste them on vanishing air of the domestic hearth. Another way they bothered me was by bothering about the war. Nothing they could do would have any effect on it,

but they would go on. And William such a solemn little boy. Ray said: 'He is shy. Don't be unkind to him. He is not so ungracious as he seems. It is so fatally easy to make young children believe that they are horrible.' But I can't stand shy people. Let them give over their self-indulgence and stop being shy. It is gross egoism. I did. And Ray's shyness. Behind it all an uncompromising, passionate, weak mania for truth. Strange people. I really like Ray very much. But more in small doses. It is like living with Mrs Be-Done-By-As-You-Did. She is as ferocious to herself. This bottling up so bad. A week ago she suddenly had convulsions after dinner, and I had to drive for the doctor. She is trying to shield both her children and her husband from a world where her Truth God does not really reign, and she tries to be Spartan about it. The bore is that she has a bias for these wretched children. It is the one thing in which she is not true. She would kill me if she knew I knew this. This is an absolutely untrue picture of her, for it leaves out the one essential thing about her, which is that she is dying of cancer. Take this in and she is the greatest hero in the world.

Note added in the margin:

Now that Ray is dead, Bunny in the R.A.F.V.R., Richard training for the sea-rescue service, and poor William half-abandoned by everybody, I can only plead that I was half dead from 'flu when I wrote this. In fact I have never met a greater woman than Ray—of whom I still think or dream nearly every week. The irritation which shows in this entry is at least proof that I felt deeply about all of them, even in the influenza.

An earlier note shows that he did not always feel irritated by a mania for the truth, even in social currency:

2.xii.38. Stayed with the Garnetts ... We had a lovely week-end, very bracing to have to talk truthfully.

Tim's strange view of me is recorded also in the Sheskin Journal.

David Garnett ix:39.
T. E. Lawrence remarked with irritation that he was over-educated. In the course of our drive to Sheskin I found that: (i) he remembered more about heraldry than I did just after finishing

Boutell, (ii) that he knew more about the petrol engine than I ever shall, (iii) that he knew as much about the Irish language as I do, and he had read all the Fianna stuff, (iv) that he had read all the Irish history I have. This for a mere tripper to a man who has spent the last eight months in Ireland, and I thought not idly, was a stunner. I would lay long odds that he has some acquaintance with any subject ever likely to be mentioned: often a very good acquaintance.

I need scarcely say that Tim's view of me was wholly mistaken, but it was certainly genuinely held. He admired me as a scholar far more than as a writer, and this is a clue to our relationship.

Tim's irritation accounts for the gap in our correspondence until 1940. But I must have written to him mentioning a flight I took far out over the Atlantic in a Sunderland flying-boat to escort an incoming convoy during a tremendous gale in November, because he refers to it, and to another flight which I took over the North Sea, in a postscript to a letter in February.

1940

After a gap of four months Tim wrote enclosing the manuscript account of his visit to Inishkea, which was later used in *The Godstone and The Blackymor*. I sent it on at once to Cyril Connolly who published it in *Horizon*. There was some delay in packing up and sending him the books of the Irish Text Society he asked for in exchange for my doing this, as they were at my mother's cottage The Cearne and I was spending every spare moment at Hilton because Ray was dying of cancer.

I dont know your rank, for the address of this envelope.

February 4th, 1940   *Healion's Hotel, Belmullet, Co. Mayo*

Dear Bunny, I am wretched to hear about Ray. When you left her behind you at Sheskin, she had a dreadful attack of some sort, and we had to get the local doctor. She was unconscious and did not remember about it: we did not tell her more than we needed: and I did not write to you about it, because I thought it would be unwise to trouble you until you could get at her. The doctor said that she must come home to you and was quite fit to travel. So I asked William to tell you about the attack as soon as your family was re-united. I hope he did.

There is nothing I can say to you about her dying, except that *I* dont believe people do die in the full sense of that word. I believe in the law of conservation of energy, or something of that sort, and I dont think the electric current has gone just because you switch the bulb off. On the whole I think I had better not write to her at all, unless you tell me she is in need of letters, and then I would write a chatty letter about my God-stone—except that I hate being chatty in such circumstances.

When I asked you if you could, after all, send me a few of the Fenian legends, it was à propos of my Godstone. I have been following him up ever since I ran across him—it is a perfect detective story—and I am going to write a paper about him for a learned journal called 'béaloideas'. It is the first time I have stumbled across an opportunity to do original scientific research, and I spend half my time interviewing aged dotards who can't speak English. In the end I think I shall make it into a short brochure, about as long as Beaney Eye, beginning with the bit I sent you and then following the Godstone trail through my diary to heaven knows what astonishing conclusion. The more people you interview, the more his story grows, and (extra-extra-censorable-whispered-under-the-table-with-bated-breath) I *may* have stumbled on an epoch making anthropo-literary discovery. The Godstone's name was the naoinoz (pronounced neevoag) which is generally interpreted to mean naoin-óz—The Holy Youth, or Saint (naoin) Young (óz). But the astonishing thing is that Inniskea is connected with the Atlantis legend—there is supposed to be a regular inhabited country between it and Innisglora, seen once in seven years. Now Oisín was taken to Tir-na-n-óz (in the Wanderings of Oisín) by a lady called MAIN, and, as you know, Tir-na-n-óz was the land of perpetual youth. I could make out quite a good case for my Godstone being the golden-haired young main herself (main-óz*) and Inis-Cé being none other than the island of Tir-na-n-óz. This would mean, in plain terms, that the story called the Wanderings of Oisín originated in Erris and was based upon Inis-cé, *where Oisín's Queen was still venerated until seventy years ago!*

Naturally I can't go into the whole affair in a letter—I have depositions from old men who saw the naoinoz, and answers to questionnaires I put out in the schools and all sorts of material—I have been to search the Dublin museum—I am in correspondence with the Irish Folklore Commission etc—but this is the reason why I want to read The Wanderings of Oisín carefully. The whole of this country is bound up with the Fianna.

The bit in your letter about flying over Atlantic and N. Sea made me feel so lonely.   love from TIM

I have taken Sheskin.

March 14th, 1940   *Healion's Hotel, Belmullet, Co. Mayo*

Dear Ray, It seems a long time since I wrote to you, and I'm afraid I generally dont write to people unless I'm cadging. I tried to cadge some Irish books off David last time, and now I want to ask you for a snapshot of myself. You are the only person who photographs me. A person writing articles in the 'larger weeklies' wants to write one on me, with informal photograph. It is *not* important. Dont trouble if a bore. I really

* Also pronounced 'neevoag'.

58

dont hanker much after the larger weeklies and I have come to disbelieve in Publicity, but if you happen to come across a print of me as Stout Cortes or the Bearded Lady, you might send it. Dont look for it specially. I am still bearded, but no longer stout. Our bishop in Mayo is strict about Lent and only lets us have one meal a day—apart from that, you may have 10 oz. of bread, but no butter for tea, and two days a week with no meat. As I have also been teetotal since Christmas Day, you would not know the old hulk. I am thinking of becoming a fashionable gigolo. On St. Patrick's Day (next Sunday) I drive to Meath (D.V.) to be capsized as a Catholic. Do you remember how you once detected me proclaiming that people were more beastly than nice on a monday and then I said on tuesday that they were more nice than beastly? Well, so far as I can discover, this is natural to me. I dont find much reason for supposing that I am even one person for more than a few hours together. It makes it almost impossible to explain about being a Catholic. There is one disgusting person in me who is quite atheistical and is doing it simply because it makes it easier not to be massacred when living among Catholics. There is another one who walked about the fields all Christmas Day, weeping with joy. (I told them I wanted to be capsized on that day.) Presiding feebly over these rowdy elements, I think I detect a 1% leaning towards Catholicism. So, after thinking about it for a year, I am giving the casting vote for the B. Virgin. One consolation is that I flatter myself I shall be the worst Catholic in existence. It is all very muddling. And probably of no interest to anybody except myself. Anyway, I couldn't explain it all at less than novel length. I tried hard for six months to get a lease of Sheskin etc. and, when I had the agreement in my pocket, I discovered that old Peter Joyce did not want me there. By having an absentee landlord he was getting the use of the 3 fields, also £50 a year for upkeep of lodge and garden. So, rather than hurt him and incidentally make a bad neighbour, I have dropped the whole affair. Now I am trying to buy outright another lodge called Kilteany, which is on the river bank lower down. It is not so beautifully situated, and is partially fallen down, but, if I get it, it could be pulled round. The river is at the door. I have caught five salmon in it since the season began. There is a ruined church beside the grounds which was built in a night by the agency of some well-disposed sheep who carried the stones a coupla miles from Tristia, on their backs. One of the best pools in the river is under this church. Another pool is called *druim an Aipreann*—the Mass Pool: in the penal times they said mass in the next field, under the sky. I have caught a fish in it. There is nothing there but sky. Just below the lodge water, the Owenmore runs into the sea. Very good for night fishing in July—sea trout. It is a fine place for the wild geese too. If I can get this Lodge reasonably, I shall keep a cow and some pigs. I shall have a married couple to look after me, and I shall make the man dig potatoes all the time. Then I shall want to do some tree planting. I wish I had Bunny to advise on this. I want some cedars in one place, and miles of fuchsia hedge. But can I have peaches? That is what I want more than anything, and the soil is sort of clay, though it is bog all round. I am going to have a gillie who talks only Irish to me, by contrast. What day dreams! Probably it will all fall through. And then I shall put in a motor for electric light and to pump the water, and I shall have a little rhododendron avenue—we call them Rosy-dender-Rums—which the woodcocks come into in frosty weather. My next neighbour is a darling: we adore each other and he is a dreadful fuss-pot (same age as Peter Joyce: batchelor: simple) and will not let me fish alone. He stands on the opposite side of the river from me (has no waders) like a hen whose ducklings have taken to the water and talks incessantly and once he managed to hook us together, back to back, with two salmon flies. He says I am the nicest gentleman he has ever met, and he sings songs to me, and tells me stories in a high voice, breaking off every now and then to giggle and exclaim 'This is a good one, this is!' They are stories about *tricks* mostly, in which the hero is Solomon or O'Connell. Often they both occur in the same story, but he says they did not have moty-cars in those days, he thinks, but only jaunting cars. I shall have a little chapel in my house and dining room, sitting room, 5 beds, bathroom, lavatory, kitchen, big hall. There are outbuildings for the cow and the car.

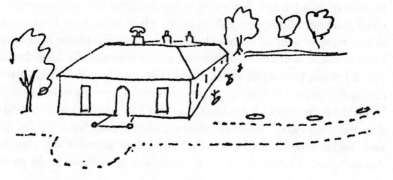

It is a brick house (plastered) with slate roof and ivy all over it. Brownie is very fond of it, too, which is a good thing. She is worried by all the negociations, however, and runs about between us, while we are bargaining in our strange yapping voices, in an agony because she cannot help. I expect Bunny has told you about my island. I am deeper in it than ever. When I am living as a millionaire at Kilteany I shall have a motor boat at the mouth of the Owenmore, so that I can go over whenever I want. I have found a dozen thurrows on it, a church long prior to William

 Conqueror, and several early Christian grave stones. One is like this. The wonders of the place are such that it is no good at all trying to describe it. Until 1876 they venerated a sort of false god called the Godstone or naoinóz.

love from TIM

Five bedrooms makes a nice number for entertaining the Garnetts in. P.S. Book 3 of my Arthur cycle is going to be a *cracker*. Book 2 was hopeless.

Dear Tim, Both Bunny & I enjoyed your description on camping on the island with the god. He ought to have sent the books & will, & I will send a photo as soon as it comes. I am glad you have found another House I like the look of it from your drawing & description & you have caught 3 salmon there but you must pull down the ivy unless the house would come to. I cannot write to you without telling you the truth which is that that the fit I had at Sheskin was the beginning of an illness from which I am now dieing in real ernest & I hope quickly. Don't answer this if you find it awkward write to Bunny. It gives me pleasure to think of them (B, W, R) staying in your new house & catching salmon. Forgive Will I never objected to your believing one thg one day & one another, far better, than being a consistent Catholic. I hope there are days when you don't believe I am damned. I am frightened of many things but not of your God. I am writing this in the middle of the night. I have just had an injection & should be changing from restless misery full of pain to calm, peace, relaxation like puss—to sleep—but the effect of the injections are wearing off I'm afraid. I would have liked to have read your Arthur books.

love RAY

Dearest Tim, Ray wrote this and a letter to Will the night before last. Last night she was very bad & the chances are that she will be dead before you get this.

I have been with her whenever she was free of the nurses & not asleep, for a month now.

She has been longing for death the last few days. Last night she could not sleep till nearly 4 in the morning & I went down & talked about different people's characters to her & she discussed them rationally & then when I mentioned William cried out in a tone of joy:

'There he is! Oh William is here & lifting up his head to look at me.' After a time I talked about your new house and how you would be sure to have horses and ride since Ireland is a country of horses.

That pleased her & she fell asleep, but fighting for breath in her sleep terribly.   Love from BUNNY

Dearest Tim, Ray died on Easter Sunday—a fortunate & peaceful death. I was with her most of the day. She was very bad as one lung had gone out of action & the other was filling up.

But for the evening the doctor had ordered a big dose of morphia. I put puss on the bed: he sat very quiet & Ray stroked him while I talked to her. But she said she felt very strange & her hands grew very cold although I was holding them. Then she lost consciousness, & as she did so the tired out heart which had been working under an enormous overload, beat more & more feebly & she died almost imperceptibly so one could not be certain within 2 or 3 minutes.

The last words—Love Ray—on the letter to you are the last she wrote.

I am going up to London tomorrow & shall see the boys at the weekend. Richard was more or less prepared but it was a very bad shock to William I'm afraid.

I shall try & let this house. I hope the Air Ministry dont recall me. I feel as though I want to lead my own life.

Ray was very eager to read the latest Arthur book & so am I.

Well I'll write again. Please understand that when I send my love now I mean it very much.   Yours BUNNY

Dear Bunny, I have been away in Meath for a week, so I only found the 3 letters when I got back here this evening. I can't imagine what you are feeling—or rather, I could but dare'nt—so I dont know what to say to comfort you. All I can think of is that, if it had not been for what you were able to do for Ray, her death would have been quite dreadful. But because of your work it was immeasureably bettered for her, and you can know that you did not let her down, but, on the contrary, that you were splendidly useful to her. She was magnificent to send that photograph, and to attend to my affairs in her last letter. I did not in reality want the photograph a bit, but used it as an excuse for writing to her, because you had told me to be careful. I shall treasure her marvellous letter. She was one of the grandest women, and you helped her to be grand, and kept her so to the end. So that is all I can say.

I was thinking that you may want to get away for a bit. If you would like to come here, my purse will stand up to it. I can get you plenty of fishing (but it is too early on the W. coast) and some extraordinary archaeology—on which I expect you are, as usual, a better authority than I am, although I have been sweating at it for the past six months. If you came, it would mean staying in this hotel, because I am not getting that house at all. I told Ray about it, for something to tell her. But the hotel is clean and comfortable. If you preferred the Boyne, I could come back to Meath and we could stay with the McDonaghs. But the Boyne is bad this year, and I think you would find it dull in the mass. (One day on it is good: but more than one day gets tiresome.)

If you are not feeling like making up your mind about things at present, just leave this letter unanswered. I shall know by not getting an answer that you are not coming, and I have no plans of my own which would be interfered with either way. If you do feel like coming, I could— at a stretch—drive over to Dublin to meet you. The only trouble is that it would be straining my petrol ration a bit. I would prefer not to do so unless you were feeling badly. But if you were feeling badly, I would prefer to do so. The alternative is to catch a 'bus from Dublin to Ballina, or a train if there is such a thing, and I would be waiting in Ballina.

Another thing is that, if you do come, you can please yourself about bringing gear or not (fishing gear) as I have enough for two—even a telescope gaff! Most of the fish are slack at present, but they mend very well on this short river and are quite amusing to catch. The great thing would be for you to get out of the war atmosphere—among other things —for a little time. But there, I am trying to persuade you in my own interest. You know that to have you here, in whatever condition, would be the greatest blessing for me there could be, and that I shall love you whether you come or not. You are very lucky to have so many people to love you. When are the boys' holidays? I have a guess that they would not like to come here. But no doubt they are able to make up their own minds. Bring them or dont bring them. Answer or dont answer. Arrive heralded, with great accoutrements, or unheralded with nothing but what you stand up in. The river & the hotel are always here.

love from TIM

If you do come, you may need an exit permit: if you do need an exit permit, you may find they want to see this letter of invitation before they issue one—so keep it pro. tem. The second page would do.

Ray once told me, with some irritation, that everybody loved you.

N.B. Unless you are feeling in need of change, put off your visit until May, June or July (July for sea trout)—only come if you want immediate change rather than the best fishing.

April 13th, 1940   *Healion's Hotel, Belmullet, Co. Mayo*

Dear Bunny, ... That you call me now an Irishman is for the first time a source of pride rather than amusement to me. For I am beginning to understand them—us. I dont quite feel in a position to lecture you on the subject—you always turn out to know more about my own subjects than I do—but, in case you have not discovered these things, I want to say them. A. There is a gulf between Englishmen & Irishmen so wide that they might as well be Hottentots and Esquimaux.* Only the Irish realise this. Because they realise it, they have had to clear the English out. And the English *must* go: out of the six counties as well. It is not a matter of justice or anything of that sort. It is a matter of the Unconscious, or whatever you choose to call it.
B. Irishmen differ from Englishmen in being much more sensitive and apperceptive (as women differ from men) and are aware of more than the apparent logical facts in any given situation. I have never had such a

* Or MEN and WOMEN.

tonic for my sensitivity as I have had since I began to bargain for domi-
ciles, fishing rights etc. in the west. (They are much less Irish in Meath.)
A little while ago I suddenly woke up and realised that I was a blunt
bayonet among stilettos. The tip is to do nothing hastily. We are a nation
of Burleighs. The thing is to sit back and wait for the relevant facts to
turn up, and always to be sure that we live in the Unconscious much
more than the English do—a good place to live in. You will never know
when we are laughing at you, because we dont laugh. We sit, and watch,
and encourage you into still further and more ridiculous exhibitions, and
that is our form of humour. It is not exactly cruel humour. It is a form of
observation, the sort of detatched, replete, interested, uninfluencing
satisfaction with which I make a pet of a grass snake. You Englishmen are
as different from me as a grass snake is, and I can watch grass snakes for
hours. This is much nearer to a definition of Irish humour than all that
English bunk about 'pigs in the parlour and drakes that wont lay.' And
this results in the whole world of *appearances* being deceptive in the
west. We 'laugh at' or 'enjoy' people for being obvious, blunt, straight-
forward, honest, bluff, English. We call that being shallow. We prefer to
have an outer *appearance* of honesty, or simplicity, under which God
knows what darksome reptile-pits of interest and innuendo are abysmally
writhing. Simple Paddy, the man with a clay pipe in his hat and a pig on
the end of a string, is the stalking-horse of *appearance* under which there
prefers to advance a universe, an infinity of unfathomable depth. We
never tell the truth or accept any of your bourgeous simplifications. We
are rampantly primaeval, unrepentant, subtle, sensitive, feral. All the time
you are talking to us, we are dancing round you in ring after serpent ring:
we have thrid round every word before you have mouthed it. (I dont
mean in a Shavian way—not at all: he is just a windbag from the Pale. I
mean in a witch-like way, in a womanly way, in an unconscious way:
magically.) This is why we believe in magic, why we believe in changes
of shape. The hare is only a hare in appearance. Dont let's be shallow and
Anglo-Saxon and deceived by the hare. Let us sit back, tempt it with
poker-face to be more and more of a hare, until it finally gives itself away
in perfect exhibition, and then we shall see what it really is. This marvellous recognition of 'appearance' is why the Irish are the best actors in
the world,* why they believe in the supernatural (life is only an appearance), why they tell lies (truth is simply toadying to appearances), why

* and also the best poets.

they can give the most perfect sympathy to concealed sufferings. You see, they are *really* observant. They look beneath the appearances. And, since they do not live in the *apparent* world (where Englishmen make politics) it is why they are considered a hopeless nation for politics etc. You know how a woman often can't put what she wants to mean into our masculine words? That is the West. You can tell me about the political rights and wrongs of landlordism or Home Rule or anything else: but these are the rights and wrongs of a logical world, a male world, a world of appearances. We just dont live there. Unless your pal Churchill will try to deal with Ireland in the same way as he tries to deal with his wife, he will never deal with her. And my information is that illogical wives are not necessarily to be neglected. Your only hope is to stop patronising us —to stop that infuriating, dense, self-righteous shoulder-shrug with which you refuse to quarrel with a woman. The real Irish is incomparably more subtle, grown-up, aware than the Englishman. The real Irish is an almost terrifying giant: not a thing to be condescended to. We are savages. Are you civilised people better than savages? I think you are just duller.

C. The proximity of a great Empire like the British one has a bad effect on us. It gives our stupider and more eastern elements an inferiority complex. The fools in Dublin find themselves forced to measure themselves against the British yard stick (instead of chucking it out of the window, as they ought to do, and measuring themselves against their own subtly magnificent ancestors, the cannibals.) This means that the English-MAN is not only trying to rule the Erin*woman*, but that this female is rendered doubly dangerous by having an inferiority complex. She is twice more deadly than you wretched saxon males. Dont forget it. When you come over here you are *not* to condescend to us, you are *not* to make up some logical little theory about us, you are *not* to be in a hurry. We dont intend to be bustled or pitied or neglected. Just mind your p's and q's, my friend, and remember that you are in the presence with a P. Then sit down, be quiet, wait, be humble, try. Know that that simpleton, whom you have just rewarded with a sixpence, had previously read your heart like an open book. Recollect that his ancestors ate one another in historical times, and will again, I trust. Keep your mouth shut, and your eyes open. You shall see what you shall see.

D. Spontaniety of the Irish. The thing which Irishmen (like women) most loathe about the Saxon is his ...

66

April 22nd, 1940

Here my revelation ends. I was going to proceed with a long lecture about cold-bloodedness. Irishmen can fornicate or murder spontaneously (a sudden spasm ended by repentance) but Englishmen look in their bank accounts and decide that they can afford to keep a mistress in a business-like way. Such logical behaviour revolts an Irishman to the core. There was a lot more to say. But I got sleepy and went to bed, and, on reading it over after ten days, I wondered why I had ever bothered you with the subject in the first place. Thank you *very* much for the Irish books: one is just what I wanted.

Write to me again as soon as you know about coming to Ireland ... God, how I wish you really meant coming over for a long stay, so that we could be a little pacific together. It is difficult trying to be a creator in the present world, all alone.   love from TIM

My second Arthur volume, called The Witch in the Wood, is just out in England. If you have not already read it, dont, but wait till I can lend you a copy when you are in Ireland. I shall then ask you to do me a favour. The book has a few merits in parts, but there are many parts much too vulgarly farcical. I have read it through so often that I can no longer distinguish. I want to appeal to some man of decent feelings to blue-pencil the shoddy passages for me—particularly the Evelyn Waugh, P. G. Wodehouse bits. If you will do this for me, I will cut out all the parts you object to, and substitute others, before the book is finally published in one volume with the rest of the tetralogy. The present publication is only in the nature of artist's proofs. You need not take much trouble, but only read it and make bluepencil marks as you go along. Would you do that?

June 2nd, 1940   *Butts Intake, Low Row, Richmond, Yorkshire*

Dearest Tim, I heard on the wireless last night that restrictions are to be placed on going to Eire except for work of National Importance & I cannot imagine any visit there could be for any reason except pleasure.

So after so many delays my visit must be put off & my fishing also. I have wanted to write to you, but feared that we might start a quarrel over the Irish—you being so very Irish while England has my bones.

But I love Ireland, and of all the Irishmen (or women) I know, I love you the most. Much the most. Please write to me & tell me what you are discovering & that you are happy.

I only hope that Ireland will escape invasion now, as she did in the time of the Romans. Unfortunately Hitler has a predilection for attacking the weak & the Irish are not well-armed. There seems therefore a fair chance of your having an army of Germans to deal with before we have.

I resigned my commission in the R.A.F.V.R. for various reasons: I could not be sure of being allowed to be with Ray till the end, & it was impossible to tell how long she would live. Also the work seemed frustration & despair. Now we have this grand new Government I regret having left. But there is no going back & I am living up here now. I am trying to let Hilton furnished. Find me a tenant, do.

I scrubbed the floor this morning & the flagstones look so nice & clean. I make bread. I listen to the wireless set I bought at Ballina. I am, like you, trying to write as I think it is the most useful thing I can do. A book on Air power for the U.S.A. is in the Air. I wish it were on paper. I am beginning to feel rather old my dear Tim. So please write a friendly letter to a poor Englishman, who cannot help his lack of religion, of the Gaelic, etc, etc but who really loves you & sends his warmest love to you, to Brownie & to whatever hawk, badger, otter, or young girl you may be distressing her (Brownie) by having a flirtation with.   Yours BUNNY

Please tell me if I have not put enough stamps on—for the future, if any.

June 14th, 1940   *Healion's Hotel, Belmullet, Co. Mayo*

Dear Bunny, I wrote you a long letter on the 4th of this month, in answer to yours, but got dispirited with it and tore it up. These are hard times for writing letters in. I had rather make a bona fide speech than carry on these strained conversations à trois. If it goes on much longer I shall get hysterical, and begin including the censor in the conversation—you know, ostensibly to you, but half of it to him. And then one could speculate about the life and appearance of a censor, and what their private lives are like and all that. And finally madness. Damn the whole thing. One might as well be in the condemned cell, with a warden present: chewing gum, or cutting his finger nails. Byron seems to have stumbled on the proper attitude, when the Austrians were opening all his letters from Venice. He always put in something nasty about Austria. I have just been reading his letters, such a ruined man! But I wish I had his *go*. However selfish or

postured he is being, he does it with such a flaming passion for the thing—
the lie, or the treachery, or the pose—that you can't help loving him.
Warmed both hands before the fire etc. No, he sported in it like a sala-
mander. What a pity you did'nt come to stay in Erin. Know that last
sunday at Pollatomish—where you caught the sea trout last year—I had
three sea trout of 2 lbs, 4½ lbs and 5 lbs. Do you remember the lovely
quiet hills and sand-dunes there? Pollatomish (Ordnance Survey spelling)
means the Pool of Peace. I finished my 3rd volume of Mallory a few
weeks ago, and sent it off to America with a regular 'Ite, missa est.'
Please God it will get through all the censors and submarines eventually.
I put a St. Anthony stamp on it. If it turns out to be a good book, as I
suspect it may, it will be due to Ray. Some things she said at Sheskin
made me think in an improved way, and particularly to settle down to
read the Russians. It will be through them, but particularly through Ray,
that Guenever has turned out to be a living being. Ray was impatient
with me for not attending to my women: I have attended to Guenever
with something more than respect. With fear, almost. And I have put one
of Ray's remarks in verbatim. 'It is so fatally easy to make young children
believe that they are horrible.' (This à propos of Lancelot.) My next job
is to re-write The Witch in the Wood almost entirely, and then, after
vol. 4, I shall just saunter off to Olympus and sit down between Mallory,
Chaucer, Milton, Tennyson, with a cold shoulder for the Pre-Raphaelites.
Perhaps it was Parnassus. Why on earth do you want to write a book
about air power for America? I feel a personal sense of outrage that a
person like you should waste time with such trivialities. Write another
Grasshoppers, if you like, based on your ocean flights in war, but for
God's sake keep out of politics and statistics and such baseness. As a
matter of fact, what you *ought* to do—it may either enrage you to be told,
or make you madly laugh, for such are the proper reactions to the truth—
is to go on writing hundreds and hundreds of books like Beaney Eye.
You should take all the countless incidents of your life which make
significant wholes, and realise each separately in a little book. Siegfried's
line is the one for you: and you would do it just 73·04% better than
Siegfried. (I put in the decimal for the censor: I hope it will cause him
to soak the whole letter in invisible-ink-detector, and roast it, and
photograph it upside down, and count the vowels, and take away the
number he first thought of.) But that is what you ought to be doing, and
not writing about air power for America. In any case we have made the

air a disgraceful thing, even apart from the madness of wasting creative genius on controversy, or whatever books on air power are called ...

Ireland is in a most amusing condition just now. Everybody has noticed in the last 3 days that there is a war on: it is too ridiculous. We are going about making speeches in which we exhort each other to join the volunteers in order to protect the country from invaders. But we prefer to keep up the fiction that we dont know who the invaders are going to be—it might possibly be the English? the French? the Esquimaux? the Pawnees of Sarawak? No public figure has yet mentioned the Germans by name. Lord Dunsany said to me six months ago that we are like children on the beach at Howth, quarrelling about what shape our sand castle is to be, while all the time the tide is coming in. Last week the Senate was discussing Irish accents while the dail was arguing about a hospital which was not going to be built. I wonder if I wrote to you about Dunsany? I made friends with him when I was in Meath. He is not a patch on his wife, who remarked in a tone of acute nostalgia, à propos of a Daimler which they had once owned: 'Ah, that was a splendid car. It was simply riddled with bullets.'

Dear Bunny, I cannot write to you about anything sensible. The only thing is to pray that it will all be over eventually, and then we must meet and *bask* in a sea of sanity. How long is it since you laughed—I mean from amusement? The last time I laughed was in 1938, at my cottage, when a perfectly filthy little fox terrier who was persecuting Brownie (then also in season) piddled on an accumulator which was standing by the front door, thus making an excellent connection. Now I put funny bits in my letters to you, while everybody is being slaughtered every minute, but it is a mechanical habit. I dont suppose Voltaire laughed, when he said 'Les flammes, déjà'. How can I strike a right note when it is all done through a third party, or how write from the heart? I think the heart is the only thing worth anything in our failure of a race, and you can only open that to one person, or to everybody, but not to intermediate numbers. *Please* write to me soon. I am lonely. It is the unreality of this war, of this life, of this letter, which is killing everything. You say that you are feeling old, Bunny, and ask me to write that I am happy. Well, I am not. I feel mechanical. One makes the movements of speech and writing and fishing and all that—jokes too—but inside the thing which is moving about you might as well put up a notice saying Not At Home. There is a crack of light, however. I really believe that if we could have met, or should ever meet again, people would come back to the empty rooms for a minute, and talk out of the windows. I should look round, blow the dust off the furniture, and push the shutter across: At Home. Then we would be most surprised to find that we were there. It is something to look forward to.

I have found eight pairs of Phalaropes.
I have been writing poetry.
I am tea-total, thin, brown, bilious.
That is the end of the news.   love from TIM

September 16th, 1940   *Hilton Hall, Hilton, Huntingdon*

Dearest Tim, It is a long time since I wrote—but one lives such a curious waiting existence that it is hard to think of any continuous way of life, & to write letters needs that. (Yet people write on journeys, don't they?)

I haven't been in London since the bombs so can't tell you much. But I gather things are surprisingly normal. The general feeling is that the Germans are pretty helpless; that they will crack up within the next year. We are giving them a really bad time on the Ruhr. We are confident of victory & of smashing up these damned tyrannies, but I suppose they may have a shot at invasion. So many of the bombs of which I have first or second hand knowledge (3rd hand I exclude) are duds or missed by a mile or fell in open country. The woods behind my mother's cottage were thoroughly bombed—no doubt some German boy who thought 20 miles off London was good enough.

However to speak of other things—Since the end of the boys term I have been here keeping house for a lot of people—the big family with whom Ray & the boys had their holiday at Ventry have been here—a mother who is my oldest friend—a boy—3 little girls & a new baby. I have been cooking & washing up. There is also Angelica Bell, 22, whom I tease. She is rather like Brown, but more beautiful. Richard has left school & is going to King's this October—he will read for the Mathematical tripos. Will goes on at the same school.

We have had a lot of picnics on the Ouse & bathing. All these noisy little girls, squabbling, & jumping with their manes of hair flying behind them & the beautiful bodies lay the ghosts of the past & make it seem good that the trees should be so loaded with apples & pears & they gobble up peaches & wolf down roly poly puddings a yard long.

I am being rather indifferent about money & work & earning my living. Managing a house like this & arranging meals for 12 people—as we have sometimes been—has been enough work. Perhaps after they've gone, in a few weeks now—I shall be able to let this house. I may go for a time to Sussex as Angelica's family live there & I expect a good many people thereabouts have left their cottages empty as it's only 3 miles from the coast. However that depends on letting this house.

Well you see I have precious little news. England is very little changed but curiously enough the war has brought out the best in people. I like people more than I did in peace time. The things people are doing are worth doing. I haven't joined the Home Guard as I was moving about when it was being formed. Also I think this immense army of ours is really unnecessary. Armies & rifles are out of date in these days of bigger bombers. Isn't it astonishing the German Air Force should be so damned bad? Perhaps the Germans will conquer Ireland first, before they are smashed. I rather wish they would. Then perhaps the Irish would have something to compare us with & would become a really united people.

Here is a story to wind up with. Captain Hamish Hamilton (with whom I shared my aeroplane in the past) came to tea with his foreign wife bringing John Hayward. She looked out of the window & asked what the building in the garden was.

Hayward[1] (speaking rather thickly)

A dove-house.—& proceeded to give a little lecture on Huntingdon-shire dove houses. Mrs Hamilton stared in amazement & said

'It must be your imagination, John. What are they for. Why separate from the house.'

Hayward went on with his boring account—this was a farmer's one, but the one at the manor house at Fenstanton was a gentleman's & more elaborate etc.

Mrs Hamilton remained dumbfoundered.

'Is it—perhaps pour avoir un peu de tranquilité?' she asked.

She thought she was being told about Huntingdonshire Love houses it turned out.

It is almost as good as the trouble over the kidneys in a book written a long time ago by an English foxhunter called White.[2]

[[1] John Hayward, the crippled bibliographer, had been a friend of mine since he was up at King's College Cambridge. He spent the war in Cambridge in Lord Rothschild's house and Jamie Hamilton kindly brought him over to see me.—D.G.]

[2] See Chapter V, *Earth Stopped* by T. H. White (Collins, 1934).—D.G.]

When is your next instalment coming out Tim? We often think of you & talk about you & the household here reads all your books at once. When peace comes I shall celebrate it by fishing with you in the best stretch you can find anywhere. Love from us all to you & Brown & to any creature of the moment—you may have about you.

DAVID GARNETT

September 22nd, 1940   *Healion's Hotel, Belmullet, Co. Mayo*

Dear Bunny, Thank you for writing. I only hope you are right about the Germans cracking up in a year. Here the feeling is definitely more pro-British than it was twelve months ago, but still apathetic. The attitude is (1) 'If only they would settle', (2) 'Ireland cannot help by joining in any more than she can by staying out: indeed, she can probably help more by staying out.' We are quite powerless. The 'if only they would settle' attitude is weakening, as people realise that settlement with such a party is impossible. Hitler has helped the English a little by bombing a few ships and an Irish creamery: but there are still a few dyed-in-the-wool national-ists who hint that this was done by the English in disguise. Fortunately a bomber crashed, and was found to be full of Germans. I have rubbed it in what marvellously cunning people the English are, not only to steal German bombers and bombs for their outrages on Ireland, but also to train crews for them from childhood, so that they can only speak German. I am so Irish now that I can afford to be wildly pro-British. Also I know more Irish and European history than anybody except (if except) Dr. Hyde, so I carry all before me. Things are slightly troublesome personally, because I am always being reported to the police as a spy, but they can't make out whether I am a German or an English one, which confuses the issue. I get fits of depression about it, but not much. The boring part about it is that it hampers my movements. I can't, for instance, go out to my beloved Inniskea, because it would be thought I was re-fuelling a submarine etc., while even my hawks are interfered with. When I wave the lure round my head, a hundred zealous watchers are sure that it is semaphore. When the French fleet was still in the balance I thought there was a real chance of Ireland being invaded, so I joined our Local Defence Volunteers and offered my car. But soon it was discovered that the Belmullet Legion could only be one of two things. Either it could be the Legion minus White, or White minus the Legion. They did not want a

73

fifth column! So I was politely requested not to attend any parades. I offered to return my card etc., but was told that this was quite unnecessary. Now I am a non-playing member, and hope to have a medal at the end of the war, which is a good thing, as I dont have to attend any parades for it or do anything at all: surely the high-road towards my country's gratitude.

I dont think I have much private news to give you. My high spot this year was climbing Croagh Patrick in the great midsummer pilgrimage, and being mistaken on top for St. Patrick, by the Archbishop of Tuam. I will send you the full account of this one day, like my Letter from a Goose Shooter. It was a great moment, and I hardly like to put it jokingly, though the temptation is frightful. I suddenly found myself behind the altar, closetted with the Archbishop of Tuam and the Bishop of Galway. However, I really will not betray my pilgrimage. We were all in deadly earnest, and it is my duty to continue so. The only way I could fairly tell you the story would be at full length, in one of my typewritten extracts from diary.

Another good bit in my diary is the day I spent with a Nigerian Witch Doctor, curing the local peasants of rheumatism. Forgive me for calling them peasants: there is no correct descriptive word in English. I will send you this story also, one day. He was a genuine Cannibal, called Lewis Lascelles, and we became blood brothers. I fear he is in prison now.

I wonder whether this war ever will end, and whether you will come to Ireland then. I should so like to dose you with potheen and show you the Fairy Fire. You wont believe about the Fairy Fire unless you see it. I have looked back on a mountain lonelier than Sheskin, at midnight, and seen my footsteps behind me flaming as far as you could see. And I have a pair of pampooties (the most insanitary footgear in the world) and a bawneen. My dear Bunny, you cannot imagine how ridiculous I look. Particularly with the beard, which is, of course, one of my main claims to being a spy.

The grouse shooting has been hopeless this year, and the fishing not good. But I caught two salmon last week. I am going back to Doolistown, Trim, Co. Meath, on October 1st, to settle down for three months to the last volume of Arthur. Vol 3. comes out in America in October. It is better than Vol 2. but still not perfect. I have completely re-written Vol 2. (The Witch in the Wood) so that when they all come out together I hope it will be a good epic.

I am jealous of this Angelica Bell, 22.

Brownie is well and happy and much more beautiful than any woman could be. Besides, she does'nt talk. When she dies, I shall become a Cistercian.

Forgive me for writing such a long letter. Nobody has written to me for a month, so I find it difficult not to write at length in answer. It was a great moment to find your letter in the rack. This letter is shorter than it looks. We are only allowed by the censors to write on one side of the page—to save paper, I suppose.   love from TIM

If you are in Sussex, and happen to be near the place, my mother lives (I believe alone) at MOUNT PLEASANT, BURWASH, SUSSEX—unless she has been blown up. If you did happen to be near, you might drop in on her? There was some talk about whether she ought to migrate to the Buckinghamshire cottage. You might be able to advise her. I dont know the conditions, or even the regulations. She is a Witch, so look out, if you go. Probably she is a poor old witch by now, and probably I ought to be ashamed of myself. I am. But I have tried to get on with her, and every year or two I try again. We communicate by letter. I am in one of my ashamed periods, and that is why I am trying to use you as a cat's paw. But only if you are near, of course. She must be nearing seventy, and is alone. It is because she has chased away her husband, lover and son, by her own efforts. But this does not alter the fact that she is 70 and alone. And then there are the bombs.

I have omitted numerous passages in the war letters which follow and have marked the omissions by a few dots. The vast majority of these passages deal with plans for my coming to Ireland to fish, which proved impossible, and with fishing generally.

Other omissions deal with negotiations which I undertook at Tim's request with his then publishers Messrs Collins and his future publisher, Jonathan Cape. Many of these passages are vituperative and libellous and all of them show Tim to have been incapable of understanding the difficulties of English publishers in war-time.

December 6th, 1940   *Doolistown, Trim, Co. Meath, Eire*

Dear Bunny, ... Would you like to send me a Xmas present? (Doubtless not—but I would pay for it.) I can't get in all Dublin a decent box of pastels. Do you think there would be any left in England? They are made in France, by Lefranc, Paris. If I can't get any, I must stop drawing. I have got very good at it lately, that and knitting. And another thing— this you have *got* to do for me, by every moral law there is—will you or will you not, once and for all, tell me name and title of this mythic work which you alledge to have read about Mallory having raided a convent? I think Mallory himself may be coming into my fourth volume, as a character, and obviously I *must* know. You planted the filthy doubt, which has never given me a single night's rest since, and it is up to you to do something about it. If you do not, I shall put the Great Curse of Ireland on you, which I learned by accident in the West: it is infallible, frightful, brief, final and hideously suggestive. Nor can it be recalled. And another thing. So far as I can see, my fifth volume is going to be all about the anatomy of the brain. It sounds odd for Arthur, but it is true. Do you happen to know, off hand, of a pretty elementary but efficient book about brain anatomy *in animals, fish, insects etc*? I want to know what sort of a cerebellum an ant has, also a wild goose. You are the sort of person who would know this. Now dont forget there are four things in this letter: the Irish holiday, the pastels, Mallory and the cerebellum. All here just wags away as ever. Nobody knows where Greece is, or which side she is on. The Pope is praying for peace, is our latest war news. It would do you such a lot of good to come in February. I have a dozen of claret, a dozen of burgundy and a dozen of madeira. The fire crackles, Brownie hunts mice, the salmon are spawning, and here we are in the 18th Century. If you came, we could go and pull Lord Dunsany's leg—it is a flexible one. And we could go and talk nonsense in Dublin, where the best nonsense is talked fastest. I am sure you ought to come out of your bomb-showers, and that you would enjoy it as much as I would enjoy, for a little, to be in them. You will say the last part of this sentence is nonsense, unless you think about it. love from TIM

December 16th, 1940   *Claverham Farm, Berwick, Sussex*
Dear Tim, I forget when I wrote last—but not from here. Your letter with its appeals & threats came this morning & I am hastily setting about your behests ...
(3) I have ordered a box of medium pastels to be sent to you from Lechertier Barbe, Jermyn Street. Let me know if they arrive safe.

(4) Sir Thomas Mallory: ... Well ... well. I haven't, I think, read Prof. Kittredge *Who Was Sir Thomas Mallory?*. But I read a pamphlet, or a paper in a learned publication, which I found at the London Library, which was concerned with his birthplace. At all events what sticks in my mind was that during the Wars of the Roses Sir Thomas was a bit of a freelance, that he raided a nunnery. The girl he was after was not specified. And I fancy he robbed a bit & anyhow was stuck in prison for ages which turned him to reading about Arthur & writing his book. If the London Library has not been bombed when I next go to London, & if the books have not been buried, I will discover the sources of my information.

But curse me at your own peril, as I shall be useful later on, & if I wither away or turn into an Ogham inscribed stone, you will have lost a friend.

So much for you—now for my news. October was a mad month at Hilton. I spent it in showing ridiculous people (at least 25 parties) over the house which I was trying to let. My word, it was funny. I was horrified by the possible tenants, & the tenants were so horrified by Hilton Hall that they fled. Finally it became a race between letting it & having it filled with children whom I should have had to look after. Indeed I only stopped its being filled up, by saying it *was* let. At the last moment I got an excellent Widow Sidgwick (whose husband was the publisher) who beat me down in price & seems an ideal tenant otherwise. Richard went over to see her after she moved in & found such mediaeval confusion that he expected to see rushes on the floor, which was actually covered with wicker baskets occupied by numbers of dogs & babies, for the widow's sons & daughters are married. Crucifixes & Communist tracts testify to a mixture of credulities and religions, & one of her lap-dogs travelled to Hilton Hall in her Naval Son's full-dress cocked hat.

Having let Hilton furnished at 3 gns a week I had to find somewhere else to live. As all the furniture vans in England were streaming from s.e. to n.w. it seemed reasonable to go in the reverse direction & I have therefore taken an empty farmhouse in the flat land in sight of the Downs. It is not bad—lonely with no village or cottage near & a large pond & 2 small ones. Angelica is living with me: her family are about 4 miles off. Richard & William are here now; Richard arrived resplendent in purple scarf & socks which signify that he rows in the King's College boat. He is pleased with himself because it came in 13th out of 43.

He has taken easily to Cambridge & enjoys it immensely, is reading mathematics.

He will be 18 in a few weeks time & is curiously more grown up than I was at his age. Will is flying aeroplanes of his own construction, while the Germans fly ones of theirs some 20,000 feet higher up. We have had very beautiful air battles—one sees parties of enemy aircraft—sometimes 30 or more, come in, & headed off by small parties of our own—often so high up that the naked eye can only see the aircraft when they wheel & catch the sun ...

My only first hand experience was travelling with the lorry which bought some furniture from Hilton. We set off back as darkness was falling & drove across London—altogether 120 miles back, in pitch darkness during a pretty hot air raid. As we approached London guns & bombs lit the place up like violent summer lightning. The difficulty is of course being frequently turned off the main roads to avoid craters or time bombs & wandering in the dark mazes of side streets. One never knows what one will find—Pulling up short at the sight of a taxi which had plunged head first into a vast hole, one descends to ask the way & is lucky to find an old lady taking her dog out ... before retiring for the night. In daylight things are very different. The shopping crowd still surges along Oxford Street.

Well—what am I doing? Richard is binding books—Angelica is doing pictures of St Michael & of the Virgin for the local church, the interior of which is being decorated—I am digging the garden & I mean to work —I must work. But an invincible repugnance makes me shun all effort. I think I have only been saved from some sort of collapse by living with the young. You did it at Stowe of course—but that was different.

By the way Richard has found an admirer of yours John Fay at King's.

I say—about fishing. I'll come & fish with you as soon as its possible. If we knock out Italy this winter, this may mean in the summer of 1942. Well I'll find out about Malory & write again soon. Let me hear all your news.   Yours with love BUNNY

1941

Dear Bunny, A splendid box of pastels arrived today, with 9/6 marked on them, and no bill. So I am assuming that you paid for them and sending ten bob, which I am sure will not cover the postage. Thank you for troubling with my little things. I traced the pamphlet about Mallory, but can't obtain it: it was itself a contribution to some learned journal, so I shall have to wait until the B. Museum is functioning again, and go there and read it. I can't think that it was more than conjectural ... Your letter about keeping sane by living with the young made me very happy: it was the only thing to do, I mean the only good thing. If Will has not gone back to school, will you ask him about carrion crows in Ireland? I said at Sheskin that there were none, but was shouted down by Will, whom I believed implicitly. But I still havn't seen any, only jackdaws, rooks, hoodies, ravens and choughs. Is Will quite sure? I wonder what Angelica is like. It is difficult when you can only picture a piece of green stuff off a cake. Was she the person you saw the pigeon with, which you wrote about in the Statesman before the war? Do you still write for it? Does it still come out? If the censorship is at all strict, it must be frightfully cramping for their grumbles. How is your book about air power going? I am still cross with you for writing it, and you are still cross with me for being cross with you, but that doesn't alter the fact that your proper duty towards Man is to go on writing more and more Beaney Eyes. People dont realise how frightfully interesting their own lives have been, if they would only look back. Just because something has happened to them, they assume that it is the sort of thing which happens. But everybody's life has at least a dozen of the most extraordinary situations. You would think that mine has been a tedious existence, and so did I, until I examined the matter dispassionately, and found that I had been (a) arrested by the fascists, on suspicion of trying to murder Mussolini, (b) not arrested by the English, for tying a donkey to Rudyard Kipling's front door, (c) shot at by an unseen assassin in a London fog with a ·22, (d) mistaken for S. Patrick by an archbishop. At my prep. school I once pushed a boy out of a first floor window—he broke his leg— and when I was about 24 I committed, in one night, burglary, assault, trespass, breaking and entering, and sacriledge. And all this does not touch the fringe of what must have happened to you, which if you truthfully savoured it over as in Beaney Eye, would be read some centuries after all these bloody aeroplanes had blown themselves to hell. However, it is you that writes the books, not me. By the way, can you tell me if anybody has written a famous book about war? I dont mean Clausewitz—how to fight it—but somebody like Sir James Frazer. I want a book (not fiction, like Tolstoi) about why people fight and all the sidelights and statistics. André Maurois mentions a Frenchman called Lapouge, whom he states to have written something of the sort. Have you read it? Has anybody written a definitive book about War, like Frazer's about magic? Do be a dear, Bunny, and send a p.c., if you can put me on to anything worth buying. My Death of Arthur is going to end up as a treatise on war. No news here. Love to you, Bunny, and to this green person off the cake.

from TIM

February 17th, 1941   *Claverham Farm, Berwick, Polegate, Sussex*
Dearest Tim, I was delighted to get your letter exhorting me to write about my own life & giving me such good reasons. So I sat down to write a letter which I never finished. It was entirely about crows. Since writing it I have discovered something really important & not solely out of a book, but with a putrid & putative crow in hand.

Let scholasticism come first:

Don Quixote who you will remember was well read (went mad from it) said:

'You may as well say there was no Hector or Achilles nor a Trojan War nor twelve peers of France, nor a King Arthur of Britain, who is now converted into a crow ...' Pt. I Bk IV Ch. 22.

In The Amateur Poacher, p. 44, R. Jefferies says Don Q stated the English will not kill crows & surmises this is a mistranslation for Rook or Raven, as we have always killed crows. Had Jefferies never eaten Rook pie?

Probably you know what Arthur became—perhaps a Cornish Chough.

However as regards Ireland: Carrion crows are rare vagrants: bred in Mayo in 1890, interbred with Hoodies in Dublin 1935.

It is obvious to a geneticist that Hoodies & Carrion Crows are the same species—simply a unit colour character present or absent. They interbreed freely. The reason they do not do so more is because as Mrs Cornish wife of the Provost of Eton remarked to a schoolboy having tea at the Provost's: 'Pity the fate of the Carrion Crow. He is mated for life.'

It is to be inferred that she was speaking of her husband. Waterton used to make carrion crows into pies which he gave to his guests saying it was pigeon pie. So much for scholasticism. Now for the bird itself.

William trapped several rooks & what we thought was a crow in the holidays. The crow was ringed, let go & shot stealing chicken food. The dead bird was brought to me. It was a Juvenile Rook. Juvenile Rooks are identical with Carrion Crows, or at any rate with Juvenile Carrion Crows until towards the end of their first winter. The only certain distinction is that the 2nd primary of the crow is shorter than the 6th whereas it is longer in the Rook. They have same nasal bristles, feathered face etc.

Between Jan. & May the young rook slowly goes bald under the chin & round the base of its bill & cheeks.

So if William saw carrion crows in Ireland they were rooks & if you see any they will be rooks too.

You say nothing about salmon, or of shooting in Ireland. Yet you have Brownie, gun, & rods. How many snipe have you shot & eaten? The salmon must be coming up the rivers. As for me, I have been writing The Air War & have almost finished what I can do alone out of my head. I am now going to the Air Ministry for help. If they give it, I shall try & finish the book in two months, so that the Americans can publish in the early summer.

On the other hand the Air Ministry may be aghast at what I've said & veto it.

However if I finish it I may possibly try & get permission to visit you in Ireland, if you have not been conquered by Germany by then. I fancy my visit, if it takes place, would be in May. It is possible the Air Ministry may want me back, but the book would have to come out first so as not to be the work of a serving officer. But this is all very doubtful. Richard has been sitting on King's Chapel Roof waiting for bombs & reading Swift's Instructions to Servants. Well Tim, I long to see you. Please write again soon & tell me your mood & that you sometimes catch a fish.

It gives me a vicarious thrill to imagine your minnow swinging across the water & going plonk into the Boyne.

Angelica sends greetings to Brownie.   Yours ever BUNNY

Ash Wednesday [1941]   *Doolistown, Trim, Co. Meath, Eire*

Dear Bunny, ... Thanks for your data about carrion crows. Don Q's remark about Arthur shall go in the book. As for hairy beaks and length of primaries, I never noticed any carrions flying close enough for me to measure them. My own method of distinction is simple, if crude. When, in England, I saw *not more or less than two* big rooks in a field, I said they were carrion crows. Also the carrion lumbers slightly in his flight. Have you seen any Great Northern Divers lately? (Yah.) And I may add that it was not only William who hooted me off the stage when I said there were no carrions in Ireland. The whole family of you rose up from the table and belaboured me with tea pots for the space of five hours on the subject. I now bask a little in your modified and evasive apology.

I am beginning to like the idea of your Air War.

Just say the word to yourself—Killaloe. It is as nice as the word.

On the other hand there is Trim—but April, April, April.

love from CORPORAL TRIM

Tuesday April 1st, 1941   *Claverham Farm, Berwick, Sussex*

Dear Tim, ... Virginia Woolf committed suicide last Friday. She was Angelica's Aunt & we saw a lot of her. She was ill, felt she was going mad & could not face it. She had been out of her mind once before, many years ago.

Angelica & she were particularly devoted to each other and they kept up a perpetual flirtation & teasing of each other which was very charming. She wrote a few letters—went down to the river & her body has not been recovered—probably never will be as it is close to the sea.

Another death is that of Ray's mother—but that is not to be regretted. She did not expect it, & it saved her from a miserable illness ... I feel very unsettled. I hate doing so little in this war. But I did less in the Air Ministry on balance than I shall have done if this book sells & has a good effect. However it is a very bad book—a patchwork badly put together & badly written.

It has been raining all day today so my letter reflects the grumpiness one feels after hearing the rain driving for 12 hours on the windows. By the way a few nights ago I saw a most extraordinary thing. My first impression was that it was the end of London. There was a terrific grey-green glow over an angle of 30 or 40° to the North rising above a bank of clouds. Hundreds of distant shafts of light arose, like distant search-lights. Suddenly I realised it was not Man's work—but the Northern Lights. I had never seen it before & it was wonderful. I fancy you went to the Arctic in the middle of summer & won't have seen the Aurora Borealis there.

Well—I will let you know directly I have finished my book. I don't know whether I shall bring Angelica—probably not. It would probably be easier in every way not to, & in any case it may be difficult to bring her.

I shall be glad when I get my book out of the way. Love to Brownie

Yours affectionately BUNNY

P.S. This letter has been hanging about for a week in the hopes I would write a more agreable one. But alas—no.

June 4th, 1941   *Claverham Farm, Berwick, Sussex*

Dear Tim, Forgive me, please, for not writing before. I have been think-ing of you a great deal, because of your letter & your book which I have received and read. It is the most *profound* of your books: the only one which touches serious things & reveals you yourself except for passages in England Has My Bones. (How I wish England had more than them—your living presence.) I was immensely impressed by it & also the surprise which a revelation of anybody's character gives, has been with me a lot. Why?—Why?—That is what I have been asking myself. By which I mean why is what seems so straight and moral a path, difficult, tortuous, & impossible for you.[1]

However that is not the question. What you want to know is how it compares with Sword in the Stone & Witch in the Wood.

Well—Sword in the Stone is like Wood Magic. It is poetry: it is for children & we are all children & happiest when anyone can make [us] believe we are. Sword in the Stone is genius in a dozen episodes & is a superlative Punch Christmas when it isn't genius. The Witch in the Wood is sometimes good—nearly the real thing. Often padding. The Illmade Knight is *serious*. It is one of those complicated things—a revelation—a sermon for a few—hidden under a camouflage. The bookjacket set me thinking who you are *really* like. Perhaps you won't be pleased if I say the Kipling of your generation. There is the same curious shyness, secret

[1 My reference was to Lancelot and Guenever's love and not the war.—D.G.]

83

quality in his best work. The same damnable quality of genius. The difference is that Kipling was VULGAR—perhaps only because of his date & that you have not that taint. Also Kipling was a beastly sort of cad, whereas you are a serious person.

That's enough about your work. Your illness is more important. Yet I have faith in your size & vitality. If you go blind you will be a Homer. But I would rather you remained a wise, wily Odysseus. So do, for goodness sake, stop drinking Poteen or whatever you did to make yourself so ill.

My news is a spider's web of trouble with a few flies in it.

My book—five months sweat—came back PASSED BY THE CENSOR today. It goes on the next clipper & $2,000 comes back to me. It is, you know, a technical work written because I can't stop thinking about the Air War & can't take a hand in it. Nor can I say anything really worth saying. However I'll send you a copy & if they go on bombing Dublin when they are looking for Belfast, I dare say some of you Irishmen will be taking an interest in the subject.

Besides that I am writing a pamphlet on the Battle of Greece. It is rather like a description of why one lost the game of chess one played with Capablanca after giving him a Queen and two Knights. As a matter of fact we did damned well in Greece. Indeed we did as well as the Greeks & no words could say more. It has been most interesting doing it as the War Office people laid all their cards on the table. My trouble is that I never was in Greece & that it is impossible to make military movements seem other than moves in a game. They are not. My chief trouble is that I'm being turned out of this farm in a fortnight & have nowhere to go & lots of furniture to store.

I suppose your mother doesn't want to let her house—or know of any empty houses near?

Richard says he has done badly in Part I Maths Tripos. He is rowing in May races & I posted him a pair of purple socks to wear on the occasion.

I have another small job on hand after Greece and by the time I have found a new house & moved into it, the boys will be on their holidays. My visit to Ireland must be put off, anyhow till the autumn. I so much want to see you.   Yours affectionately, BUNNY

Dear Bunny, You have written me such a lovely letter that I cannot help answering it by return of post. Indeed, I dont feel unpleased when you compare me to Kipling—only shy, because I know it could not be true. Puck of P's Hill (which is within sight of my mother's cottage by the way) Rewards & Fairies and Kim are three of the greatest books in the world. I stood outside the hospital in London, where Kipling was dying, on the night he died. I just stood there for a bit. I dont know why, and can't say that I felt anything in particular: or at least it was not a feeling with any known label. It was one of these modern feelings. 'Am I being dramatic? What is death anyway? There isn't any God. Why stand here? etc. etc. etc.' I must have looked at the great barrack of a wall half resentfully, also blankly, confusedly, self-consciously: I was thinking of myself more than of the little beetle-browed dusky man snuffing it somewhere inside. But the fact remains that I stood. There were no other people in the side street and I had not gone there on purpose. He was a great and good man. Did you know that I was born in India and could speak Hindustani before I could speak English? You probably have to be like that to understand Kim properly: it is one of the books which is absolutely true to the feeling of a place. To explain what I mean I must say that it is the *opposite* of books about Ireland by Dorothea Conyers and people like that. God, if I thought I was like Kipling I would hop round the room on my hands.

I have written to my mother, asking if she knows of local cottages. She would be most unlikely to let her own. The place—which reeks of everything in Pook's Hill (a local hill) and Rewards & Fairies—is one of the most beautiful valleys in Sussex—in the Weald—but I really cannot advise you to put yourself in my mother's power by proximity. You wonder why straight & moral paths are difficult, tortuous and impossible for me. Go and see my mother. However, I have written to her. Every time I have to write to her even, it is like being mildly crucified.

Now Bunny, I am going to be absolutely selfish, because I want your help. If you had not written so much about the 3 books, I would not have liked to bother you, and you need not answer this for months, so long as you answer it in the end. I want to be told frankly about The Witch in the Wood.

The position is that the final epic, which will be called The Once & Future King, will have five books. (1) The Sword in the Stone, boyhood and animals. (2) The Witch in the Wood—that bloody bitch Morgause. (3) The Ill-Made Knight—Lancelot & the middle years. (4) The Candle in the Wind—final bust up with the sons of Morgause—none to blame except because of her—ending with the aged Arthur weeping and smashed on the eve of his last battle with Mordred. (5) The Book of Merlin.

The last book, number five, is, I hope, the crown of the whole. The epic theme is War and how to stop it (I stand on Tolstoy's shoulders, as G.B.S. claimed to do with Shakespeare's, in this respect) and number five solves the problem. You see, the Round Table was an anti-Hitler measure. It began by trying to control Might-as-Right in individuals, by harnessing it to worldly ends: then, in the Grail, it tried to harness it to spiritual ends: then, in Book 4, The Candle in the Wind, it recognises that Might-as-Right must be quashed altogether, instead of harnessed, and Arthur turns over to abstract justice—he invents 'Law' (out of Canon, Roman & Customary) and is prepared to sacrifice both Lancelot & Guenever to the ideal. This works, so far as Might in the individual is concerned, but, no sooner has he got it settled like that, than Might in the congeries, collective Might, War, pops up behind him. All his life he was trying to dam a flood which broke out in new places. This book brings him face to face with the final theme, and ends with him broken.

Now we come to Book 5, a frightfully tricky bit of writing because *it goes back to the animals* of Book 1. The trouble is not to let it be puerile. I have resisted the temptation to turn him back into a boy by magic, but he has *got* to visit two more kinds of animal, Ants & Wild Geese, which he does, and I have tried to keep him on the level of the great king he has become. Merlyn and all the animals of Book 1 are in the badger's sett of Book 1 (which turns out to be the hole into which Nimue put him) and they explain about War from the biological point of view. At the end, having discovered to my own satisfaction all about Might by glancing at the 250,000 other species beside man which have had to face the problem, Arthur goes back to his battle and comes to his end. I insinuate in the last paragraph that he was not taken to Avalon or buried at Glastonbury, but that he is back in the badger's sett, waiting to come out and help us with Merlin and all of them, if we ever let the time come. See legends of tumulus at Bodmin—where I situate the sett.

Now, Bunny, if The Ill-Made Knight was at all good, it is because you & Ray made me think straighter at Sheskin. You may have spotted the quotation from Ray which ends Chapter 10, about the young children, and the remarks about Anna Karenina, because you made me read the Russians. I have read the whole pack of them now, and, as you have noticed, they have done me good.

Well, you have got to help me about The Witch in the Wood.

Morgause is the villain of the piece. (I may mention that she is my mother.) This is why I have had such awful difficulty with her. I have already written that book four separate times, sometimes taking her seriously, sometimes trying to palm her off under a patter of farce. I shall have to write it again.

What I want to know is: Can I take it as it stands and cut it down and make it more dignified (all through the epic I am turning 'donts' into 'do nots' and chastening my style) or must I wholly re-write it with Morgause as a serious, darksome witch?

God, how I wish I had you here, and could make you read the later books and explain the trouble.

You see, Bunny, I have suddenly discovered that I am doing what Geoffrey of Monmouth, Mallory, Spencer, Hughes, Purcell, the Pre-Raphaelites, Tennyson etc. did and what Milton thought of doing. They called it The Matter of Britain. You get even the most extraordinary unlikely people meddling with it—Aubrey Beardsley and your friend Don Quixote for instance. A man who copied out the Morte d'Arthur in morse code would still be an important literary figure. It is the theme which makes it so.

This is why I am sweating myself blind—by the way, my eyes are better—trying to get it straight. It is odd, but I feel responsible to *it*, not to myself.

Can you tell me anything about The Witch in the Wood? Anything. Not compliments, for God's sake.

Mordred, who finally broke the Table, was her son.

Gawaine, who helped to break it because he was stupid, cross, clannish but fundamentally decent, was her son.

Agravaine, a swine, was her son.

Gaheris, only stupid, was her son.

Gareth, a dear, was her son.

Agravaine murdered her, because he found her in bed with Sir Lamorak at the age of 70.

The clan also murdered Lamorak—and they had murdered his father Pellinore.

She was a celt from Cornwall, and her husband was a celt from Scotland. (In the serious re-writing I was thinking of doing an immense amount of stuff about the gaelic blood—the feral, subtle, treacherous Pict.)

All her sisters were witches—a common trait in female gaels.

Damn! Obviously I can't explain in a single letter. God bless you, Bunny. My mother will write direct if she knows of anything.

love from TIM

P.S. I was courting a barmaid at the time of Kipling's death, I now remember. I once made her blush for 10 minutes without stopping—but she didn't wriggle. Stood outside the hospital on way to her bar. Strange mixture.

P.P.S. Yes. Our reaction to having Dublin bombed has been quite funny.

P.P.P.S. Good about your Air War, & Greece. Thank God they have the sense to get it done by genius.

August 11th, 1941   *Garden Cottage, Alciston, Berwick, Sussex*

Dear Tim, You will think me a bad friend since you asked me to give you advice & I have neglected to reply. I told you I had to move & I may have said I was busy writing things. When I got this place I found so much to do that I continually have put off the re-reading of your books necessary. Today it has rained and I have read the Sword in the Stone. Unfortunately I brought the presentation copy which is English & has the Anthropophagi chapter & not Morgan Le Fay which is much better.

I will not give you my advice until I have read the Witch in the Wood & the Ill Made Knight again. But here is what Richard says: Much of the Witch is very good & the book can be cut by about one half. The Ill Made Knight however is *too compressed*. It has too much Malory & not enough of your solidity. You have not visualised it, or built it up out of your own experiences to the same extent. He therefore wants you to expand the Ill Made Knight & cut the Witch in the Wood.

We will send you our respective views on what should be cut & what expanded shortly. But I think I agree with Richard's thesis—that some expansion is needed to maintain a certain unity of treatment & also for its own sake. There is not enough of *you* he says in the Ill Made Knight— if I repeat it, it is because he does.

Well—now I will break off to tell you of my own life. I am getting heartily sick of Sussex. However here I am. This place is a bungalow, about 20 years old or more, thatched & spacious & built of weatherboards outside & asbestos within. There is a studio next door. I was told I should have the whole place but there is a family next door in the studio who wont go.

The landlord tried to turn them out—so I am regarded with hostility as an evicting interloper. The man is a loud mouthed blusterer of the usual Sussex labourer type to-day. There is a Germanic stupidity in them. The woman plays the wireless all day & scolds her children—and I feel depressed. I also realise that if they are got rid of, the studio will be commandeered by the army.

Meanwhile there is no room for Angelica to paint or to put up a visitor, or to store beehives.

We have bees—five little lots which I am trying to feed up. We have also 2 British Blue Shorthaired Cats—Brother & Sister descended from the famous Champion Gentleman of Henley etc. He is called Carrabas & she is called Gray-malkin. In a few days we shall have fowls bad luck to them—which is the best way of getting eggs.

I have been working furiously in the garden & now am getting the place really ship shape—& shall have some vegetables for the winter.

I dont know when my book[1] will be out—any time now. I left out the chapter on the Russo-Finnish war since it was not very polite to our new Allies. I will send you the book when it appears—or have it sent which I believe is now a necessary precaution taken by the Censorship.

Richard failed in his Part I Maths Tripos. That was because he was inspired with an enthusiasm by his maths master but not taught how to attack his subject. At Cambridge he was too much alone & rowed & enjoyed himself, & was only 17. I think he will now leave Cambridge & go into an Aircraft Factory until its time for him to be called up— probably next July. He will then either be exempted, or easily go into the R.A.F. with the sort of knowledge which will make him useful. There is a hope his maths will get him into the Research designing dept.

William shot a woodpigeon stone dead with an airgun slug through the head the other day & we had pigeon-pie with some beef added to it. A good shot.

I am thinking of writing a play which has taken shape in my mind.

[1 *War in the Air. September 1939 to May 1941* (Chatto and Windus, 1941). —D.G.]

Unfortunately I don't know how—but I suppose I shall eventually find out if I try. It is a very good subject—& like some of Pirandello's plays has a double subject—the drama of the present develops by unfolding a drama of the past, about which opinions change. Changing attitudes to that alter the whole relationship of people today—It is called The Blood Test[1] & the subject is whether two young people are brother & sister or not. By the time they have proved they are not, they don't care a damn for each other, having found out too much about each other's characters & practically shattered the whole older generation who have been put through third degree inquiries ...

However I won't describe more. I went fishing in the estuary of the Cuck with the boys the other day. We caught plaice the size of one's hand (smaller) but the mullets & Bass were not there. I shall come to Ireland directly the war is over I think, for a holiday. I think my morale is rather bad just now—having finished my various jobs—& the War going away from us. But really things go well. Far better than one would have thought possible. Hitler has doomed himself—but we must see the doom is a comprehensive one.

Do write about yourself. Love to Brownie.

Yours affectionately, BUNNY

August 28th, 1941   *Doolistown, Trim, Co. Meath, Eire*

Dear Bunny, It was nice to have a letter from you, and to hear about your projected play. It sounds much more like what you ought to be doing than writing about air wars—rather like the kind of situation which might have developed in the later life of that unfortunate kid at the end of NO LOVE, if his father's life had been a bit more promiscuous. But of course I ought not to begin guessing from the scanty sentences you put in your letter. The only thing that worries me a bit is that it has got to be a play. There is such a lot of non-literary hanky-panky in the theatre, such as knowing when to end Act II with a situation which will keep the audience interested through the boozing interval, or leaving the whole climax to the kind of grimace which the leading lady makes in Act IV. I tried to write my fourth Arthur volume as a play, but all competent authorities, such as Noel Coward & R. C. Sherriff, assured me that it was childish, which it was. It seems to me that play-wrights are not

[1 This play was written in October, 1967.—D.G.]

really writers. Look at Browning and Byron etc. producing utter tripe. For that matter look at Shakespeare—did he succeed as a novelist? However, you are the least advisable man I know, so I daren't risk putting you in a passion, and anyway you may succeed. I hope so.

This letter of yours. Richard on the Ill-Made Knight is good, and I will try to do something about it i.e. will go through it, inserting bubbles of visualisation here and there, like putting the fizz in soda. When he says that there is too much Mallory and too little me I dont think he is being quite fair. Malory states the actions and some few of the conversations, but he does not pursue the motives and characters behind them, which is what I tried to do. In any case I never pretended to be more than a foot-note to Mallory: it is a kind of literary criticism of him. As for the Witch in the Wood, I have cut it down by ¾ and altered her character by ceasing to satirise her—whether for good or ill, I dont know. She is a straight witch now, and above all a Gael.

I have finished books 4 and 5. All that is necessary is to get the new Witch typed out, insert some visualisation in the Knight, and possibly wait until I have a cable from America to acknowledge receipt of the sum total. I may be able to get round the last of these hindrances some-how: by leaving copies with a bank or something, with instructions to send them to America at tri-monthly intervals. Unfortunately there are only 3 copies. In any case I shall be free by Xmas, possibly much earlier. Then I want to do something about the war.

Bunny, can you help me about this? What ought I to do?

I offered services to the British Council before the war and to the Ministry of Information at its outbreak, thinking that I could combine those services with finishing Arthur, but they did not want me. Damn this ink. Also I joined our local Home Guard on the collapse of France, but that is not a serious occupation. On the face of it I ought to try for some intellectual employment in England, though these seem difficult to get without being the nephew of a duke. Can you get me anything to do which is not utterly frivolous? In the Air Ministry or for propaganda or anywhere? If you can't, I shall go to Belfast and volunteer as a gunner on merchant ships. There is a decent lack of the stupid forms of discipline in that line, as the gun teams are units of three men with no officers to bugger them about. My attitude is that I refuse to be a half-and-half: for instance, to take a commission in the army or something like that. If people will not use razors as razors then I think the razor has a right to refuse to be a lawn-mower. It has a right to insist on being a steam-roller. Either I must have a serious occupation as a razor, or I will be quite insane as a garden-roller-able-seaman-cum-lewis-gun.

In case you can think of any useful work, here are some things about me: I am 36, I took a First at Cambridge, I once could speak Italian rather fluently and fly an aeroplane very badly indeed, I am a best seller in America where I have sold getting on for a quarter of a million books (believe it or not—by the way, have you seen Walt Disney's Fantasia? I can't see it here. I think the prehistoric sequence in it comes from the Sword in the Stone. Does it?) I have broadcast and been serialised by the B.B.C., have a contract with W. Disney and I am in this year's Who's Who. Also I suppose I know a good deal about Ireland, if there were any honourable employment in that direction.

Failing rational work, as I say, I shall just suit my own inclinations and go on convoys.

The only thing which will hurt like hell is leaving Brownie. It will hurt so much that I must not think about it.

I was rather sorry to hear about Richard's tripos. On the other hand it may be a good thing. Unbroken success in early youth—believe the schoolmaster—generally fizzles out, while the people who get a smack in the eye when young often come back terrifically. Besides, he was finding out about the physical lines, rowing and so forth, particularly about enjoying himself, which is the most important branch of education. Perhaps it was the best thing he could have done. Is he eight foot high yet? It is infuriating to see the race improving like this! It makes me jealous of the brutes. And why should they know more than I do?

Are you stuck in that cottage, or could you escape to Burwash stile? Your only hope, if stuck, is to fight the neighbours tooth and nail. They will consider you an upper class aggressor whatever you do, so you may as well be one. It is what they would prefer. Put on your hob-nail boots, and grind the faces of the poor.

By the way, I have another subject to bother you about (or you could bother Angelica) and that is:— Do you remember an oil painting in the National Gallery which shewed some 15th century knights in armour having a battle? I want it for the end papers of Arthur. Their spears were all beautifully parallel. I have a visual recollection of it, but can't remember the artist's name, date or whether it had a title.[1] It must be 13th, 14th or

[1 Obviously Uccello.—D.G.]

early 15th century armour (plate or early middle period) as I do not want the Bayeux-tapestry kind of mail, nor the later gothic or milanese. In the Ill-Made Knight there is a little sketch of a knight dated 1380 or so, who is more or less what I want. I would like a splendid battle scene, as the epic is really a book on war, and how to prevent it. Also it is a book on the next peace. I think I shall have to send presentation copies to Roosevelt, Churchill, Ghandi and Chiang-Kai-Shek. I would, if I thought there was the least hope that they would read it. Also Stalin. But I suppose they are illiterate.

I heard a thing on the wireless called The Battle of Britain. It said that this was done by So-and-so in collaboration with the Air Ministry expert. Were you the expert?

If I did get a sensible job in England, which would be kinder: to bring Brownie or to leave her with the McDonaghs?

As for the island of saints & scholars, we are just the same as ever. In the eastern counties there seems to be a microscopic leaning towards co-operation with Britain (largely because their candles, tea, cigarettes, flour etc. are giving out) but in the West no such thing. One brave man who generally talks sense—Dillon—has stated in the Dail that Ireland's present policy is a disgraceful one, but he was howled down. It is much that he should have dared to say it. My friend the Bishop of Galway has denounced the 'agents of a foreign power' who are seducing the upright, innocent, trustful young men of Erin to take their *capital* out of the country in order to be exposed to physical and moral dangers about which they have not been told. Anglicè: he has denounced the English for allowing starving Irish labourers to earn £5 a week in England without liability to war service. One other piece of grim humour is the Catholic Herald, which is still busy denouncing Russians & Englishmen, quite regardless of Vatican broadcasts, and the prize Bun of the year goes to the government, which actually censored a message from the Pope! Shortly after this achievement there was a hysterical squeal of rage because an Irish bishop's pastoral letter arrived in Northern Ireland a week late (uncensored) owing to the English censorship. But I must stop this sneering. What a glorious (and distant) day it will be, when people can talk politics or religion without snarling at each other. I fear we shall not live to see it.   love from TIM

P.S. On reading this through, I feel much less heroic than when I wrote it. Why can't I just come to England without leaving Brownie at all, settle down in the country near you, and join the home guard? Would they let me at 35? This would be the ideal solution, because Brownie needs the country and I wd. be able to do some more writing in spare time. But Bunny, I dont know anything about conditions in England. I still think that I can help civilisation better by making it than by defending it, but I want to shew that I am prepared to be blitzed for it next winter, on account of certain conclusions in my epic: in order to stop the mouth of vulgar criticism. If I can stop it without too much sorrow to my heart I wd. be quite glad to take the easy path. I once spent 6 months in the Brompton Hospital for consumptives, and now I am wearing these filthy spectacles, so I really can't see why I should offer myself for the regular army, when they wont use me for what I am good at. Even if I was on a convoy, I probably shouldn't see the bloody aeroplane which blew me up.

Can you think it straight?

How you must hate the egoism with which I trade on your good nature. It is because I am grievously conceited and think that I know more about everything than anybody else—except you.

September 7th, 1941   *Alciston, Berwick, Sussex*

Dear Tim, I was delighted to get your letter which interested me very much. I also have news. Angelica has been having bouts of exhaustion & I took her to Lord Horder. He at first thought it was some poisoning so when Angelica went to be called up, she said at her interview she would get a medical certificate. Horder now finds there's nothing wrong with her, which is a great relief to me. Meanwhile her old schoolmistress wrote & asked her to come & teach—so to avoid bother & because she is rather attracted by anything new, she has decided to go. An hour after seeing Horder & this being settled, I was offered an important & well paid job—it is not definitely settled but will be in a few weeks. I shall be working as personal assistant to my old chief at the Air Ministry.

Well the point is that if I get this post I shall be able to use you in a sensible way doing work for which in my opinion you are admirably qualified, & which is most worth doing. So if you are still of the same mind next Christmas, come to me.

This revolution in my life means giving up this place, storing furniture, & sending William back to school for another year. Richard is not

94

due to be called up till next summer. He is leaving Cambridge & going into an Aircraft factory in two or three weeks time.

I shall probably live with some friends or in a furnished room in London until Christmas after which I hope to find some reserved occupation for Angelica near London & shall try & find a temporary home for us outside from which I can easily get to my work.

My book came out yesterday. You can wait to read it till you come over.

We have got Benedict Richards here which is fun. (Ray & the boys were camping with the Richards family before they came to Sheskin.) On Wednesday William is going out shooting with Clive Bell & Lord Gage's keeper. I bought a magnum which is a bit heavy for him, though lighter than yours. William has been reading up the etiquette of shooting in Burke's Steerage & also a passage in Earth Stopped—which is as funny as anything in The Sword in the Stone. I don't know if you remember it— but the shooting party in which a gun goes off when its owner is smacking someone over the bottom with it.

The business of giving up a place when one has been working like the devil for 2 months in it & the vegetable garden is looking really lovely, produces complicated emotions. I may cry over my rows of winter lettuces, endives, seedlings under cloches, etc. But I shall not regret Sussex, for I really rather dislike it and it will be pleasant to live where one is not disliked by one's next door neighbours. But the chief thing is that the work offered me is what from the very start, in Sept 1939, I wanted to do & never got a chance to do. All that winter our efforts were stymied & now when things are really being done, I have the chance to go back & take a responsible share in it. I think that the separation from Angelica will do neither her nor me harm. She is a bit too dependant on me and it will toughen her.

The bees fortunately hibernate: the real problem are my two pedigree British blue cats: now growing out of kittenhood. It is possible William may take them back to his school. One of the masters has an owl there— one of the brood of a nest discovered by William who pulled out the parent & ringed her, when he was only expecting to find owlets.

Richard has written some devastating notes about the Witch in the Wood, with which I am not in complete agreement. They do not spare an author's feelings. The real thing was to change Morgause as you say you have. It is always a mistake when one feels an author is venting a personal grudge on a character. I felt that about you & Morgause.

95

Don't rush off on a convoy without giving me a chance to make use of you as you should be. However your postscript shows you are thinking straight. It is no good talking about the army. They do not accept T.B. cases with uncertain eyesight. Well much love to you & my greetings to Brownie.   Yours BUNNY

September 14th, 1941   *Doolistown, Trim, Co. Meath, Eire*
Dear Richard, Bunny tells me in a letter that you have written some notes about changing The Witch in the Wood, which he does not send me because they dont spare an author's feelings. I have no feelings as an author, except to do my best for the book. If you still have these notes, will you send them to me? Now is my last chance for improving it.

I have been through the Ill-Made Knight on your advice, putting in little bits of scenic effect—stained glass windows, september corn fields and all that sort of thing. It was quite true that the book lacked visualisation. I dont think I have put in enough even now, but I am afraid of distracting from the main object of that particular section, which was to deal with Lancelot & Guinever as characters. One reason why you said that there was too much Mallory & too little me was because I have kept referring to Lancelot by his proper name. It gives a sort of Mallory atmosphere, where there is a plethora of proper names. Now I have put 'He' instead of 'Lancelot' wherever I could, and you can't imagine what an un-Mallory-ing effect it has had.

Dont write me any actual insults in your notes about The Witch, not in my private capacity,* but say exactly what you think about the book. I have, in any case, cut out everything already, except (1) the Unicorn hunt (the boy's part of it—the grown-up part is out) (2) the Questing Beast imbroglio, shortened by half or even more (3) the Conversations between Arthur, Merlyn etc. about inventing the Round Table. The Queen herself only appears on 3 occasions, each time as a serious villain, not guyed. She appears (1) Boiling a black cat alive, (2) Beating her children, (3) standing in the moonlight with a bit of a dead man's skin, which she intends to use as a love charm. I have put in, to balance the cuts, (1) a lot of Celtic stuff, to give the Orkney atmosphere (2) more conversations with Merlyn about wars, aggression, race hatred etc., and (3) the Battle of Bedegraine as a serious battle.

There is one reason why I may not be able to agree with all your
* I have feelings as a *man*, if not as an author.

96

criticisms, and that is that I know what the contents of the two subsequent books is, while you dont.

A lot of people hated the Unicorn Hunt—and I have cut out the grown-up part of it—but if you think about the murder of Morgause by Agravaine and co. which came in the next book, you will see why the Unicorn can't be cut altogether.

It may be the same with some of your criticisms. Parts of Book Four, which you have not seen, depend upon bits in the Witch, which may therefore have to stay.

What I have done to the Witch, to put it in one sentence, is to cut out the Evelyn Waugh.

It is much shorter. Only 150 pages.

How are you and how is William? Did he hit anything when he went out with Lord Gage's gamekeeper? If not, tell him that the first time I went out on a regular shoot, aged 19, I did not hit anything all day. Suicide would have been a sheer pleasure that evening. It was rather a formal kind of shoot—all the top drawer was there, and I was shy. This sort of thing makes no difference. It was not because I was a bad shot. It turned out afterwards that I was quite a good one.

Have you turned into a frightful rowing man? I have knitted myself some Leander couloured socks, which I wear to shew that I never rowed in my life. It is useful to have these labels. But I think Bunny once told me that you have some socks of the same colour, so perhaps I am only wearing them out of envy. I was always rather jealous of you. The first time you saw me, which you wont remember, you came into the room and looked at me for 10 minutes and went away again without comment. I have been in an inferior position ever since.   love from TIM

P.S. That Irish saint is out, together with all his stories, and the children now talk in a Gaelic idiom, instead of like children at an English prep. school. I am afraid, in short, that most of your notes will be about things which have vanished already, but I would like to see them for all that, in case.

September 14th, 1941   *Doolistown, Trim, Co. Meath, Eire*

Dear Bunny, I will take any job of any sort which you consider ought to be taken: anything to get back to England, but particularly to work for you. How splendid!

If necessary, I can get finished with my book in 3 weeks, in a sort of way. Ideally speaking I would like a bit longer for a last revision—after forgetting about it for a week or two—but if an emergency arises I can come to your whistle in October.

Dont trouble to answer this until you have something definite to say, but, when you have, do try to be definite. I dont even know what this job is.

They would have to pay me enough to live on.

Can you manage, if matters do turn out as you hope, to send me some official offer on office notepaper? I should need something to shew to guards, consuls etc., and in order to provide self with identity card, ration card, gas mask or whatever are the currency of life in England, before I could scramble out of this island.

Then there is Brownie. If it is a job in London which I have to live with, I shall be forced to leave her here. If it is the kind of London job which allows of living in the country, I shall bring her with me and settle down at a little pub I know at Finmere in Bucks, which is wholly in the country (no village even) but about two yards from a main line station which used to run morning and evening business trains in the piping days of peace. If, best of all, it is merely a writing job which does not need to be done in London, we will go and live with my mother or near Stowe or anywhere where Brownie can be happy. I do hope, by the way, that there is some method of gas-protecting Brownie. I am perfectly sure that Hitler will try some absolutely filthy trick as soon as he gets desperate, so that I dont know whether it would not be better to leave her here in any case. Your advice would help.

I am very excited and pleased about coming. Keeping in Ireland to finish the book has been like bracing oneself against a current.

Also it is rather fun to be offered a job without knowing anything about it. I cannot even guess whether I shall have to cut off my beard and dress up in a uniform, as you did.

You might try to give me a little time for getting identity card etc., when you do send for me, also remember that censored letters take about a week.

I have written to Richard, asking for his insults about the Witch in the Wood. As an author I am level-headed about insults.

No news. This is not a letter. Just a general benediction.

You wont trouble to answer till you need.   love from TIM

98

I shall salute you every morning and stand at attention whenever you speak. As a matter of fact, I suppose I have been doing that ever since I knew you. Except about those Great Northern Divers. Dont trouble to send the Air War book. I have ordered it from Figgis, a very nice Dublin bookseller, who knew your father.

[*Undated*]   *Doolistown, Trim, Co. Meath, Eire*

Dear Bunny, I am still eagerly waiting for news from you with one ear, while I scribble corrections in the epic with one hand, but meanwhile I have been able to detach one eye to read The War in the Air from beginning to end twice. It is a very good book and I feel humiliated that I should ever have complained about your writing it. While I was prosing away about some heros who were mythical even in the Middle Ages, you have adroitly identified yourself with the living epic behind my back, curse or bless you. The only criticism I have to make is that you ought not to have tried to be up to date. At Chapter 15 the strain of digesting current events while at the same time hamstrung (bad metaphor for the digestion) by the necessities of concealing information from the enemy, has begun to prove too much for you. Also I think it a pity that you have not yourself been in the Middle East during operations. You ought to go there now. You will, of course, have to be the official Historian when we have won the war, and, as such, you ought *now* to be visiting Cairo, Iceland and possibly Singapore. I have two other minor criticisms: the first, that you dont quite seem to have realised the main reason why we shall win this war, I mean the main strategic reason. It is that England has, in the last four hundred years, made one inspired subconscious guess. We have grasped the fact, without realising it, that the country which puts off its re-armament longest, while remaining just able to defend itself, is the country which wins. For the first country to arm itself lays out its resources upon arms which have become out of date by the time that the laggard is beginning to spend. The other criticism—mere carping—is that really you great men can't let us small ones down by writing bad grammar. The population, on p 106, is 'trained what to do'—God between us and harm. Your chapter about Poland reminds me that I was at Dunsany Castle at the time of the collapse of that country, and a young man of 30 who was present—I have an idea that he was a Dunsany nephew, perhaps a Fingal—said in an Oxford accent: '*I dont want to be unchivalrous*, but

99

really I *do* think the Poles might have put up a better show.' So they gave him a post in the Ministry of Information.

Do you remember how I once nearly invented a revolving Lewis gun? Since reading and pondering over your book I have had several inspirations of the same or better sort. I can't write them in a letter, and, even when I see you and tell you about them, I suppose the moment of inertia of the English war machine will be such that it is impossible to get anything done about them. Still, I would like to try.

Now a message for Richard. He is a first rate critic, and I had reinserted St. Toirdealbàċ on his advice, before you added yours. I have also put back the drinking scene. King Pellinore's poetry has had to stay out, in spite of his plea for it, because of exigencies of structure. It is like packing a trunk. I have ignored several of his remarks about The Ill-Made Knight, which he does not really understand. When he complains that the Grail business is told in oratio obliqua he is paying me unintentionally the terrific compliment of assuming that it *could* have been told in oratio recta. In fact, I have 'sold' him the Grail, to a certain extent at any rate, by means of my oratio obliqua, and, when you reflect that the Grail story entails a personal meeting with Jesus Christ, you will realise what a hoax I have been hawking. Does he seriously expect me to start telling the public, in propria persona, that Lancelot met Jesus trapesing about with the wretched pot? Such things can only be said by one's characters, for whom one takes no responsibility whatever. And in the same way, he misunderstands my attitude to Galahad. Personally I consider that Galahad was a pain in the neck. But I think that Lancelot was so nice that he would have been willing to apologise for him as well as he could.

I am hoping desperately that when you have read my last two books you will think that I have helped in the war effort almost as much as you have with the Air War. Or at any rate in the next peace effort.

If you dont get me a crashingly useful job, I am going to try for being a ferry pilot.

I think I shall post the epic to Collins next week.

This is only a letter about your book.   love from TIM

October 24th, 1941   *Doolistown, Trim, Co. Meath*

Dear Bunny, I am waiting with anxiety to hear from you. If your hopes have fallen through, or if you cannot mention an approximate date until which I ought to wait, can you help me to become a ferry pilot? I want to know what age I must claim to be, and how many hours solo I must claim to have flown. I want very much to talk to you about air strategy, and to be in England. To get there I shall have to produce a letter stating that I am wanted. I am rotting here, now that the book is finished.

love from TIM

October 31st, 1941   *Alciston, Berwick, Sussex*

Dear Tim, If all had gone smoothly with me I should have written to you long ago. But I have been engaged for two months in complicated negotiations to get the job I wanted and to get a good salary with it, or if it were uniformed, rank which would command a decent wage.

I have at last got the job I want, though I fear not the salary I want. Meanwhile I have another job offered & my simple plan is to recommend that you should be offered it. Whether there is any likelihood of my succeeding in this I cannot say. It depends on the sense & open mindedness of two men who will both be annoyed with me for having chosen the other string for my bow. As a matter of fact you are infinitely better qualified to do the work than I am.

I dont think there is much chance of your getting taken on as a ferry pilot. You see there are thousands of pilots who are better & more experienced than you, there are Americans too. And since the price & value to us of a Fortress is considerable, they don't take any chances with pilots without many hundreds of hours to their credit. It is absurd to expect me to recommend you as a pilot, when I've never flown with you, & my opinion on the subject is worthless, to people who have been flying for 20 years & have the pick of the pilots of commercial airlines, & of the R.A.F. There are so many other things I can recommend you for: So I shall go with Burke's Steerage in one hand & England has my Bones in the other. If I fail in this first attempt dont despair. It has taken me two months to get my own job & even that is not yet signed & sealed. My job will mean my keeping office hours in London.

Richard has enlisted in the R.A.F. as motor boat crew in the Sea Rescue Service. He goes on Tuesday & I fear will have a beastly time until the preliminary training is over.

Angelica has been back for a fortnight as there was a case of infantile paralysis at her school & all the children were sent home. She goes back on Monday.

If it is any consolation to you, I am in just as feverish & bad state of mind as you can be & am longing to begin work. Meanwhile vague nitwits ring me up in chorus to ask me to write films or learned articles for the American Press on the most secret items of our defences (All I know about them is that!) It is the aftermath of my book which has apparently done better than the publishers expected.

Love to Brownie.

I will write again soon. How I should like to catch a salmon next year!

BUNNY

November 22nd, 1941   159 *Clifford's Inn, London,* EC4

Dear Tim, In my last letter I referred to a telegram, but I did not send it as your letter saying the form had come to hand arrived before I sent it off. Now the only thing is to wait & see—but I greatly fear there will be no job coming to you through Peake. You must therefore consider fully (i) whether you really want a job (ii) What sort? I dont see you enjoying plain schoolmastering which is very easy to get & for you particularly easy. On the other hand active jobs which don't require brains seem to me a mistake for you. So my advice to you is to wait. I have been in my job now 9 days & it is obviously too soon for me to begin to see just how you could be useful. But great developments will obviously be taking place in many directions, & there is bound to be a demand for someone who is vigorous & intelligent. So please send me the particulars about yourself which I ought to know but don't—(age—languages—etc.)

I am already beginning to be hard worked, after some days of twiddling my thumbs. I am exceedingly lucky—in a central position & enjoying myself & so far liking & liked by my masters who include the sort of General nobody could believe existed—the ideal Englishman but infinitely more logically minded than any Englishman's ideal of himself. There is also a man whose book you quote from in Has My Bones (not me) on records of killing animals. We are in an excited state of mind as it looks as though we have pulled it off in Lybia. Altogether I feel excited & pleased to be back in the boat.   Much love, BUNNY

Dear Bunny, I have had 2 letters from you, the second of which, dated Nov. 22nd, admits hearing from me that my application form to the R.A.F.V.R. had been sent off. I have also heard from the Headmaster of Stowe, dated Nov. 25th, that he has forwarded the form to Air Commodore Peake. I have heard nothing from the latter.

I note that Peake is likely to have disposed of the job by now.

You ask me to make up my mind whether I really want a job. Well, of course I dont. I never said I did. I am safe, well-fed and surrounded by Brownie. Naturally I dont want to leave her in order to be starved and blown up. But unfortunately I have written an epic about war, one of whose morals is that Hitler is the kind of chap one has to stop. I believe in my book, and, in order to give it a fair start in life, I must shew that I am ready to practise what I preach. Intelligent people will understand that I am stopping Hitler much better by writing such books than by coming to England. But I have come to believe that people are not intelligent. I have come to dread the kind of damage which might be done to my book by people like Godfrey Wynn or Beverley Nicks, if they chose to hint a slander at my private courage. The epic is a sort of Caesar, and I, as Caesar's wife, must be above suspicion.

Nor do I believe that I can, in fact, help the 'war effort' appreciably by coming to England. People are not supposed to be intelligent in wars (only Germans are allowed to be) and I know quite well that the moment of inertia of the higher-ups will effectively quosh my own intelligence. Look at yourself. If having a healthy neo-pallium went for anything, you certainly ought to be an Air Marshal. You have been in it from the start. Yet there you are, keeping 'office hours' in London, and I dont mind betting that you are still a flight lieutenant.

No, I never said I wanted a job and I never thought I would do much good by having one. I am only thinking of my book.

When the chance of this job of Peake's turned up, I was pleased, because it seemed not utterly futile. I was going to accept the job of describing training on the sane condition that I might be trained myself. Damn this pen. Then, when trained, I was going to insist on going into battle *once*. Obviously a training is not finished until you have done what it is for. After that I was going to drum my chest in a good book, under the thin pretence that it was the R.A.F.'s chest I was drumming, and, if I had survived the experience, I should have considered that I had not been wasting time.

Now you ask me to make up my mind whether I really want a job. Well, I did'nt *want* any. The Peake one would have slightly made up for leaving Brownie, and, considering what my duty is (to the *book*, not to any bloody nation) I was very pleased to hope for it. It is my *duty* to have a job in England, before the book comes out in the spring. Dont talk to me about wanting.

Peake is evidently going to fall through. You mutter about coming to England (a) as a schoolmaster or (b) as a flying instructor. It would be futile to come as the first, and, as for the second, I am sure I have wholly forgotten how to fly.

I am finding this difficult to explain.

A. My only reason for 'wanting' a job is for the book, not for England, Home or Beauty. I need not have this book-defending job before next spring. B. Had I been able to get a sensible job, like the Peake one, it would have been worth coming over at once. C. But if it is to be school-mastering or managing the rears bumf, I may just as well stay here till spring. In fact, I agree with you that I had better wait (till Spring) in case you can get me something sensible to do, and, if it is still lacking by then, I will come over as anything to do with the latrines.

Now, Bunny, you ask for my particulars. I will send them in a later letter if you insist, but *can't you get the completed form from Peake?* In the first place, you would then have the whole thing signed and sealed. In the second place, you would take a load off my mind. By implicitly following your instructions, I find myself in the position of a man who has applied to be a pilot-officer with (we now suspect) no definite employment following it from Peake. Suppose he absent-mindedly sends that application on? I may find myself at any moment bidden to an interview, accepted, sent to some foul saluting school, and employed for the rest of my life as a bottle washer, while some happier lad basks in the favours of Air Commodore Peake. For heaven's sake save me from this.

Finally, *very important*, will you please send me your proper rank and office address, as I want to address an official memorandum to you, upon another subject. I can't explain this as the paper has run out, but I MUST HAVE Rank & Official Address. love from TIM

P.S. I am sorry if some of the above seems to contradict my recent claim to be rotting in Ireland. I made it when I was trying to whip up enthusiasm for leaving Brownie. What I now mean, after thinking about your question for two days, is that I am anxious for a sensible job (though I shall hate having it) but I am less anxious for a silly job (which I shall hate having more) while it will be my inescapable duty to have a job of whatever sort next spring—however much I hate having it.

1942

Dear Bunny, ...[1] I have been reading a book called Siamese White, which you recommended. I am almost certain that this man must have been my great-great-great-great-great-grand uncle. My great-great-grandfather was a person called Jem White, who was a pal of Charles Lamb's, wrote a book called Falstaff's Letters, and, according to Charles Lamb, 'took away half the fun of the world when he died'. He was the chap who gave an annual dinner to chimney sweeps. Jem White's father, according to the D.N.B., was a Samuel White of Bewdley in Worcestershire. Note that his name was Samuel, that his property was in the west, and that his son Jem probably met Lamb at the India House. It seems to me quite probable on the face of it that he was a son or grandson of Collis's George White, named after Samuel the pirate (who only had daughters) and possibly, inheriting some of the western property bought with the plunder of Siam. My family has served in the East since time immemorial, which also points that way. If I survive this war, I shall try to follow this up at Somerset House, for Collis's Sam seems an ancestor to be valued.

... I am filling in the time by writing a sort of Treasure Island book—a cross between that and The Island of Dr. Moreau—which deals with the most thrilling rock in existence, namely Rockall.

Have I caught you out over a bit of general knowledge, Bunny, at last? If you already know about Rockall I shall give up, like T. E. Lawrence, and say that you are over educated.

Brownie is fat and well, and has developed a baffling phobia about pheasants. When we shoot one, she snatches it up and runs off home with it, however far away we are, to give it to Mrs. McDonagh. Sometimes she buries it on the way. She sends her love with mine,   from TIM

My dear Tim, ...[2] I have not finished reading Book Five, but shall send my appreciation in a day or two. Of course the appreciation has little

[1 The first two pages of this letter, dealing with his relations with the publishers Collins and Cape, omitted.—D.G.]

[2 Portions of this letter about Cape and Collins are omitted.—D.G.]

bearing on the business problem you have entrusted me with, which is rather a sticky one. I will do my best. But I hope you will not be cross if I say that the problem is not easy, & that this arises partly from the fact that you are out of touch as the result of living in a neutral country.

Collins was really rather wiser than he guessed when he said in his letter of Dec. 23: 'Such subjects should really be written about some time afterwards so that they could be seen in perspective.'

The fact is that the space between London & Trim exactly equals a certain distance in time & so for all practical purposes the book may be considered to have been written in 1955—or ten years after we have won the war.

A good deal of the book which will seem obviously true in 1955 seems to us in London today to be superficial, or irritating. The condemnation of man as stultus, impoliticus ferox etc makes us cross. We think so vividly & so continually of our chaps on rafts, washed about for a week, or a month; of the men digging out the living plaster covered mummies from bombed houses, of aircraft crews beating out fires with their bare hands. And we do not feel man to be what you describe.

But this should have waited until I can write a criticism of the whole book.

But if in such passages you are a dozen years removed from our spirit, you are also rather out of touch with our economy. There are 2 practical points which face every publisher today, & it is these I suggest which have influenced Collins far more than anything like Waldman's report ...

(1) There is practically no paper for books.

(2) A publisher can sell all the books he publishes provided the price is low, i.e. if the books are short.

The publisher who wishes to keep afloat must therefore use his paper in making the largest number of copies of the smallest number of short books.

... I will do my best to get you out of this tangle which is due to time space as well as to inherent vices of publishers & literary agents. I send you my warmest love. I wish to God I could come & show you how to catch Boyne salmon on the reflex minnow as I did in Feb. 1939. Love to Brownie. BUNNY

P.S. I am glad you are writing a Treasure Island Book about Rockall. That is splendid news. Rockall was an obsession of mine when I was about fourteen years old & I have only once read a good account of it. So apparently I am as you say over-educated. I wish I felt so ...

February 11th, 1942   *Doolistown, Trim, Co. Meath, Eire*
Dear Bunny, Curse you for knowing about Rockall. I thought there were no books about it at all, except proceedings of Geographical Societies etc. However, you are incorrigibly informed about everything and I here renounce all effort ever to know anything which you dont know already ...

I am sorry you think I have underestimated the decency of homo sapiens. Perhaps by now you have got to the later chapter about Gollileo etc. which may make up for it. The point I tried to make was that ants or any other animal would drift about on rafts, dig each other out of bombed buildings, or beat out fires with their hands, just as decently as you say homo sapiens does. However, I must wait for your final judgement.

By the way, before posting to America would you correct my facts about *ration books,* if I have mis-stated them too grossly?

There are several minor adjustments which I shall have to make in proof.

I am glad you are writing again. I think you are about the only person I know who can write about his ancestors and make them absorbing. Was the Jesuit martyr a collateral?

Tomorrow begins the salmon season and I am in the midst of twisting up traces, cleaning reels and all the other fun ...

I enjoy very much getting letters from the Foreign Office, stamped with lions & unicorns. Do you walk with a slight, distinguished stoop, swinging an eye-glass on a wide black ribbon?

Since writing the above, I have looked back over my Arthur book to refresh my memory. I always have to leave a book to cool for about six months before I can judge of its *tone.* Well, I find that it is simply crammed with little pomposities of style, unnecessary adverbs and gaucheries, particularly where Merlin is talking. All this will be remedied in proof, by cutting and toning down and making simple. That was why I wanted so badly to have a Collins (or Cape) proof to send corrected to America. That also is why I feel very doubtful about sending it to America at all in its present state. Oh damn all these censorships and post offices and torpedoes to hell! Perhaps the best thing would be to have the 3 typed copies made and send them to me here to correct, and then I would send them back to Putnam's agent in London if only I knew his name & address, and he could do what he pleased with them. It is only little faults of taste (puerilities) which have to be snipped out. The structure and intentions are sound. It just needs a blue pencil ...

Brownie sends her love to your umbrella.　　　　　love from TIM

I am shamefully grateful to you, Bunny, for all the trouble you are taking: I can't say anything sensible about it, except that I wish it was I who was taking the trouble for you.

Tim White had second thoughts about the following letter [16.3.42] and never posted it. It was found after his death by Sylvia Townsend Warner, who posted it to me on June 8th, 1964.

March 16th, 1942　　　　　　*Doolistown, Trim, Co. Meath, Eire*

Dear Bunny, I hate to keep pestering you like this, but it would so help if I could get something definite fixed about my book on one side or other of the Atlantic. The Air Mail is discontinued and it took nearly *4 months* for my M.S.S. to reach Putnam's (mainly through bungling in the Irish Post Office). This means that it is a life's work to get and correct proofs from America. Unfortunately I suffer from what I can only call a *visual critical sense*, so that I can never pull my books together properly until I see them in print in proof—up to that stage all the puerilities remain in them—and as this book means so much to me I do feel I ought to get it right before sinking into the war. I am sure that things will blaze up very soon—in the spring—and I would like to have my little bone safe buried in the right flower bed before it is too late. So if there is any hope of hurry in relation to Cape—I thirst for *proofs*—from anybody—before the spring—I would be so glad to hear something. I am sorry I am bothering you. Of course I am quite at a standstill and can neither write to my agents nor to Collins—and hardly even to Putnam's—until I know how the Cape business stands and whether Cape decided to post the final letter in the file to Collins.

I am in a most peculiar and lamentable state about this war, in which my head and heart are utterly at variance. In my head I dont—I'm sorry—approve of it as much as you may think I ought to. Indeed, I dont at all.

But in my heart the most dreadful things happen. Last week I got a list of old Stowe boys who had been killed. I read Squadron Leader A.B. C. ... , D.S.O., D.F.C. (posthumous) and with great difficulty I suddenly would connect this with C. ... , A.B., mi., in some long forgotten list, and then after that there would be a sudden flash of a picture in which a fat little affectionate creature looked at me with eyes of trust, holding up its hand perhaps and asking to Please, Sir, it had bust its pencil or etc. And there were scores of them, such decent kids, born after me and dead before, and I had taken trouble with all of them and loved them, and they had loved me. I have always been shy of telling you what a good school-master I once was. Well now, it was to have one's guts knotted to keep suddenly recognising under Flight Lieut D.E. F.... , missing presumed dead, a little half remembered brat with bright eyes of *trust*.

If I can get my book fixed in a proper proof-corrected state I really dont know what I will do. It will be either to refuse to fight at all, in a stubborn manner, or else to skip the border into Ulster as a private soldier. I have sincerely tried to get intelligent employment and rightly failed—for no intelligent man can be employed in this war, except you, who are the exception to all rules—so I will either be an intelligent poco-curante, if my head wins, or I will be a private soldier if my heart does. If the private soldier (or seaman) business turns up I want you to remember afterwards that I had no intellectual excuse for being martyred—indeed I shall consider myself an intellectual traitor—but that it was just that I could not bear in my heart to be parted from these poor little devils that loved me because they knew I would protect them from being caned, although I have not been able to protect them from being shot to pieces.

Please excuse me for writing almost hysterically, but the lists have upset me and I want very much to face this issue while I can—i.e. before the whole thing is taken out of my hands, perhaps next spring. *Nothing* can be reasonable to be done before I have settled the book, which is my reason of being. I have of course done my best to get hold of American proofs, but I see little hope of them, and so I am bothering you to know whether there is any hope with Cape.

Since the beginning of the salmon season exactly 3 salmon have been taken by all competitors on the river above Navan. It is the worst year ever known and that is saying the hell of a lot. I had a slack this afternoon, who was hooked, played, gaffed in the tail, unhooked and back in the river in 5 minutes, which I'm faintly pleased with, as it was almost a thread line and a 10 ft rod.

The issue of *Horizon* which you helped me into has been banned, confiscated by the guards and for all I know burned by the common hangman! The Island of Saints and Scholars! (The priest I told you of in my last letter has been remanded at liberty on bail.)   love from TIM

April 16th, 1942   *Doolistown, Trim, Co. Meath, Eire*

Dear Bunny, I hate to keep pestering you like this, but until I hear something from Cape all my affairs are at a standstill ...

Can you remember the weights of the Boyne salmon which you caught in the spring of 1939? I am trying to persuade myself that they were slacks—I can't quite remember that one on the floor of the car— because it is so unnatural that you should have been so lucky ...

I have been ill for some months with some sort of slow melancholic poisoning—a septic throat? Not due to drink, which I am off. It just gives you the black dog on your back.   love from TIM

It is not often that Tim was so honest as he is in the line: 'I am trying to persuade myself that they were slacks.' He soon succeeded.

April 22nd, 1942   *Doolistown, Trim, Co. Meath, Eire*

Dear Bunny, How lovely to hear your voice on the wireless. I scampered down to the kitchen to spread the alarm and all trooped up and sat in chairs round the wall, with hands folded in their laps, as in church, to listen while you told us about mice. Afterwards, Mrs. McDonagh said: 'That will give you your health now, Mr. White, now you have heard Mr. Garnett.' (All know you are my chief hero.) And Paddy went back to the kitchen as silently as one of your mice, but with an important expression, as if he had received the sacrament. Nobody knew what the devil you had been talking about.

You did it well. When you were doing Jefferies you sounded exactly like yourself. When you said 'dinner' I could see just the way your hair is over your ears, and also you eating, and also (this will madden you) I could remember some remarks of D. H. Lawrence about you as a trencherman. But when you came to your own brief comment, like all truly modest people, you faltered. You began to talk with unnatural clarity, as if trying to convey some vital message to several deaf charladies over an atmospheric telephone. Indeed, as far as we were concerned, this was exactly your position. Have you any idea of the real Irishman, I wonder, and can you imagine that Paddy can't count beyond ten? Still, we adore to listen to anybody we have met in the flesh. Some time ago, a musical cattle dealer visited us, and told that in 3 weeks time he would be on Radio Eireánn. Punctually to the day and time we all folded our hands in our laps and listened, although what he was doing was classy beyond words (Jelly d'Aranyi—or however she spells herself—would have had trouble with it) and all the music we knew was There Are Three Lovely Lassies in Bangor. Afterwards Mrs McDonagh said it was loverlay—and meant it. You got the same reaction. Oh, Bunny, if only I could hear you even once a week. I really do feel saner tonight, and Mrs. McD., like all women, was quite right.

Brownie became anxious and recognised you—you wont believe it—by rushing about the room, jumping up into my lap and looking *away* from the wireless. Dogs are much more tactful, tangential, than we are.

Please let us know if you are ever going to do it again. It was pure luck catching you. I shall send this to the B.B.C. like real fan mail, in the hope of making you do it again.   love from TIM

April 23rd, 1942   134 *Clifford's Inn*, EC4

Dearest Tim, ... Really I must say your remarks about my salmon provoke a smile. You of course didn't eat them! They were both clean run fish like the little 3rd one.

The first one, from the Blackwater, weighed 19¾ lbs in Dublin so we can call it a 20 lb fish. It fought me magnificently & stirred the envy of old Mr ——the Dublin harbour official. The Boyne fish weighed 17 lbs & though darker was as full bellied & ate as well as the first. It also fought hard—but there was no difficulty as there were no sunk rocks in that flat stretch of river. In the Blackwater there were rocks & rapids everywhere & a weir below.

Incidentally I hooked three other salmon while I was in Ireland that time, & owing to my inexperience I lost them at once.

Now let me tell you something more urgent than to defend those fish— they can be vouched for by all who ate them (Jonathan Cape included)

I own a stretch of salmon fishing of my own.

Really I dont know whether it ranks as financier's water, hotel water, laird of the ilk or worm water. I fancy it is ilk water.

The story is this: In 1940 I invested on expert advice £440 in Richard Thomas 6½% preference. I sold out a few week ago for £1150, & thought I would invest in land. In the Times I saw some farms to be sold in Northumberland. So I went up there ten days ago—inspected them and bought one called Ridley Stokoe on the N. Tyne for £2,200. It is let to some perfectly delightful people who wish to remain there the rest of their lives & are quite happy about the rent. There is 2/3 of a mile of river. One pool about ¼ mile long is reputed good & the story is that the local General who has hitherto rented the shooting once got five fish out of it in one day. Naturally I'm eager to repeat the performance. It is 338 acres—about 200 of which is grouse moor. There are plenty of grouse and below the crags there is an oakwood in which I was surprised to find pheasants. Mr Hedley says there are a number of them. At the moment the farmer & his wife (who talk English rather like foreigners because they roll their Rs) have some women sheltering from air raids on Newcastle. There never were any air raids on Newcastle judging from the appearance of the town—but no matter. After the war there will be three bedrooms to spare & one will be able to stay there, eat Mrs Hedley's bread spread with Mrs Hedley's butter & supplement it with Hedley mutton (there are 200 sheep bound to the land) together with trout for breakfast, pheasant for luncheon & grouse for dinner one day & salmon the next. Perhaps really one will have the good creatures spread round the year in their seasons, but at the moment I like to think of them all together. Will you come & fly hawks at the grouse, shoot pheasants & watch me gaffing salmon—at the earliest possible opportunity?

I hope to get nearly a week there shortly & a full week there in September.

Well am I wise or crazy? Anyhow that is what I have done & I don't regret it.

I am overtired & overworked but my work is good & worth doing.

William has mumps poor chap. Richard has been doing odd jobs waiting for his training in the R.A.F. Speed boats to start. He seems very cheerful. Very much love to you & Brownie   BUNNY

May 10*th*, 1942   *Crown Inn, Falstone, Northumberland*

Dear Tim, ... Angelica & I were married on May 8, in the presence of my sister-in-law (Ray's youngest sister) Frances & her husband, and William. Richard arrived that evening & we all came up here by night with sleepers. The woman at the inn here makes wonderfully good bread with a mixture of brown flour & oatmeal—the best bread I've ever eaten. The river is almost empty—the chance of catching a trout is very slender.

There are curlew, rock doves on the crags, wood pigeons in the birches, pheasants searching for acorns, rabbits everywhere. The first thing we saw was a mounted figure coming through the wood below the moor with a dog fetching in a sheep with lambs. When we got to the farm it turned out to be Mrs Hedley, the farmer's wife. Today it is drizzling & cold. Torrents of rain might lead to my catching a fish but would be hard luck on Angelica who hopes to sit under a sheltered rock & paint. Love from all of us,   BUNNY

May 16*th*, 1942   *Doolistown, Trim, Co. Meath*

Dear Bunny, What larks you kids do get up to. I hope it will always be a very happy marriage indeed, but without knowing anything about Angelica except that she paints (good) I can't say anything particular. All I know is, if you have picked as good a one for your second, as I'm sure you have, then you are the superman I always knew you to be. It is only since Ray was dead that I have known how intensely she impressed me (more than any woman I ever met) and I wonder very much whatever Angelica can be like. Anyway she is a lucky girl. Perhaps if I knew her I should say you were a lucky man. All we others can do about it is the harnessed angels hand on sword business—which we do, Bunny, with all our hearts. Please think back to May the 16th at 11 p.m. your time, when I am toasting you both in a dram of Irish with two candles to write by and Brownie in the chair, so that I have to crouch on the edge of it. Brownie urges me to propose it in Italian—a good wish which begins with Acqua fresca, vino puro—but as the rest is rather direct I am afraid to. On the whole we have agreed that we could wish neither of you much better than the equal of our own fidelity to each other, and so we do.

Good about your farm and the fishing on it. But for heaven's sake dont build hopes on the story of the colonel who caught 5 salmon in one day. It is a story told of every pool in the British Isles, and the proper answer is What did he do on the other days? Brownie and I are longing to visit you there, but she wont misbehave when she does. Her 3 seasons in the west have made her a first class setter—one of the best I have seen in Ireland. It is only in our private Meath walks—not on the mountain—that she gets crazes about carrying things home etc.

... In rewriting the last book I am stopping the poor old King from having to visit the ants & geese in his own person (he is too old to be sent on these undignified errands) but I am introducing these visits by a trick (of reminding him of the past). I am also cutting much of Merlyn's unseemly levity and making the whole *sadder* ('sad' in the Elizabethan sense of serious.) I am also cutting the self-conscious introduction to book 2. On the whole I think it will come right in the end.

Did you see any curlew's nests on your moor I wonder? There is a bog near here where I have several, as well as snipe. I think these and various plover are the loveliest of all nests. It is the standing within a yard of them without seeing anything and then, with a sort of click or altering of focus or magic kaleidoscopic pass, the tight set bird with winkless eye or the four in-pointed eggs camouflaged just like parked tanks.

We have two cuckoos and a tame baby hare in the house. Not the cuckoos, of course. Did you know that wild rabbits are the fiercest of animals? A small rabbit I had last year used to bite my legs. You are named after a choleric species. This hare is a bit of a tyrant too.

Do you know anybody called Frank O'Connor? I have met and like him. He seems less madder than most living Irish writers. He is coming to stay next week end.

I wish it was you & Angelica. love from TIM

July 6th, 1942 *Doolistown, Trim, Co. Meath, Eire*

Dear Bunny, ... How are your teeth?

I have lately become a world renowned expert on ants, and Julian Huxley writes to me with humility. I have invented an experiment with A. flava, F. sanguinea and F. fusca which will shake the foundations of society. I suppose I may take it for granted that this is just another of my little bits of knowledge which you mastered years ago? But Fy, Bunny, I shall catch up with you yet. This war is helping me for one thing. I still go on learning in it, and I expect that you are at a standstill.

Surely you could invent some reason for coming over here? There is that Betjeman fellow in Dublin, who claims to know you, and he arranges visits from Our Bev and others. Can't you say you ought to write an article on Irish affairs?   Love from TIM

134 *Clifford's Inn, London,* EC4

Dear Tim, ... My teeth? I do not know to what salvage uses they are put: cribbage pegs, perhaps. However I am unlikely to see them again & have been feeling pretty wretched since last Thursday. They gave me Evipan an anaesthetic which made me feel as though I had been poleaxed. However on Saturday afternoon I shot 6 grey squirrels. They take my mother's plums etc. & were feeding on the wild cherries. I used the little 4.10.

Speaking of guns—you talked of *damascened* barrels which makes me suppose that you dont know how Damascus barrels are made. So I will tell you. About six ribbons of alternate steel & iron are welded into a bar built up like a finger of marble cake This bar is then twisted, Three or more are welded together & flattened into a band which is wound round a core rather like a puttee, the edges are welded together & the whole thing is then bored to the right size. The result is that you have hard steel & iron which until about 1870 was a stronger barrel than the steel which could be bored at that date. I daresay however you are a smith & know all that.

The only original research I have done on ants was purely chemical—an estimation of the formic acid content of the big horse ant. I trapped 1000 of them, steam distilled the formic acid out of them, turned it into lead formate, weighed it. Divided it by 1000 & presented a bottle of the lead formate with a note on the subject to the Science Museum South Kensington where it no doubt still is. I know about bees, but I don't like ants & your description of them doesn't make me like them any more.

Much love BUNNY

July 21st, 1942   *Doolistown, Trim, Co. Meath, Eire*

Dear Bunny, I have 2 letters of yours to answer. I am a lucky girl! First, I did know a good deal about Damascene barrels, but I dont know why I may not call them Damascened. There was quite a good illustrated article about them in the Field some five years ago. Second, what the devil is a Horse Ant? Can you remember the Latin name (I rather guess F. pratensis). Third, how did you trap 1000? I am constantly needing to count ants and have discovered no better way than picking them up one by one. It is no good weighing them, as the individuals vary. Fourth, I shall soon have to get you to teach me to do micro-dissections. What is the best microscope for a beginner to buy and what tools and how much should it cost? Are there microscopes with variable magnifications? I want to begin with simple things like counting joints in antennae, for purposes of identification only, but in the end I shall have to dissect brains. If this letter does not grow too long with other matters, I will tell you what I am doing with ants at the end of it ...

Now ants. The position as known to me at present, and I seem to be the only living person who has thought about it clearly, is that there are only nine animals in the world (out of some 275,000) which will indulge in spontaneous inter-special belligerence. Julian Huxley claims, and gave me permission to quote him as claiming, that the only animals other than man are the Harvesting Ants. Two years ago I began to investigate on this basis, and had built up a fascinating connection between the yearly life-cycle of a seed and warfare, when I discovered a belligerent non-harvesting termite, also several belligerent non-harvesting ants. Huxley has now climbed down about this. Forel, who was on the same tack, muddled himself by not realising that true warfare must be inter-special. He was always considering wars, say, between F. sanguinea and F. fusca, and he had the bad habit of promoting these by artificial interference. Well, anyway, I have been doing a series of original experiments with such few ants as are available to me in Ireland, and reading all I could get about foreign ants, and I am beginning to establish the platitude that wars are due to a territorial claim and to nothing else. It would be too long to go into the whole thing, but the ruling experiment is to see *how close* you can establish a new nest to an original nest of the same species. This gives you a line on the territorial claim. I find (at present: but it is still all going on) that in A. flava, for instance, you can establish a new nest actually on top of the old one or even in it. A. flava is wholly pacific. Then you get a type of ants which I call 'Evicting' ants, who, like F. sanguinea and F. fusca, will 'chuck-out' the members of the new nest up to about 4 yards or so. No sting or biting with the mandible is used, but the intruder is led or carried away and then released. (She does not resist except passively.) Finally you get the true belligerents, who fight fratricidally up to 30 yards and more. F. pratensis, M. barbarus and others come in this class.

You see that the belligerence comes at big distances (territorial claim) and the peacefulness at small distances (little or no territorial claim.)

Although this is more or less a platitude, it has its interesting features. For instance, the possession of *communal portable property within the nest* does *not* lead to war. (Huxley said it did.) There are plenty of ants who have portable cattle, honey (already potted, which makes it portable), and fungi and even grain, who do not fight, provided they make no territorial claim. *A nation can have property, though it cannot have territory.* (Note that Lapps & Esquimaux with reindeer but no defined territory remain pacific. The so-called 'Nomadic' arabs who fight do make a very violent claim to their part of the desert, but true nomads are pacific everywhere.)

I have been following this up as well as I can, making vast lists of property-holders, both gregarious and solitary, and always the same fact emerges.

If the property is not territorial, the species, whether solitary or gregarious, remains at peace. Here are some owners of property who do not fight about it, because it is not territorial property: Bower bird, Bear (property = his fat), Dormouse (stores food), some woodpeckers (store acorns), jackdaw (bright objects), two species of beaver (stored food), squirrel (stored food) mole (stored worms), honey-pot ants (stored portable honey), honey bees[1] (somewhat importable honey but also portable pollen), leaf-cutting ants (agricultural produce) and very many aphid-herding ants who do not indulge in cattle-raids like the Irish.*

Moreover, you can have peaceable gregarious species whose individuals possess more or less private property within the community (c.f. beavers) and this undercuts Karl Marx.

But if I go on about this I shall be writing you a book. I am writing a book about it, called The Insolence of Man.

The thing which I am now trying to do is to find out *why* the territorial claim is made in the first place. (If I can do this, I can say That's War—that was.) J. Huxley says it is made on account of natural stringency i.e. deserts make ants fight for their few seeds. This is not true. To

[1 Tim was wrong about bees which are belligerent, mercilessly fighting intruders and robbing weaker hives. They have no territory.—D.G.]

* And, on the other hand, as soon as the claim is territorial, you get combat even in solitary species—c.f. robin etc.

begin with, the stringency in Bond St. is the same as the stringency in Timbuctoo, for it attracts more competitors. And, to go on with, you get belligerents who do not live in any apparent stringency—for instance, of a gregarious species, T. caespitum in England, and, of a solitary species, the robin I mentioned.

This is why I want to cut up the brains of ants. They have things called pedunculate bodies in them, which nobody knows anything about. It is just a rather silly shot in the dark. What really ought to be done is obvious. If man is serious about wanting to stop wars he ought to finance immense Columbia-University-Field-Expeditions to study the eight at present known other belligerents. Mathematically speaking, surely if a mere dozen out of 275,000 go to war, you ought to be able to settle the matter by a sort of H.C.F. sum? And pretty easily? But, instead of this, man leaves poor, unassisted, ill-informed individuals like me to do the work: all he does about it himself is to squeal out 'There shall be no more war' on political platforms: and even me he forces to be a sea cook.

love from TIM

August 21st, 1942   *Doolistown, Trim, Co. Meath, Eire*

Dear Bunny,

... About bees. If you can give me a reference to any description of spontaneous organised belligerence in them, I will be very grateful. I have kept the creatures in a lackadaisical way, but know little about them. But I have considered all I can find out, and Julian Huxley positively assures me that they are not true belligerents. So did a man on the wireless.

You see, it must be *spontaneous*: it must not be the result of artificial interference by man, in robbing or altering the comb. And they must *band together* to do it. It would not be true war if everybody in England began killing everybody else, all-against-all, without organising for it. This kind of anarchical hysteria sometimes breaks out in the common vole in autumn, but it is not war.

My information at present, in spite of your letter, is that the honey bee is not a spontaneous organised belligerent but if you can give me a reference to a printed description of spontaneous belligerence in them, I will reconsider it.

God, how glorious it would be if I really could get to Yorkshire and take Brownie with me! But I simply can't believe it. I shall have to leave her here and take to coprophily. But if only the Home Guard would come off and I could see you in London on the way! love from TIM

August 26th, 1942   41 Gordon Square, London WC1

Dearest Tim, I haven't heard from you and write again because I am afraid you may have found my last letter unsympathetic, goading or critical. If so, I am very sorry & ask you to forgive me. Please write & tell me that you have. I have never meant to try and drive you into what you are doubtful about. And far more than the wish to act as recruiting sergeant, is the wish to see you again, to have a few days with you by the river or on the moor.

I am going to have a holiday with Angelica & William in Northumberland for a week or so from September 10. Richard may also come. We are taking up guns, rods, a tent to use as a shelter by day. Camping out is almost impossible nowadays because of the business of rationing combined with transport difficulties. The easy way to camp is to take a packing case with all necessary foods to cover the period of the camp.

So we shall stay at the inn again.

Richard spent a week's leave down here & is now posted to the extreme N. of Scotland. I am rather glad as it is relatively out of harm's way. He has had a good time in recent weeks sailing a good deal in whalers as well as in motor-boats. He also did a good deal of poaching & had some curious stories I have never heard before. He saw the following trick done. Two men bend down from the waist, head to head, gripping each other's shoulders. Assuming this attitude

they then slowly walk up to a number of feeding rabbits which take no notice of them. Apparently they are taken for a horse or a cow. When they are close enough they fire catapults, throw sticks etc. ...

October 18th, 1942   *Doolistown, Trim, Co. Meath, Eire*

Dear Bunny, ... I must stop about salmon. To tell you the truth, I have a fear coming over me that I shall give them up in favour of trout. You can raise a reluctant trout by skill, but no skill in the world will budge a reluctant salmon.

My latest acquisition, apart from a Pliny like yours but defective, is Edwards' Natural History in 7 vols for 10 guineas, wonderfully illustrated, mid-eighteenth century. I expect you know it. The fifth volume is dedicated in enormous letters TO GOD, and subscribed 'by his most resigned, humble creature, Geo. Edwards.' The other volumes are dedicated to the Marquis of Bute, the fellows of the Royal Society etc.

I have invented a new way of using smoke screens to land on beaches, and would try to send it you if I thought it was worth the trouble. But the fact is that if you *do* know any intelligent generals—which I still find impossible to believe—then they will have thought of the way for themselves: while, if you *dont* know any intelligent generals, they wont attend to anything I have to tell them. It depends on laying screens in a *grid*, *perpendicular* to the coast line. Think this over for yourself.

love from TIM

December 22nd, 1942   41 *Gordon Square*

Dearest Tim, I should have wrriten before but have been rather more hard worked than usual. We all send you our warm love for Christmas.

My personal news is that I am very much wanting to write having got a story in my head but I find it difficult or impossible to write when I get home at half past seven or eight.

William is here—very handsome—playing chess problems most of the day. On new Year's day we are going with Angelica to a pub in the fens for three days. Then William is going up to Northumberland for a week with his gun to try & shoot pheasants & woodcock.

Richard is in Scotland & is going out to sea nearly every day in his boat—likes it, likes the people he's with. The R.A.F. has been an experience which coming after Cambridge has done him a lot of good. He has learned to get on with every sort of person.

By the way I have bought myself a gun which I think would pass the most exacting critics & which fits me pretty well. It is more modern than William's—about 25 yrs old by Atkin (From Purdey's) Jermyn Street, but not really such an exquisite work of art.

So far I have only shot a few grey squirrels with it.

Angelica has been painting Christmas cards & we send you one. Owing to paper shortage they are done on the back of old Private View cards— The dog says it is snowing eagles.

Let me know what you have been doing, thinking & writing & reading. I read little outside my work as that means a lot. However I have read a book called Going Fishing by Negley Farson, a life of John Ray the father of British Naturalists & a story by a French boy of 9 called *La Bataille des Arbres* which is the finest bit of writing inspired by the war. The village people suddenly see the trees pulling up their roots—climbing over garden walls & going clanking off to the wars. The King rushes after & asks the King of the trees 'What shall we do for firewood?' 'Come & fight with us,' replies the King of Trees. Meanwhile the Flowers take order—some of the dahlias professing neutrality & faring no better for it. The battle begins—tree rushing upon tree, crashing their branches together. At last the battered old oak pointing to the heaps of slain says: 'There is your firewood for the winter.' I am going to translate it—no easy task & will send you a copy.   Very much love BUNNY

Catch three salmon in one day. Why don't you go to Navan & fish there?

1943

Dear Tim, I was very glad to get your letter and the M.S. Here I shall note down one or two criticisms of the matter which occur to me. (1) You are definite enough about not accepting a God in Man's Image, or a God as judge of man's importance, & I am glad to find it so. But you are still uncritically accepting an absolute ethic which happens to be vaguely Christian & 19th Century. For example you say: 'You can be ingeniously cruel or ingeniously wicked ...' Chapter 4. But wickedness, like Justice & other such concepts varies according to place & time. The young Nazi, having been brought up in Hitler Youth has a different ethic from you. That is a real achievement *in one generation*, for his schoolmasters. The islanders of Malekula having been brought up in a Hitler Jugend of their own for some 140 generations have an ethic entirely different from yours. If you want to know about this you must somehow obtain & read a book called *Narven* by Gregory Bateson, a young Cambridge Anthropologist & a son of the great Bateson the geneticist whom I used to know. Unfortunately I lent my copy to Raymond Mortimer & the Hun dropped a bomb on his house & I don't suppose I shall get the book back. I don't suppose there's a copy in Ireland unless there is a real anthropologist in Trinity College. It is very difficult reading—one of the hardest books I have ever understood, but it will put you straight on ethics as none of the philosophers can. It is also I think by far the best explanation of why one has to fight or perish— however I suppose I am almost the only person living who would so regard it.

Once you accept the idea that man creates the ethic which suits his circumstances, just as he creates the Gods needed for his culture, then you begin to see, I think, the overwhelming arguments in favour of conservatism. For it is innovations & discoveries which by altering the economic set-up, make the former ethic unsuitable. And it is the discrepancy between the old & the new ethic which lead to man's chief troubles. However I cannot swallow this argument as regards the arts of poetry, painting, music etc.

That means simply that I am prepared to jeopardise humanity for the

sake of literature though quite prepared to have called a halt at the pony &
trap & have done without the engine.

Incidentally Angelica & I have decided that one of our peace aims is a
pony & trap.

Well I have not much news except that I've been having 4 days of
lumbago—really bad. I am in very good spirits since the news is pretty
good & the Germans are having a hell of a time & will I think have an
increasingly hellish time now until the end.

I owe them a particular grudge just now as I want to be writing a story
and have no time to write or think.

After the war I want to have a gun dog. I think I should like a French
poodle better than a spaniel or a setter. I am told they are excellent—can
be taught to point & to retrieve.

Would you like to buy me (I'll pay) a French poodle puppy in Ireland
& train him for me? This seems to me an ideal occupation for you & a
test of Brownie's emotional control. In any case I should like your advice
& comments. There are two kinds of French poodles—large, & small.
The large black, brown, or grey is the kind I am thinking of. Ray's
family had a Russian poodle but I do not think they are so suitable. Very
much love. Do not think I condemn your present life. I am far from
doing so & wish to goodness I could see you for a few weeks & show
you how to catch salmon in the Boyne.   Love BUNNY

July 2nd, 1943   41 *Gordon Square*, WCI

Dear Tim, It is some time since I heard from you or wrote, & I should
like to know how you and Brownie are: haymaking—shortly to be
harvesting I've no doubt—& what books you are actually writing while I
only have time to project mine & make a note. First of all my news: in
January Angelica & I decided that with victory looming in the offing, it
was foolish to postpone the child we both wanted—the creature will be
born about mid-October if all continues to go well. It is already kicking
vigorously. If a boy he will be called Thomas Bartle; if a girl Virginia.
Richard warmly approves our action: William more silently regards it as
our business. Richard is in West Africa. he writes once or twice a week
& his letters are full of pelicans, monkeys, mangroves, plans for alterations at Hilton after the war. etc. William is in the middle of taking the
Higher School Certificate & may be called up at any moment. The R.A.F.

is so bunged up with recruits that it was impossible for him to get in. He has decided rather to my regret to join the navy—& will try to get a commission in coastal craft. I think he has been influenced in this by my cousin Dicky Garnett who is in the same branch of the Navy & enjoys it very much. I wish I felt sure William would. I am going down to see him at his school tomorrow. If his call-up is delayed long enough I shall go off with him for a holiday in the north which may take the form of a tramp from Swaledale to the N. Tyne at Ridley Stokoe. I wish to goodness grouse shooting opened a fortnight earlier!

I continue to work at my job: one gets awfully tired but naturally we are all in extremely good spirits as things go well & we know that we are winning faster than appears and that Europe will be free again. The tables will soon be turned on the oppressor. However no doubt it is better not to bank on victories, & to expect several more years of war. I can't do that & spend my time thinking of plans such as planting a cider orchard, turning the Dove house into a studio for Angelica, etc. Cider interests me a lot. I dont suppose one will ever have a bottle of burgundy again every night—& I am becoming a connoisseur in cider. Angelica's ambitions involve a pony & trap. Richard's a sailing boat, preferably built by himself. William has passed the entrance exam. for King's College & is down in their books. I hope this may accelerate demobilisation.

The only new books I have read are really remarkable—you should try & get hold of them when next in Dublin. Reflections in a Golden Eye & The Heart is a Lonely Hunter both by an American girl called Carson McCullers (published over here by the Cresset Press). The titles are not attractive but she is extremely original & gifted. I really dont know what I can tell you about my life: I go down to my mothers cottage on Sundays —look after my bees there, shoot a rabbit or a woodpigeon when I get the chance & then back to the daily round of my work. Gordon Square is a piece of green outside the windows; we stroll there: the railings are gone of course & the square is full of people lying on the grass, taking their dogs & cats for walks etc. I went to Hilton the other day. The trees are getting enormous: village boys with whom I played stump cricket have become heroes who have experienced things as strange as Arthur or Lancelot. The orchard is breast high in nettles: Italian prisoners are popular with all & are happy with us, it seems. I can't get a thatcher to mend a roof. Hornets have appeared. In fact it is a paradise down there.

Love to Brownie & to you BUNNY

My dearest Bunny, I think you or I or both of us must have extra-sensory-perception, for I wrote to you on the day you wrote to me, but tore it up. I had been re-reading Beaney Eye and wanted to tell you that I loved you for being exactly like your father, and destroyed the letter as too effusive. Also, believe it or not, I wrote and destroyed a letter about 6 months ago, asking when you were going to have a daughter. This one was torn up because on second thoughts it seemed indelicate. Anyway, I'm delighted to hear about Angelica and hope very much that she will have the strength of mind to make it a Virginia. It is high time we had some female Garnetts about.

My own news is nil. Six months ago I suddenly recognised the fact (with pleasure) that I was not a normal human being. The great thing about not being normal is that you dont have to do the normal things—go to war etc. Here had I been fretting myself to be normal for thirty years and more, quite unnecessarily and vainly. It was a great relief. I instantly gave up drinking, with no ill effects, stopped writing a diary which I had kept for years, improved in health, and discovered that I was a first class gardener & carpenter. My hair began to grow brown again and I had regular, natural stools. I have cultivated a garden of nearly an acre, which had not been touched for ten years; designed and built a green-house which now has its first red tomato in it; started an asparagus bed, also Indian Corn, celeriac, kohl rabi and several other oddities besides the usual vegetables, and I have three hotbeds made, with captive melons and cucumbers in them. I dont know if you have ever kept a tame melon. They are definitely alive but not very intelligent—about half as intelligent as a snake. Next year I hope to stop being a writer and earn my living by growing Iceberg lettuce for the Dublin market. Meanwhile I have had to keep in funds by writing one more book, a novel about Richard II which I am cribbing rather cleverly out of the D.N.B. Brownie and I are quite settled down to our new life. We dont intend to have anything more to do with human beings, except to pay the taxes which they make us pay. We never go off the farm and refuse to meet people. We will meet selected people like you, but no others. We live with animals and are equally interested in them. Brownie has become passionately fond of chickens and almost all forms of wild life, which she studies closely. She has got a favourite swallow which is nesting in my book case, she is constantly being stung by my bees—this year I took 3 swarms—and was fascinated by four woodboring wasps which she discovered in my work-shop. In fact, she has become the best kind of field naturalist and will spend hours with any wild animal. She also has a pet lamb.

Our greatest excitement lately has been the greenhouse though it bored Brownie a bit, until she got fond of collecting spare bits of wood. When finished, I was standing loving it, and particularly how the shadows of the wooden skeleton cut across the skeleton itself. Then I noticed that it could be used as a sundial. If you put half the dial at each end of the house, on the wall which it leans against, then the roof would make a first-rate gnomon. So I worked it out on June 22nd (shall have to do so again about Christmas) and painted it nicely, and then it seemed to want a motto. I thought of:

> I am a sundial
> And I make a botch
> Of what is done far better
> By a watch,

also of my mother's favourite sundial motto:

> Horas Non Numero, Nisi Serenas.

In the end, since the sun never shines in Ireland and you might just as well build a tennis court at the north pole, I combined dignity with reflection and just wrote

> They also serve who only stand and wait.
>
> Love to all from TIM

July 30th, 1943   *Ridley Stokoe, Tarset, Hexham*

Dear Tim, It was a delight to get your letter the other day. Your sundial had a great success in London. When one tells someone that a friend has made a sundial on his greenhouse and thought it needed a motto, they are unprepared. But London is very far away. I brought William up here for a holiday before he goes into the navy. It is boiling hot. The Hedleys are making hay: she driving the clipper with the two horses: he mowing those places where the machine could not go. Today we took our guns to walk round the moor & plan tomorrows campaign—for grouse shoot-ing starts on July 31st this year. There seem to be no grouse however:

we only saw 2 old birds & 2 young ones. Then when we had walked all round the moor we sat down on the edge of the crags & cooled off.

One is high up—with the moor rising at one's back & the North Tyne below & one can see up beyond Kielder, probably into Scotland. I think I shall bury Ray's ashes there. She stayed in this valley, a mile or two down the river, & often talked about it. We always meant to walk up here from Yorkshire. However I have not spoken about it to Richard or William. I buried my father's ashes under a walnut tree at my mother's cottage.

Well we sat there for a long time & the rabbits came out. A hen sparrowhawk flew by below, but William did not reach for his gun. Then a heron came over very close, leaving the river to try for frogs at the top of Thatchy Sike. But the fox I saw two days ago there & who came & looked at me first on one side & then on another, did not appear. There are two cubs: there were four—but 2 of them & the vixen 'met with an accident' said Mr Hedley.

We had lunch: did not talk but only looked. Then we heard a rabbit squeal. William jumped to his feet, peered, put up his gun & fired at something very close in the rocks below. Then he fired again unnecessarily & ran down without his gun & from between the rocks at the crag foot, pulled out a stoat, quite dead—in fact simply riddled. It was a lovely beast. Now he has gone down to the barley field where he will have arranged some cardboard decoy pigeons. But there have been no shots. Most creatures seem to live here—but there are too many corbies. They are the worst enemy, but one it is not easy to catch or shoot.

I bathed in the river yesterday. Angelica is in Sussex & is splendidly well. But the journey would have been too risky for her.

I am in the Hedleys' good books as the water supply he always wanted has been put in at great expense. It supplies the yard, the farmhouse, & four of the principal pasture fields. Hitherto they have had to carry water 200 yards from a spring & in droughts to cart it from the river.

I have plans or rather projects, for building a small cottage here. I should use the stone from an old ruin below the crags, & we could cut down some oak trees for the main beams & rafters. Perhaps, when the war is over, you will come & be the master mason & you may occasionally revert to your old self and shoot us some snipe and woodcock for Angelica to put into pies. She is an extremely good cook. Well I shall go now & join Will watching the cardboard pigeons & after that dip into the pool where by rights there ought to be a salmon. Only 58 salmon were caught with rod in the whole of the Tyne during 1942. Very much love to you & to Brownie. BUNNY

About September 5th, 1943   *Doolistown, Trim, Co. Meath, Eire*
Dear Bunny, Thank you for two letters. I have written to you since, but I lost it. Before I seal this up, I will have one last rummage and enclose it if possible.

I want to dedicate a book to you. May I put F O R B U N N Y on the flyleaf of it—I mean printed? The reason is that it is a kind of Bunnyish sort of book, though naturally not of the same quality. It is like Lady Into Fox in so far as it develops an impossible situation as carefully as possible, and it is like Beaney Eye because all the people are real. As you know, everybody in this household spends all the time howling out the rosary and we all know exactly what is and what is not the Houly Will Av God and are on intimate terms with Our Lord and the B.V.M. and the Little Flower and a great many others. One day Mrs McDonagh was explaining the nature of the Trinity to me, and I thought: I wonder what you really would do if the Holy Ghost suddenly put its head down the chimney? So I got involved in working it out, and then I began putting it in a book. The Holy Ghost had to have some object in coming down the chimney, so I made It come to warn us that there was going to be a second flood, and that we were to build an Ark. After that I became involved in the problems of building an Ark (I am using the corrugated iron hay-barn, turned the other way up) and of stocking and provisioning it, and of what will happen next. I have got about 30,000 words done, and still going strong. We are only beginning to bolt on the sides.

Here is an extract, so that you can see what you are putting your name to: ...[1]

I must stop sending extracts or I shall be sending the whole book. I think it is one of my better ones, but of course I dont know. It was worrying, at first, to write about real people, even in imaginary circumstances, because I was afraid of hurting feelings. But the McDonaghs dont read the papers and I will see to it that no copy is mentioned or comes within ten miles of here. For that matter, I think I'll refuse to have it sold in Ireland at all. The Irish sale is negligable, and anyway it would

[1 154 lines from *The Elephant and the Kangaroo* omitted.—D.G.]

probably be banned for mentioning the Holy Ghost. Though I've been careful to give It a capital letter every time I mentioned It, and not to describe It or even to report Its words. It's true that Mrs O'Callaghan observes that it be's a bit like a mop, but she does so in the most respectful terms ...[1]

Why dont you become a publisher yourself, Bunny? You know about books and you seem to be as rich as Croesus. You could take me on as a hack reader, after I have built your cottage for you.

By the way, I am bringing my own labourer over, whom you will have to pay, and the cottage is to be built entirely out of plastic glass and velvet curtains. We shall let you have no say in the matter whatever, except perhaps I will let you say how many rooms you want. I'm not sure of that either, as at present I mean to have one kitchen, one room or studio, two bedrooms and a bathroom.

How is that baby coming along?

Further to my remarks about extra-sensory perception, the last letter I wrote to you (the one I am going to search for when I have finished this) was written on the day you last wrote to me—or rather, in the night, in bed. No doubt this letter will cross one of yours, or, if not, you will have been thinking of me. I think the date is really September 8th, but I began writing last night ...[2]

I bet you couldn't write a letter as long as this.   Love from TIM

September 13*th*, 1943   41 *Gordon Square, London* WC1

Dear Tim, I was very glad to get your letter this morning & as I am convalescent after a bad cold & have not gone to work I will write to you. My writing is still a bit shaky, but you must forgive that. Please dedicate your book to me, but I should much prefer to have my legal name on the book rather than Bunny. A dedication like any other document is a commitment. If you dedicate your book to Bunny you commit neither yourself nor me. Whereas if you dedicate your book to David Garnett—there you are—you've got it on record & can't pretend there are a lot of synonomous persons. Bunnies are the commonest of creatures & I've no doubt your life is full of them. Bunny might be a pet rabbit for all the public knows.

[1 13 lines omitted for reasons of libel.—D.G.]
[2 12 lines omitted for reasons of libel.—D.G.]

I hope your book does not go on beyond the building & stocking of the Ark in the steady rain—& stops short of the Flood. In fact I think the end should be the rain coming down softly & steadily & the sun coming out—& NO RAINBOW. & the animals standing about dripping wet & shaking themselves at intervals ...

I think the samples of your story are extremely promising for what the book will be as a whole. By the way—a practical point—if you make your Ark by turning your Dutch Barn upside down, you will have to put a roof over it, as otherwise it will fill faster than you will be able to bale it, or pump it dry. I expect that is why Noah's vessel was the only survivor—all the open canoes, barges etc, filled with rain & sank.   BUNNY

About September 15th, 1943   *Doolistown, Trim, Co. Meath*

Dear Bunny, Your letter has worried me, for I *had* intended to describe the Flood. Your idea of ending the book in the rain with the miserable animals shaking themselves and no rainbow is such a good one that now I dont know what to do. The trouble is that the actual building and stocking wont take me beyond 40,000 words or so. Also, the flood I had intended to describe would not, perhaps, have been the one which you warn me against. I had intended it to be merely an excessive flood of the Boyne, which would go down again in the normal course of affairs. We were to float off from the Boyne Meadow, having frightful shaves with the various bridges, and, when we reached Trim (the Bridge you once stood on, talking about salmon fishing to a fat coachbuilder called O'Callaghan) we were to stick in the single arch for good. This, by blocking the river at a place where it runs between high walls, would have thrown the water into the Market Place etc. and the aboriginees, seeing me perched on top with my whiskers, would have concluded that I was Noah after all and that the Flood was genuine. So they would have taken to tubs, tar barrels, up-turned tables etc. and the river would have become covered with refugees. We ourselves, in the Ark, owing to a shifting of the cargo and other troubles, would have emptied our water casks and sailed away in these. The Boyne (I call it the Slane) flows into the Liffey for my purposes, so we should all have swept down into the midst of Dublin, screaming and praying and cursing one another, and there, under the impression that we were *parachutists*, the government would have called out the Irish navy, which consists of two motor boats, and, after a brisk engagement, they would have succeeded in dragging myself and the McDonaghs out of our tubs. You will think this a tragic conclusion, but no. Fearing that the whole thing has been got up by the Irish Times in order to discredit the government for there is nothing feared in Ireland so much as looking foolish, Dev would censor the whole affair (after a hurried meeting with the Irish hierarchy) and nothing would be allowed about it in the papers etc. To make me keep my mouth shut, they would give me a splendid job as Inspector of Inspectors, with free petrol coupons, but I, seeing which side my bread was buttered, would still threaten to write a book about it, unless they made me Minister for Education, which done, and I having thereupon tried to suppress the Irish language, they would despairingly buy me a seat in the Senate and retire me as quickly as possible on a pension of £360 a year.

Mrs. O'Callaghan, who will have been photographed by a news reel during the height of the panic, will get a job in Hollywood as a film-star on 20,000,000 dollars a minute—her *facial structure* will be just right to make her the next Garbo, and of course age is no object. She will also be sufficiently stupid to do exactly what the director tells her. Mickey will, I am afraid, be killed by a 12 pound vegetable marrow which falls on his head. Brownie & I retire to live in luxury in Merrion Square.

Now the danger of all this is, that the book looks like degenerating into farce—I am not sufficiently grown up myself, to be able to write about the real world convincingly.

This is why I hanker after your ending i.e. before it turns into knock-about.

But if I continue to attend to details unremittingly, even during the farce, I might be able to pull it through. And besides, if it is my nature to write farce, I had better accept my nature & do so.

Another 'besides' is that Ireland really is a farcical country—much more so than most people realise. We know that it is not fashionable nowadays to admire Somerville & Ross, or George Birmingham, because all Irish people are now known to live lives of simple dignity, on shark oil, in the Arran Islands. But Doolistown is not on an island, and we can obtain no shark oil. Our life is *exactly* like the Irish R.M. or one of Birmingham's farces, only more so. Last year a local priest knocked down one of his parishioners with his fists, because he suspected him of having a girl-friend (suspected the parishioner). Well, unfortunately the parishioner's skull cracked during the assault. The priest went off in a temper, but came back quarter of an hour later, to administer the last sacraments. We hardly liked to try him for anything, but we did not like to look as if we did not understand how to behave in a civilised way, so we did give him a formal trial, after a good deal of argument about whether he should be asked to enter the box or be given a seat on the bench. He was acquitted without a stain on his character, and we all said how sad it was for poor Father Blank, to have the man die on him like that. We think he will probably be raised to the next vacant bishopric elsewhere, as, of course, he will hardly like to stay in his own parish after what he has gone through.

And only last month several hundred Irishmen got on a pier together, to wait for a steamer or a ferry or something. Anyway, something went wrong with them somehow, and the ones behind began to push forward, and the ones in front rather naturally began to push back. All the middle ones (I think it was sixty) fell off the pier with loud plops, and it was a high one. Surely, in a country like this, my own little plot is not beyond the bounds of nature? The only part I am doubtful about is Mrs. O'Callaghan as a film star. I dont know quite how imbecile they are in Hollywood.

The more I think about it, the more I see that success or failure lies in the description of the event, not in the event itself. For instance, in the little bits I sent you, the description of the conjuring evening was one of an event which actually took place, but the description of the water divining was of an imaginary event. If I can make my description of the flood as real as my description of the water divining, it does not matter how improbable the flood is *per se*. For that matter, as my flood is only an exaggerated ordinary flood, it need not be very improbable even as itself. As for the job as Minister of Education etc. all this is in Ireland perfectly commonplace. It is also a fact that money is said to be offered for seats in the Senate.

I will certainly take advantage of your kindness in letting me use your full name. I will just put FOR DAVID GARNETT.

I had already roofed the Ark, as we had some spare corrugated sheets from the garage, and I was taking an ordinary well pump, which will be useful after the voyage as well as during it. The dangerous animals, like beehives, are to be carried screwed to lengths of 2″ × 2″ on this roof, though I foresee some calamities in passing under bridges with the same ...

love from TIM

Dear Bunny, (You can see by the calligraphy that I am translating my Bestiary—but, p'shaw, I'm not writing to you about that.)

The—this bloody pen is going to leak—you can see by the signature that it isn't from Henry James—thing I am supposed to be writing about— curse this gin—is the good of your soul. Well, I'll start again ...

Now, if you come to stay with us for a fortnight, the advantages will be: ONE, that you can delude yourself with the Boyne salmon from day-light to dark, and, if you ever catch one, you can, and will have to, eat it on the spot (I think there is some law against exporting them.) TWO, you can eat, unrationed, prodigious quantities of real food (butter, cream, eggs, honey, fresh vegetables, meat, everything you have forgotten) THREE, which might be good for somebody in your present office, you can catch a glimp (pardon glimsp—pardon, GLIMPSE) of what partly educated persons may be thinking in countries which have not been at war for five years; FOUR or FIVE or WHATEVER IT IS—one gets mixed up with the years, I suppose—you will save me from cutting my throat, which I propose to do on the 1st of June 1944, though the Irish-made razor will probably fail. I have not exchanged one word of more than one syllable (such as 'plough', 'hoe', 'steer', 'cow' etc) with one person since 1939. Even if you can see no advantages to yourself, it would be a work of mercy to come over.

Now, Bunny, for God's sake pull yourself together for three seconds, and forget about Melitopol or wherever it is, and consider this. It is now that we must begin to consider it. For, if you do decide to come (and write quickly saying so) you for your part will have to set to work on the machinery of permits, and I for mine will have to start building minnows which you can use. I have learned to solder minnows indistinguishable from those you buy at Hardy's, and you can't buy them, and there are none in Ireland, so I must have time to get them ready. I can also make traces.*

If you come, I am determined not to eat you, except between the hours of 7 p.m. and midnight. During the daytime I shall either fish with you, if you desire it—but by being 100 yards apart on the bank I can harm you very little—or else to stay at home in my garden and leave you perfectly free. Privately I would advise you to come home for luncheon,

---

* Also I must have warning to start forcing lettuces etc. to eat with your salmons.

instead of taking sandwiches, because we want to feed you like a civil person. From dusk to midnight, however, you have got to save me. We shall drink Irish Whisky in whatever quantity you care for, and I may say 'primogeniture' or 'steatopygous' or 'transcendentalism', or even 'etiolated' (see Grasshoppers), and you will say—but, no, I wont anticipate. Only, for the love of pity, come, eat, fish, sleep, forget, talk, drink and rescue   poor TIM

N.B. You will see that I am on the booze again—and, by God, this pen is going to leak after all. But it is after 6 months abstinence, and only out of misery, and because you dont come. Nor could any really drunk man write this hand after midnight, miserable and alone.

[Undated]   41 *Gordon Square, London* WC1

Dear Tim, I have left your last excellent letter unanswered—am not quite sure why. My news is that I have now a daughter, born on Oct 17, and called Virginia. Angelica had an easy labour & is already sitting up in a chair. Virginia is a lovely creature with a perfect complexion, very good hands & feet and distinctly like me. She weighed 8 lb 7 oz. Angelica spends a good deal of time poring over her as she lies asleep.

William was summoned to a coal mine & is now working at the Louisa Old pit at Stanley Durham. He is living with ardent Presbyterian vegetarians which sounds bad for food. The worst feature is that there is a frequent changing of shifts. i.e. after working for some days from 6 a.m. till 2 p.m. he was one day told to return at midnight for work till 8 a.m. This means that there is no fixed routine for meals—the whole family never sits down together—& as a result the standard of cooking goes down & dyspepsia, cocoa, & high-thinking nonconformity reign supreme. It has leaked out that William is a student of philosophy & as a result he writes that he spends his time 'disputing with Presbyterians for streets around.' William wants to read moral science at Cambridge.

My own view of philosophy is that it is a lot of words & no more, but naturally I shant try & impose such senile views on William. However I rather hope that by the time the war is over he will decide to read English, which I think is what Richard will probably do. Richard by the way wrote the other day to say that life in the R.A.F. had made him very critical of Cambridge—particularly of the bad manners & ignorance of undergraduates. He spends his time when off duty, in teaching classes of airmen calculus, in designing a new motor with a friend on an entirely new principle, & in designing the sailing boat which he is going to build directly the war is over. I fear he may drift into school mastering—the word drift is not the right one—But he is attracted by it, I think. The other occupation he used to think of was publishing, which I should prefer for him. Schoolmastering seems to involve such a lot of hypocrisy —doesn't it? But I daresay your opinion of publishers is as bad as of school masters.

I am extremely optimistic about the duration of the war with Germany, which I think will be over some time before next summer. I shall retire into being an author as soon as may be. By the way we have an Irish nurse from close to Rosslare looking after Angelica & Virginia. Did I tell you that after the war I am going to get a large poodle & train him as a gun-dog? My plans for Ridley Stokoe Hall progress.

Very much love BUNNY

November 2nd, 1943   *Doolistown, Trim, Co. Meath*
Dear Bunny, I was delighted to get your letter this morning, saying that Virginia had arrived. I wrote to you three days ago, assuming it. We have means of knowing these things in this island, since the days of the Tuatha De Danaan. I hope she will prove as good as she is beautiful, and that she will be able to stand up for herself against you in your old age, when you try to prevent her marriage in order to keep her for yourself. I hope she will not become any kind of artist, but will be happy doing ordinary things. I hope she will inherit your constitution. I hope she will have at least one more brother or sister to keep her company. I hope she will not believe in God, Freedom, Human Decency, Love, or any of the other things which dont exist. I hope she will be interested by being alive, and that she will live long and be prolific. I hope she wont be too beautiful, or indeed hardly beautiful at all. I hope she will like men in bed, but only one at a time. I hope she will never go into Parliament or speak on the Brains Trust or ever address a meeting on any subject whatever. I hope these are the best hopes for her to be happy. I now hook the invisible wire into the catch at the back of my ballet skirt, wave my wand, and disappear top right into the wings.   love from Brownie too TIM

Dearest Tim, This is to wish you a very merry Christmas & Happy New Year. I hope it will see the end of the war and our meeting, whether to fish in the Boyne, or to shoot grouse in Northumberland.

My daughter Amaryllis Virginia Garnett tips the scale at a trifle over 13 lbs and at 9 weeks old is just learning to acquire new interests & new powers. She laughs, crows, recognises people, lifts & turns her head.

I am abandoning her & Angelica for Christmas and am going to visit William who will get 3 days off. We hope to shoot a few pheasants & possibly a fox and a corbie. William is appropriately enough now working in the William pit, underground, but not yet at the coalface. His last letter on the character of the miners is rather interesting; he says:

'The miners and their grievances is a theme I have become accustomed to, from the Boss, the Under-manager, and now the fore-overman, & plenty of people who tell you the miners are suspicious. Anderson, the fore-overman, told me he was Public Enemy No. 1, which is quite false. On the contrary the miners are incapable of taking anything seriously; they cannot think but only feel and when they do, it is always for fun, or about something utterly trivial. I have only met one miner with views ... Rather than being infected with anti-capitalist slogans or feeling that these are the finest men in the world, (most of the actual hewers are hump-backed, weedy-looking men, with either no teeth in their head, or bad eyesight) I feel amused by them, not because I am from somewhere else and a different sort. (Oh, how local-minded they are!) nor because I am humiliated or bullied, but because I watch them without feeling any relationship at all to them, just as when one reads fiction. They never do anything except for fun, even when the Gaffer plays hell with one or other of them, he does it not merely to the amusement of others, but to that of the culprit.'

It will be very interesting to see William himself. I expect he will be getting pretty brawny.

I spent last week-end in a very different sort of world—at Charleston where Sheppard, the Provost of King's was staying for the weekend. On Saturday he gave a most moving & amusing lecture on Homer, in Lewes, to a gathering of local people. It was really brilliant. But his conversation was extraordinary—story succeeding story—all of them rather long. Here is one about his predecessor Provost Brooks. About the turn of the century, young Brooks & his friend McClean were the most brilliant young men to take Holy Orders. Great things were expected of them. One day the Bp of Wells said to them. 'You ought to do a piece of really important work. You should edit the Septuagint. It will take a year or two, but will give you a reputation.' They set to work, noting all the variations which have crept into the versions, since the original 70 scholars made their identical inspired translation into Greek about 150 B.C. Twenty years later poor Brooks realised the task would never be completed. His life had been ruined, and in any case a variorum text of the Septuagint was of no interest to anybody. But McClean was still full of fire & enthusiasm. Forty years later the great work was still unfinished & Provost Brooks would clutch at any visitor after lunch quavering: Don't go. Dont go. I'll telephone to McClean that I'm detained. & he would call him & say: 'The Vice-Provost has come to see me on a matter of College business. I am afraid I may not be able to come over this afternoon.' Now Dr Brooks is dead. McClean is still full of enthusiasm, he has never doubted, but his editorial powers have deserted him. He can no longer copy out notes accurately. Don't you think that is a perfect short story? Well I send you my warmest love & hope to see you before many months have passed   BUNNY

The envelope containing the following poem from Tim is missing. It may have been sent with the letter dated January 10th, 1944, or separately.

THE SILENCE ROOM
Xmas '43.

Shout! Shout! They can't hear you unless you shout.
A million Poetasters pour it out
Hourly in Biloxi and New York.
In Chicago and Hollywood the stork
Delivers one Brain Trust per second and
Prophets come quintuplets in Maryland.
They know how to think: they know how to feel:
They know all the answers for this new deal.
And, my God, dont they know the way to squeal.
So shout. Shout loud enough to mount the roar
Of Hearst's most smashing printing presses or
My Lord of Beaverbrook's. Shout till they hear,
Louder than Quintin Hogg or Shinwell. Cheer

138

Better than Stalin, Churchill or Rooseveldt.
Yell louder than any of them have yelled.
Scream how to put it right. Howl down the mob.
Roar, rave, stink, thump, assert, go holy, sob.
You havn't a hope else, in such a crowd,
In such a loudness, except to be loud.

So, my Philosopher, dont study sense.
Dont try to find out why it comes or whence.
Dont bother to work out the dark and dense
Forest of Truth. Just shout. Shout for Silence.

1944

Dear Bunny, Tight again, so I have got to send you a lecture. This time it will be entirely about self. (Did you get letter about William's Ethics and Richard's school-mastering? Our postal service is a bit complicated.)

My new year resolutions for 1944 are as follows:—

(1) The business of a writer is to recognise his own limitations, and then work within them. It has taken me getting on for forty years to realise that I can never be a Shakespeare. I must try, at best, to be a Lewis Carrol i.e. I must be content to write for children. I have therefore begun, and written 40,000 words of, a book for Amaryllis Virginia.

(2) The only object of any sensible writer is to make money. This I will do, or die.

(3) All children's books, and at least 50% of grown-up books, depend upon their illustrations. To take the grown-ups to begin with, I believe that Dickens and Surtees would have made nothing of themselves without Phiz or Boz or whatever he was called, and Leech. As for children's books, I am perfectly certain that without Shepherd the miserable Milne would have been lucky to clear 2½d, and Lear without pictures would not exist and, however much you may think this is heresy, I believe that 2/3rds of Lewis Carrol is really Tenniel. The White Queen—your idea of her—is it the picture of the lady with her hair coming down, or something Carrol made her say? Mome Raths, Borogroves etc? Would the mere *words*, that they were a cross between a badger and a corkscrew or whatever he said, would these have made their features like the Tenniel pictures? You have only to read some un-illustrated edition of Sylvie & Bruno, to realise that 80% of Alice is Tenniel.

(4) Very well, since I am going to make my fortune by writing books for children, I want an illustrator.

(5) Here your tipsy Tim draws toward a point, shewing he is not so bottled after all. DO YOU, OR DOES ANGELICA, know of any living artist who could compare with Tenniel? I did know one such, a person called PONT who drew for Punch, but to my inexpressible chagrin the wretched youth has died. I want somebody who will trouble with detail, as Tenniel did (and my poor Pont—a lovely person) and who will agree

to be treated by me as an equal. We should have to stay together, for months, while working, and he would have to insist on being paid by *percentage* on the books, not by a lump sum. (This, if he was any good, for his own good.) Now, my dear Bunny and Angelica, I do not want a 'modern' artist, and I dont want an ancient one. I only want a real person. I want somebody who, as I do, when the book deals with the 18th century, is willing to learn about that same. The book for Amaryllis Virginia is a kind of continuation of Gulliver's Travels. For it, I have troubled to find out who was the publisher of the first edition etc., and the illustrator must be the kind of person who will take the same kind of trouble (costume, architecture etc.) and *draw as carefully*. I DONT WANT A PETER ARNO. I have no objection to the miserable Arno as 'Art', but it so happens that I am myself a scholar. I want a scholar artist, and didn't somebody say that scholarship or something of that sort was an infinite capacity for taking pains? I dont mean that he must cross-hatch (though I should prefer it, as one thing is a sign of another) but I could stomach his using ink-washes even, so long as he had taken pains with them, if one can take pains with slop like that.

Now I have not seen a copy of Punch or Esquire or any other illustrated Periodical for four years, so I dont know whether such a person exists. Can you or Angelica tell me of one? Naturally I dont want somebody to *copy* Tenniel. (I keep feeling I havn't spelt him right.) What I want is a *living* Teniel, a modern one, a new one, quite different but as good and painstaking, whom I can respect and who would respect me. I would like him if possible to be young, so that I can alter him to suit myself (and him! I was always a first-rate schoolmaster, with much altruism) and he must have no arty la-di-da. I dont want grace: I want work. I work myself, dont you?

This book for Amaryllis wont be ready for her to read, until she is ready to read it, *if we can get the right person*. He will be 50% of the book. That's why you two must help.

It all boils down to this: does either of you know a Tenniel? (I take an english periodical called NEWS REVIEW, which had for frontispiece at the new year a picture by the man who illustrated much of your 7 Pillar's Shaw. It is *contemptible*. It shewed three Knights against a sunrise—you will have seen it—and I happen to know how contemptible it is because by pure chance I drew these same three knights myself—he copied them from a work called 'Life & Work of the English People' by Hartley and

Elliot—and I can see the puerile slavishness of the whole thing. Dont recommend him.)

Well, Bunny, that is all of my new year's resolutions, and, as you can see, they are mainly resolutions for Angelica. I will stop, for fear of the new sheet.   love from TIM

P.S.

The fact is that I am a slap-dash kind of writer, and therefore I do *not* want a slap-dash illustrator. There is a person called ARDIZZONE, who does quite discerning ink-washes, but, in spite of his real goodness, this is not the man for me. *I* can do the discerning atmosphere, in the prose: what we need is some painstaking person who will fill in the detail. If you see what I mean, the Great British Public is a sort of purblind institution who have to be given a detailed picture to pore over. Then they say: What a wonderful writer Mr. White is, he doesn't half make you see what he is writing about! All the time it is the poor Tenniel whom they are complimenting, but they are too stupid to know that. When I say: 'The cat sat on the mat' (illustrated with a Cheshire Cat by Tenniel), they cry: 'What a master of prose! Who would have thought of that?'

In fact, can you suggest any artist who would make my cat sit on the mat?

You see, he has to draw the mat.   love from TIM

P.P.S.   3.30 a.m.

What is more, when Leech died, Surtees stopped selling.

It is like Gilbert & Sullivan.

[*January* 1944]   41 *Gordon Square*, WC1

Dear Tim, I must apologise for not having written before but I have been very busy indeed. Also I received your letters at long intervals—The P.P.S. coming first. I invented an application to it of a purely personal nature: I was Leech—you were Surtees & nearly replied on that interpretation. Then came the next letter which threw doubt on it—then the third which meant re-reading the whole series. Well you are a queer chap. Dont you realise that you are designed by nature to illustrate your own books— just as Lear was designed to write nonsense rhymes to his own illustrations? You will at all events be far better than Boz. I have been reading Pickwick Papers—am reading it aloud to Angelica who has never read it.

When you marry, choose a child wife, as I have done. You get so much pleasure from watching her taste the well-known things for the first time, & thus live again. The idea that old chaps of seventy are rejuvenated by the society of girls of 17 is perfectly true & is proved by my experience. To recur however to the subject in hand: you have the gift of illustration: you have the patience & the time to perfect your art. You will save the %age of royalty by giving it to that staid fellow who never drinks whiskey lest his hand shake, but invests in War Savings Certificates. (I presume that is what you miserable neuters buy in your green post offices out of your profiteering)—you will be saved all that money & you can borrow it from him much more easily than from a Chelsea Artist. Anyway some of your ideas are absurd: Ardizzone only draws drunks leaning against bars—an illustrator of genius but not for your books. No the real chap for you is White. I am not trying to flatter you, or avoid looking for an illustrator, which I will do if you insist. I am serious. You can, if you try, illustrate your own books far better than any of the chaps around the place now. Moreover several artists lives whom you would drown in the Boyne would be saved.

My news is that, as I may have told you before, I have been elevated in rank, have a slight increase in salary, a secretary, a wonderful extra telephone which moos like a cow and has an extra switch for all the great ones, and as a result I work non-stop from ten to 1 & 2-30 to 8, like an automaton, very well, & enjoying it all. I really am trying to put my shoulder to the wheel.

Our news is that our lives are altered by the advent of a lovely slinky, wild beast—perhaps wolf—girl of 21, who has come to us with her illegitimate baby, as a cook. She is extremely beautiful & according to Angelica very nice. Her baby comes tomorrow. We live in luxury—dont even cook breakfast. William continues well & sane Richard lives in a world of dream boats, ocean-going yachts designed by himself. Love to your Brownie wife   BUNNY

The first half of the following letter, about fishing, is omitted.

March 25th, 1944   *Doolistown, Trim, Co. Meath, Eire*
Dear Bunny, ... Could you lend me your Pliny? Mine is defective. As a lend it would be safe, as I value you more than a Pliny, but the danger is

143

the wartime postage. Think it over. I need it badly, for the notes to the Bestiary I am translating. You would have to send it through a bookshop, I believe.

I dont know how you married men get on in the spring, but we barren stocks are subject to some kind of sap business. Every spring I find myself helplessly building a nest (i.e. greenhouse or something of that sort) or nourishing cuckoos (i.e. bees, asparagus, fruit trees etc.) We have had four stunning days of sunshine (nearly 90° sun temperature today) and my poor old head is awhirl with fig trees, peaches, tomatoes, asparagus and the bees. A bee has just walked out of my trousers on to this paper, and there is another still inside. I like them very much. We have a warm south-west wall, where they go to pleasure themselves when off duty, have a great wash and brush up by twos and threes helping each other—I suppose you get a bit sticky after mucking about with honey all day—and then go to sleep.

A terrible tragedy has happened! I took the bee to the window, as he was bothering me, meaning to let him out after, and in a minute an enormous spider had sprung upon him. I heard a buzz and went to see. He was already quite numb and the spider was stroking him with its forelegs, while holding him down, like mesmerism: I am ashamed to say that I interfered—but only because it was happening in a crack of the sash, where I could not properly see. The bee is paralysed, though I have cleaned off the web stuff, and can only move his antennae. All this in 20 seconds. The spider has buzzed off. He is a monster. I did not know they took bees. I must stop. It is time to go and hatch something.

love from TIM

The Arts Theatre has commissioned me to write a play for them. Shall I?

May 6th, 1944   *Doolistown, Trim, Co. Meath, Eire*

Dear Bunny, I want to know why people write such a lot of cock about fishing: about the lovely weather and the enormous trout they caught so cunningly and all that lie? (Goes out, kicks cat, looks moodily at wind vane, comes in, slams door and continues.) A factual fishing story would go like this.

On Monday, while fruitlessly salmon fishing, you notice a really big trout rising further up the river. On Tuesday you go back with a trout rod and find him still rising, but it is blowing a gale in your face and you can't cast. On Wednesday you go again in good conditions, crawl twenty yards through cow dung and wild irises, and hook him beautifully on a Grey Flag. The hook comes away immediately afterwards and, on packing up to go home, you notice that the point was off it all the time. On Thursday it is blazing hot and still as death and glaring sunshine, so it is no good fishing him. On Friday he is taking the Green Drake, which are in very small quantities. You hover on the bank all day, waiting for a good hatch, which does not come. The fish is undecided and choosy and there is no ripple. On Saturday there is a blizzard blowing down stream. But you go all the same, because you know that all the bowzies from Trim will be combing the river during the week end, and you dont want to have him snapped up under your nose. You spend the whole day in the blizzard, waiting for it to abate, which it does not. On Sunday you go down early in the morning and hang about until 6 p.m., but the wind is across you, there is little hatch, the fish is on the opposite side of the river. At 6 p.m. you begin to swear. You have devoted 56 hours to this trout and you go home to tea in a passion. At 7.30 p.m. a friend knocks on the door, saying he wants to shew you a fish. He spends one hour telling you how he caught it. He is one of the Trim bowzies, of course, and, when you look at the wind vane, you notice that it has changed to South, which is the only quarter from which the fish could have been covered, and the only quarter from which it has not blown in the past week. He has merely strolled up the river, noticed the fish for the first time, the wind and a batch of mayfly coinciding favourably—half an hour after you left the river, after your 56 hour vigil waiting for this—and he has hooked him at the first cast. The trout weighs more than 3 lbs. You admire it, listen to the story of its wonderful fight, get rid of the man somehow, after heartiest congratulations, go upstairs, strangle yourself with a 4x cast and stab yourself to death with fish hooks. (Throws pen in fire, pours bottle of ink on Brownie, kicks cupboard door, which breaks, and continues.) Why is my life like this? Who has put this on me? How can I get my hands round his neck? Is it God? God, how I would strangle him if I could catch him. God damn and blast and hell and shit and onions.　　　love from TIM

Yes, and what's more, since I know of another big trout in the vicinity, we may be perfectly sure that next monday there will be a water spout, next tuesday there will be an earthquake, next wednesday the river will be frozen over, next thursday there will be a cyclone, next friday there will be a succession of tidal waves, next saturday there will be a dust storm and next sunday there will be a volcanic eruption with continuous falls of lava, except during the half hour when I go home for tea—a two mile walk each way—when the other trout, of six pounds, will be caught by a small boy with a bent pin.

Iniquity on high.

May 27th, 1944   *Doolistown, Trim, Co. Meath, Eire*
Dear Bunny, You will be relieved to hear that the troubles of my proud and angry dust were not from Eternity after all, and did fail. In short, this is a fishing story which you will have to listen to, even if the bombs are raining on your head. Oh, how I wish I could tell it in full. But we great men who accomplish things are supposed not to talk about them. We have to be terse about it. I must—but I'm damned if I will. I shall tell it as fully as I like ...[1]

There was no rise at all, it began to rain at 10.30, your time, and we decided to come home. Just as we were leaving the river, we saw a fine rise. My bowzie had no fly tied on at the time, and I had my whisky bottle fly. (A true Green Drake dun, but tied with wings extended, as in picture.) Consequently I fished him first, hooked him nicely, and the fun began at six minutes to eleven. At just one minute past midnight we netted out a healthy young salmon of 8½ lbs.

If I were not, as you know, the most modest of men, I should write to the Field about this—not because I caught and killed the salmon in about an hour on a 2x trout cast—others have done this often—but because it was on the *dry fly.*

It says in Taverner's book on salmon fishing in the Lonsdale Library that this has never been done in the British Isles, that it is done in America, and that some famous Yankee fisherman was brought over to shew them how to do it in Scotland, but he only rose one fish and did not hook that...

You are being written to, my proud Bunny, by the only person you know who can absolutely state that he himself has killed a salmon on the mayfly. Best of all, *I knew it was a salmon* when I began to fish it. From start to finish I was trying to take a salmon on the dry fly, and did so.

[1 Two and a half pages omitted.—D.G.]

146

The bowzie quarrelled with me throughout the hour of battle, believing the quarry to be a trout of 2 lbs and upbraiding me for not pulling it out.

Well, Bunny, there it is, the great event.

> His servants He, with new acquist,
> In peace and consolation hath dismissed,
> And calm of mind, all passion spent.

love from
The only man who ever caught an Atlantic
Salmon on the Green Drake.

[Probably early September, 1944]   41 *Gordon Square*, WC1

Dear Tim, Your complaints are justified & I enclose a letter which has been hanging about & which shows I had you in my mind. Unfortunately our holiday turned out badly. My lumbago increased a bit & got much worse during 3 strenuous days with William at Ridley Stokoe. It was a failure as a shooting holiday owing to the absence of birds. William however shot 2 brace of grouse & I missed an equal number. The trouble was that a fortnight of rain & snow came at hatching time—& also what birds there were had gone off to the high ground to eat knoops (cloudberries).

I could scarcely dress myself or walk to the station with a very heavy rucksack the last day. Travelling conditions were bad. I had to stand from Newcastle to Darlington in a jam of people & had both Will's rucksack & my own. Then stand again in the bus for 17 miles out from Richmond. Then climb the 600 feet up from Low Row. Unfortunately I then felt I must paunch 2 rabbits & bury the paunches & while digging a hole was seized with agonizing cramp. I clung in agony to the spade so as not to fall. William helped me in & to bed & I have been in bed ever since—over 3 weeks now. I had ruptured a cartilage in my back, and am waiting for it to go back into its place, which the experts predict will occur in about 10 days time. Butts Intake was an awkward place to be in: William had to go back to his mine and Angelica was left to look after me and Amaryllis. She had to do every damned thing for us both, do the washing, buy the food & carry it up from the dale far below us. At first I wasnt so bad & even plucked & drew grouse in bed, but then the cartilage jammed itself into the roots of the sciatic nerve & for several days I was in agony.

Sometimes I couldn't stop a scream. I can manage the pain which makes one moan easily, but the big pain is terrifying & one gets too frightened of it to move. But one *must* move, or one's legs set rigid & then there's no escape. I lay for 36 hours holding my leg with both hands making tiny little movements, in agony, but keeping off the big pain most of the time. It is horrible to see the face of someone you love when you scream & to know that if the big pain goes on you can't stop yourself. The local shop yielded Aspro. . . The local doctor gave me a sort of toning & fixing photographic mixture, which I had great faith in. I luckily found a bottle of Potassium Bromide—not a good pain killer but better than nothing & after swallowing 60 grs. got some sleep. The local doctor was charming. He told me what all the former inhabitants of the Dale had died of. He had been there 40 years & was dressed in the fashions of 1900. Luckily I have a doctor in London who is a specialist on this misfortune. I wired & wrote to him, he diagnosed the trouble & sent an ambulance to pull us out. First I had to get from the bed onto a chair. Then the chair was carried downstairs while I sweated with pain & fear. Then I transferred myself onto the stretcher & 2 grey, elderly & un-attractive blokes staggeringly carried me about 500 yards to the nearest metalled road—where the ambulance was. Swaledale had never been so lovely: the sun shining, clouds racing, a fresh N.W. wind glowing hard down the dale. There were a hundred kinds of green between the fields by the wandering river, and the higher slopes which were slate & purple with heather. Tommy Appleton had come up to carry the luggage. His two collies worried each other, biting each others ears in play. He helped carry me, & the odious attendants exploited him & a stream of dismal cockney wit flowed from them. I felt very emotional. I had not been able to see anything out of window but a stone wall for 16 days. Every sheep bouncing up hill, every curlew or lapwing's cry moved me almost to tears. But particularly the sun & the wind & the great view. I had very little pain on the journey—which was wearisome & exciting. The worst was spilling some of my urine out of the undersized bottle provided (it held about a pint) on to the stretcher. Eleven & a half hours later I trans-ferred myself to another chair & was carried up & am now in our great bed looking out at the plane trees ...

Well my future is unfortunately going to be a good deal affected by this back of mine. I shall be up & about in another 3 weeks or less—& shall then have to wear a piece of armour to keep the cartilage in its place.

I shall never be able to do the following things—dig, row a boat, mow, run, jump, tumble downstairs, or fall down. Nor can I safely carry a weight. On the other hand I can fish, stand all day in water, sleep in a damp bed if necessary, drink as much as I like (as long as I dont fall down) eat what I like etc. Having my tastes, I shall have to learn to be extremely cunning, like an old Fox which has lost its leg in a trap, & continues to get the young rabbits & game it wants. For example—I shall not be able to walk up in line across a moor, as I should have to go too slowly for the other guns. I shall have to ambush or hide behind a natural or artificial butt while Richard & William walk up the moor etc. Swimming is all right. Luckily I don't care for any games. The real deprivation is picking apples in trees, carrying weights, moving furniture, using an axe. Also I was going to build a house doing a lot of the work myself, at Ridley Stokoe. If I ever build it now, I shall only be able to do bits like pargetting, carving wood etc. While I was in bed I designed this house in every detail & William has made me a paper model of it. Richard may get home soon—he tells me he is yellow, gaunt & parti-coloured. I hope he gets a long leave. He is determined to have a boat for the rest of his life & has plans of exploring all the Scottish sea lochs & the Baltic. I hope you will join us & we will catch some sea trout.

Your tonsils sound a rather casual matter to me. It is a big operation having them completely taken out & will do you an immense amount of good—mentally as well as physically. Probably it will stop you worrying about your glass-eye painting. I am not at all attracted by your wasting your time in such a way. I dont think you are a painter or have any particular taste for it. The less you have to do with art, theories of art, & religion the better. On the other hand the more you have to do with writing & with animals the better.

That reminds me that whichever of us first crosses from Ireland to England must bring an attractive young donkey, female preferred, with him. Angelica is most anxious to keep a donkey and good donkeys are hard to get in England, whereas they are still I suppose about six a penny in Ireland.

I think before we decide about our fishing holiday together, I shall have to see how well my new exo-skeletal arrangements do their job. But I understand they are pretty efficient. Also when we have this holiday will depend partly on when I get free of the war, when we move back to Hilton, & what Angelica is doing at the time, as well as on when the fish are running up whatever river it is. I am just going to look out the Costello on the map.

Well you must forgive me sending you such an inordinately long letter. I think of you often, & always with affection & look forward very much to seeing you & introducing you to Angelica & Amaryllis, who will probably be able to walk & talk quite freely by then. She is an attractive pumpkin.   Yours ever BUNNY

September 14th, 1944   *Doolistown, Trim, Co. Meath, Eire*
                                                          P.S. I see you spell it cartilage.
Dear Bunny, I was horrified to hear about your lumbar regions, though it will probably do you good to be ill and in pain for some time, if it doesn't last, which one supposes it wont. People need chastening about once every ten years, because then they are so much more thankful for being well. I dont quite understand what was the matter, as you say it began with lumbago and then a cartiledge slipped and pressed against the sciatic nerve. If I have this right, presumably the cartiledge will come right again in time, with this shield you mention to hold it in place, and will not be more than an inconvenience. The 'lumbago' which it started with wont however ever come right, unless you attend to me. You have a childlike faith in doctors, who have always been the most notorious fools in all the professions, so I am probably lecturing you in vain, but my conscience bids me tell you that you can cure your next attack of plain lumbago in three days, and cure it for good, by using Phenylchinchorinic acid. It is manufactured in Germany under the trade name of ATOPHAN, is a poison, and must be taken with extreme care. Now do be a sensible fellow and take it, or persuade a doctor to give it to you when you next have lumbago. I fear that you will think me like Horry Walpole, with his bootikins for the gout, and his James's powder. Perhaps I am. Anyway I should have insisted on giving Horry a course of Atophan.

The only bright side to your affliction is that now you can't build the new house and will consequently be able to give me the money instead, which will be horribly necessary soon, as I am getting more penniless every day, and dont care. It is dreadful to be a pococurante. All I have cared about for the last six months is painting, at which I can never hope to earn a living, partly because I am a fairly good painter, pace your letter. Anyway I can paint quite as well as Duncan Grant, though I can't paint like Graham Sutherland. By the way, was it a portrait of your Angelica in the Penguin book of Duncan Grant?

If I bring a donkey couldn't you arrange to keep me and Brownie with it as pets, instead of all these Jews and poodles that you go in for? I can't do anything except do my best. That is, I must do what I am interested in or life wouldn't be worth living, and besides, what one did wouldn't be worth doing. Unfortunately it is rather an uneconomic way of going on, as people only begin to pay enormous sums for your work after you are dead, like Blake.

Yesterday I made friends with a person called the Duc de Stacpoole and am now going in mortal terror lest I should receive a letter from his wife, inviting me to tea. I should have to answer the letter and dont know the correct form of address for the duchess of a duc without a 'k' in him. I mean, what are they? Are they dukes or ducks or what? Are they in De Brett or the Almanac de Gotha or where? Are they related to the coralline de vere stackpool?[1] Shall I just say 'Dear Duchess'? If you know the answers, pray haste and write, haste post haste, or I shall be sent down to the servants hall.

I am enclosing a letter about the Costello river. Shall I pursue enquiries about its financial aspect?

I would be just as glad to come to England to stay with you, as my sole object is you, not the fishing, but I dont know whether I shall be able to afford the fare. Here I live free if I want to, as I luckily gave the McDonaghs plenty of money when I had some.

Dear Bunny, I am really writing this letter only to amuse you, in case you are still in bed, and as I have absolutely nothing whatever to tell you about, it is heavy work.

I will tell you about our hen. It is a symbolical hen, like Ibsen's wild duck, and it stands for everything that goes on at Doolistown. It really exists, though you will think I am romancing. It has no covert feathers on wings or tail, so that you see the quills of primaries and train: its head is bald: its body feathers are stuck on back to front. Paddy says it is a 'Guinea hen'. It is coal black. It runs about in rather an agitated way, and no wonder. This hen symbolises the fact that if you look in my

[1 Henry de Vere Stacpoole, author of *The Blue Lagoon*. Tim is referring to his books *The Ship of Coral* and *Green Coral*.—D.G.]

right-hand beehive you will find it is full of wasps: that if you look in the front hall you will find it is full of wild bees: that if you look up any of the chimneys you will find they are full of jackdaws: that the only chimney not full of daws has a tribe of cats in it, who have come to live there and gone wild (they come out at night to raid the larder, but rush up the chimney again if anybody opens the door, and they are smoke-proof, and Mrs. McDonagh says they are the Holy Will of God): and it symbolizes the fact that De Valera's only comment on your war is that we must all talk Irish.

My book situation at present is as follows:

(1) I have the whole Arthurian epic unpublished, and anyway I want to wait seven years to re-write it.

(2) I have finished rather a nice book which is dedicated to Amaryllis. It is about a decayed palace like Stowe where a small girl finds some Lilliputians which had been left behind by Swift.

(3) I have finished the book about the Holy Ghost at Doolistown, which is dedicated to you, but I am uneasy about it. I am in doubts about calling the hero Mr. White, and about some other matters.

(4) I wont publish The Insolence of Man, which I sent you once, but I have written one act of a play for the Arts Theatre, which is about Ants and embodies most of it.

(5) I have translated half my Bestiary, can read monkish Latin with all its abbreviations, and know more about nature in the middle ages than anybody except a person called Druce. I shall finish this in 20 years.

(6) I am playing with a book of adventure, like Stevenson, about Rockall and a biologist villain aged 130.

(7) I am thinking of starting a book called 'Extinct Family'. It might be rather fun to invent a noble family, establishing itself under Richard II and going on through the centuries, with which I am fairly well acquainted, until the last earl gets shot down over Hamburg. But not written like Hugh Walpole!

Talking of shooting down earls over Hamburg, when I was a schoolmaster I used to teach a nice, bouncing, naughty, gumptious little boy who was known as Cheese. His name was G. L. Cheshire. I hear from the wireless that he has now got the V.C., D.S.O. twice, and D.F.C! He is still alive.

On the whole, I think I will put 'Dear Duckess', as she is a bit fat.

You say my tonsil was a slapdash operation, but we Irish are a hardy race, have our babies under hedges etc., and it was really considered rather pansy of me to stay the night in hospital. Needless to say, there are no modern refinements. A rusty guillotine is used, with half its parts missing, and your first meal is tough beef.

It was interesting enough for two reasons. I happened to diagnose my own affliction by doing a painting. It was one of a series of four dealing with the Resurrection (a satire) and it was of Hell. I made it a red tunnel with two gloomy demons sitting in the foreground and myself in a cauldron of molten metal, yawning. The idea I thought I was expressing was that after you had been roasted for a few million years the proceedings would lose all interest for all concerned. In the roof of the cavern there were two hemispherical rocks, bluish and mucous. When finished I re-collected that I sometimes psycho-analysed myself in these fanciful pictures, so I looked at it to see if it had any message, and perceived at once that the tunnel was my throat, that I was holding my mouth open (yawning) as a hint, that I had painted Hell because I was feeling hellish, and that the rocks were my tonsils. I went at once to a Dublin specialist, who confirmed the diagnosis, and was home in two days, minus rocks. The amazing part of this story is that I came round in the theatre and was shewn a tonsil and, although I had never seen one before, it was exactly like the ones I had painted! I suppose ones unconscious mind must see one's inside? The other interesting thing was having the nitrous oxide. I am always a very resigned sort of patient and scrambled onto the table so calmly that all present fell back in amazement, saying how well I was behaving—they praised me to my face, in fact, with their courtly spanish grace—and I sucked up my N_2O like a baby at the breast. The surgeon said to the house surgeon, as I was going under, 'How did those pictures turn out?' The house surgeon said: 'They were a failure.' The surgeon said: 'Why?' At this point all contact was lost with the outside world, so the people inside my brain had nothing to do but repeat the last received message again and again. 'How did those pictures turn out?' 'They were a failure.' 'Why?' 'How did those pic?' 'Were a failure' 'Why?' 'How pic?' 'Failure.' 'Why?' 'Howpicfailurewhy?' 'Howpifailywhy?' etc. etc. Mean-while, and this is the interesting part, some sluggish and rather inarticulate overseer of the telephone exchange, although unconscious of external stimuli, continued to reflect and to observe the internal condition, and, while under the anaesthetic, I realised that if you could measure the time taken by the above conversation, from 'How to 'why?', you would know the time taken to lose consciousness, and perhaps the time taken by the act of death. At this point the repetitions changed to 'pitintothis—pitintothis—pit into this—SPIT INTO THIS', the lights went on again, and I sat up with a mouthful of blood, saying thickly '*Very* interesting. Its a question of thousandths of a second.' They thought I was raving, but I was really trying to tell them about measuring the act of death, which I had thought out when unconscious. I find this interesting, would believe that people have tried to speak after having their heads cut off, and suspect that for some short time 'dead' people remain cumbrously conscious, but only internally.

I am growing boring.   love from TIM

September 20th, 1944   41 *Gordon Square*, WC1

Dear Tim, 'The river is in good order for fishing & salmon have been seen' writes Robert Hedley from my farm. And instead of reducing me to a state of melancholia in which I devise epitaphs for my grave under a slab of rock on High Crag, it fills me with eager interest. Since the day before yesterday the world has changed—though my condition becomes slowly more distressing—my left calf flaps like the belly of a gutted fish. A surgeon has seen me, pricked me with pins for witchcraft, and is going to cut me open, break open my spine, pull out the bit of cartilage which has jammed itself into the great nerves, & then cover up & make all good as best he can. He says otherwise I might spend ten years in bed. If the diagnosis is correct & the operation is successful, I shall be as good as ever I was, if not better, in a two or three months from now. Able to carry a bag, paddle a canoe, & get into a bus, or dig a dish of potatoes without fear of a week's agony and months in bed. What will be disagreeable is the week or two of re-educating my flabby & bruised muscles to function again.

The complexion of things has changed also because a telegram arrived from Richard to say he was back & would shortly be with us. What a welcome the poor boy will get! Almost as soon as he has set eyes for the first time on his sister, we shall be asking him to give her her bath, make toys for her, keep her entertained & fed. He can go out & buy food, cook it & serve it up to me. We have a bottle of champagne for him, but also there will be a bedpan that wants emptying. Angelica is almost dead beat with looking after me & often when she lies down beside me, I think of the dying parents in Caldecott's Babes in the Wood.

There are many infuriating things about being ill, but soon one becomes resigned: the geese at Scearn Bank, the mother cat who had run wild & got a nest of 3 kittens, the sweet corn wasting its sweetness, the figs devoured by starlings, the pears by wasps, the tomatoes ripening unpicked—the greengages—a whole tree of them wasted. Details of this sort have poured in from my old mother—but they have not moved me at all. Instead I was making lists of what needs doing at Hilton. Now however I am able to take an interest in all the occupations from which I had been told I should be cut off for ever. It is therefore disappointing not to have received your inclosure about the Costello River which I cannot find on the map anyway. You speak of being poor & I was afraid you might be suffering the penalty for having become a neutral of your own free will. If you add to that handicap, that of becoming a psycho-analytic painter I am afraid you will starve unless you let me publish extracts from your letters.

However I won't moralise any more since I shall be pretty broke also—having served my country & paid a surgeon to make a hole in my back: the first unremunerative & the second ruinous.

Lack of money may affect my plans to come to Ireland: but on the other hand you never know about money—it may turn up, magically, when wanted. Anyhow the house is once more being planned: Ridley Stokoe is a place to stay at & live in & not a sort of mausoleum surrounding my ashes. Did I tell you about it? It consists of a single straight stone building of 2 storeys with a stone roof—15 foot wide internally with scullery, kitchen, hall, & library all in a row, & 5 bedrooms upstairs & on one side of it huddling into it, a squat square stone tower containing staircase & bathroom on 1st floor and a square studio with big windows on the second. By the way there is a magnificent view there of the N. Tyne river & the border hills all round from Kielder to Otterburn. The real snag are the chimneys which are close copies of 14th century ones at Nether Levens Hall in Westmoreland. They have to be pretty tall to carry the smoke over the tower roof (the tower is 3 storeys with almost flat roof. The house 2 storeys with gable roof). William has slightly heretical views about the planning of the stairs but I shall enlist Richard on my side. Well—although you may not plan the house, you can come & do a lot of the work: cut down oak trees, saw them up in saw pits, cart stones down from the moor & the ruin to the site, plan the drains, put in the septic tank.

As a reward for this you will be able to forget the war and the Irish, and become one of the Border people—learn to play the Northumbrian bagpipes (the Border music is very beautiful quite unlike the Scots.) Then you will probably kill a salmon in my pool which is a thousand times harder & more exciting than in the Boyne, because there are so few fish, so little water, and so many rocks. And you will find some way of making the grouse congregate & nest there, the blackgame return, the pheasants hatch out larger broods. All this will keep you working for me & perfectly happy. In return Angelica will give you oil paint & turps & dirty rag for you to make your horrible pictures with when the fit takes you. By the way she is the same Angelica who appears in a rather saucy hat in the penguin. You also get a back view of her as a young girl playing the piano in the same collection. Well very much love—I am very glad to have the list of your actual & projected writings & will try and make out a list of mine   BUNNY

September 26th, 1944   *Doolistown, Trim, Co. Meath, Eire*

My dearest Bunny, I wish you had told me when this operation was going to be, or, if it is not over, that you would tell me when it is going to be? I will write to you every two or three days until I hear again, but you are not to answer so frequently. If you have a wish to write, write a book, which will be just as nice for me, and nicer for other people.

I dont know what to say about the operation. It sounds terrifying, but I suppose it is a good thing on the whole. i.e. at the very worst the surgeon could hardly do more than paralyse your legs—I can't see how he can kill you—while he may restore you completely; so that it seems a reasonable gamble when the alternative is being crocked. You have a first rate constitution, and should be able to stand up to almost any surgery. In fact, the more I think about it the less upset I feel, because it is obvious that killing simply doesn't come into it, nor paralysis either. He will either make you better or leave you as you were. You are young and strong enough not to be made worse.

If you have already been done, dont write yourself, but ask Richard or Angelica to send me a post card. If not, dont forget I shall be holding my thumb for you, turning over my silver, looking at the new moon, pursuing piebald ponies, and doing everything possible. I will get Mrs. McDonagh to throw the whole weight of Catholic Ireland into the scale, so you may be sure that when they are wheeling you into the theatre Trim will be ringing from end to end with masses, rosaries, novenas, stations and special intentions. We are starting now.

When you do feel well enough to write, you must boast your fill about the operation. You will find that it is an immense pleasure. Say how brave you were, what you thought about so coolly. Give all the ghastly details. Dont be modest or afraid of boring. I shall hang on every word. Besides, when I publish your correspondence in nine volumes, ten years after both our deaths, think how interesting it will be for posterity.

Invalids and convalescents are a special class of people, who understand the same interests. I have spent 18 months of my life in various hospitals and beds, so I am the very man to appreciate anything you want to say. I am a conoisseur of anaesthetics (as a recipient) and shall feel real sympathy for your remarks about ether. We can hob-nob about the preferability of locals (or the reverse) and give each other reminiscences of nice times we have had with nitrous oxide.

I do hope you will go to hospital and be able to appreciate it. I mean not to a private ward but a public one. It is so good for one to be with suffering humans—they behave so much better when they are suffering that it makes you like them again. I would never choose a private ward any more. And the routine of being woken up to be bed-bathed at about 2 a.m., after being kept awake by the larks of the night nurse till 12.30, while the ward is continuously swept, banged, washed, dusted, tidied, visited by processions of matrons, and the beds made, and being woken up the moment you do go to sleep in order to be fed: it is all splendidly restful if you take it the right way. The whole secret is to acquiesce. Then you will find that you are sleeping like a log, weller than ever before, and just kept healingly interested by the va-et-vient of the time table.

It is splendid never having to decide what to do, at any moment of the day.

I will answer your letter the day after tomorrow. This is only to cheer you into battle, if in time. Brownie and I shall visit the local wise woman after lunch, where we will arrange to have everything done that can be done: blessing stones turned clockwise, red flannel tied to scapegoats, and the rest. For miles around, till we hear again, everybody will be hopping up and down, gathering dew, reciting spells, standing on one leg with our fingers in our ears.

It can't fail to be a success. Best love from TIM

September 26th, 1944 *Doolistown, Trim, Co. Meath, Eire*

Dear Bunny, I have been thinking about your troubles as unselfishly as possible, which isn't very, and it really seems to me that you have only one possible course of action. That is, to come here as soon as you can walk. Just think of the following points. We have a double bed for you and Angelica, and no doubt you possess some portable receptacle for the pumpkin. We have no meat rationing, nor hardly any rationing except tea, and we have all the farm stuff like butter and cream in profusion. You will need to be built up. We have a horse and trap, even a donkey. We have a maid. It is not so much you, but Angelica that all this is important to. If you go to Ridley Stokehole or any of your other country seats, Angelica will still have to empty bedpans and cook dinners, with which you are killing her, but here she needn't look at a single duster for however long you stay. Dont you think she had better have a rest cure? The more I think of it, the more sensible it seems. Quite apart from being away from flying bombs and so on for a few weeks, apart from sufficient food and freedom from housekeeping, it is particularly fortunate that I should be entwined in painting at the present moment: I know I am inclined to hold forth and lecture, like Brougham or Macaulay, which makes my mental pressure tiresome to people when they get it full blast, and would be exhausting for an invalid. But I am quite silent when painting, and could happily paint with Angelica all morning, leaving you to read or write in my little study. There must be at least 500 books to browse on. After lunch we could all three go out to our miniature bog to shoot a partridge that lives near here. You can walk across the whole bog in half an hour, and to begin with we would only lead you out for about that time. I have two guns, and the partridge will be in season next month, if he lives till then. Or we could drive round the local repulsions in the pony trap. Or make Angelica go for a ride on the donkey. Then there would only be the evening to Broughamise in, and we would try to get some whisky—which is very difficult to get. It, and cigarettes, is about the only important thing we are short on.

I can see no objections, except Richard. Of course you will not want to leave him until his leave is over, and if he came here he would have to sleep in Trim, as to give you the double bed I shall myself be sleeping on the floor, and sleeping 5 miles away is quite out of the question without a bicycle. So the thing must fall through unless Richard's leave is over, which I conclude it may be, by the time you can walk.

Other objections, such as out-door sanitation, are trifling, unless the pumpkin is liable to die at any minute, which would be a bore, as the doctor is also 5 miles off.

Now do think this over seriously, and apply for an exit permit instanter.

Financially speaking, I can sell my famous watch to pay for you if necessary, and, if not necessary, you can pay for yourselves. I pay Mrs. McDonagh 3 guineas a week, and 5 guineas between the two of you would be ample, and where in England could you get unlimited butter, cream, meat, for 5 gns? The whole point is to relieve Angelica from housework for a short time anyway. If you keep her at it she will betray you with a clerk of Oxenforde, after persuading you that there is going to be a deluge and hoisting you up in a barrel. These young wives ... So beware, Bunny, and come to stay at once with your sincere well-wisher

ANON.

P.S. *September 27th*, 1944. I suppose I signed it Anon because it was becoming a threatening letter. We write and receive so many in Ireland that it grows habitual. However, I lift the cloak of anonymity to add that if Angelica comes she must bring her own paints and canvas, as these are difficult to get.

The moment I told Mrs. McDonagh that you were going to have an operation she instantaneously and without my suggesting it commenced a Novena on your behalf. It was a reflex action. This means that for the next nine days she will add a special bit to the rosary every night, and she began it ex cathedrâ, in church, yesterday afternoon.

I myself believe that the operation was successfully performed on the night of Tuesday 26th (second sight) so it will be eight days wasted.

Now to answer your letter.

The letter from the Costello River, which is near Galway, was to the effect that Dr. So-and-so had caught 65 salmon in 11 days in June this year.

Even if the alternative is starvation, I utterly refuse to saw planks for you in a sawpit. I have lived in the 12th century quite enough with my falcons & bestiaries, without reverting to it in the building trade also.

Nothing can express my disapproval of sawpits. It will take you ten years to saw enough planks, in which time, by writing books, you could have earned enough money to deck the Queen Mary with bought ones. Even if you hire two men to saw, at 40/– a week each, they will not make as many accurate planks in a week as you could have bought for the money, and they wont be flanged, and they wont be seasoned, and I doubt whether you have enough trees that are straight. However, its no good remonstrating with romantics. I also sneer at your house. You say the tower is 'on one side of it'. If this means at one end, it will look like a toy church. The tall chimneys to lift the smoke over the tower will be absurd. In short, you will regret your headstrong behaviour when you see the house that *I* am going to build in Sussex, with no chimneys, wind-chargers all over it, electric carpets, and so forth.

Dont you wish you could reach me with that hatchet?

I have examined Angelica carefully in the D. Grant, and approve of her. Now tell me whether the satyr in plate 6 is you, and is plate 20 Ray?

If I dont have to saw in pits or see too much of the outside of this house, I shall be delighted to do all the other things, including learning the bagpipes.

It is a funny thing that you have been thinking about being buried on High Crag. Brownie was very ill last week, and, after having been up with her two nights, I tearfully arranged the details of our own funeral. It was to be on a high moor called the Brown Hill at Beldorney in Aberdeen-shire, and, although I wasn't going to have anything written on it, I was going to have a recumbent statue in Aberdeenshire granite—a copy of a young faun,* about 8 years of age, amusing himself with a small bear or badger and a honeycomb, which I saw 20 years ago at the Louvre, and at that time loved.[1] Do you know it? He is lying on his tummy, poking the honeycomb with a stick to feed the animal, and he has a most charming smile. Brownie has recovered, so now we are saving up to get the copy made.   Love from TIM

September 30th, 1944   *Doolistown, Trim, Co. Meath, Eire*

Dear Bunny, I shall have to rattle my poor old brains, if I am to keep on writing till the news comes that you are better. Are you remembering

* He is a satyr-fawn, with goat legs. He is amused.
[1 I have searched the Louvre in vain. Perhaps he is in the cellars.—D.G.]

with pleasure that sweet-sick smell of ether? Are you counting the hours till it will stop hurting when you move? Or quite better already? Or querulous? Or wanting somebody to love you? When I had my appendix out, which was done very badly by a drunk surgeon, I had one of the stiff nurses to lull my first hours: the kind that thinks it is more bracing for you to be scolded when miserable, instead of being petted. Consequently, when I was visited by a loving female for the first time, I burst into tears. I have been reading a lot of old memoirs and letters lately, people like Greville, Horry Walpole and so on, and was interested to find that this idea about men not weeping is quite modern. In Horry's time all the males spent half their lives in floods of tears, and on the very slightest provocation. It was de rigueur for funerals and all that, but also fashionable for readers of novels and in the House of Commons. When you had your irreparable quarrel with Edmund Burke, you simply cried your eyes out. When you wrote to thank Grey for sending you his Elegy in the Churchyard, long before the Romantic revival, you assured him that you had sobbed from the first stanza to the last. Even as late as the 1850's you got the Duke shedding a few manly drops, at the funerals of his comrades. Personally, I think it is much more natural to cry than not to. I think our present fashion is affected. Shall we try to alter it? Here we are, two literary men (pauses to catch flea on waistcoat: throws it in the fire) with the unbounded influence of our pens. Can't we start a Lachrymose Revival? The Renaissance of Tears. I am sure Sir Philip Sydney used to cry, when he felt his 'heart moved, more than with a trumpet.' I always cry on hearing military bands, seeing large crowds being generous (e.g. cheering King George V at Lords cricket ground, or things like that) and at the successful conclusion of any great endeavour, such as winning the Grand National or the China Tea Race or the Second World War. Why not? And why shouldn't you, if you are feeling miserable for a few hours? I wish I were in London to visit you, and let you weep on my shoulder. But a nubile female would be better. Try Angelica.

Bunny, when you feel like writing, will you tell me all you know about that great house at which you were staying when you told me the story about the variorum edition of the Pentateuch (or Septuagint?)? It was either Penshurst or the other one beginning with P—Petworth? (Catches second flea on sleeve.) I am passionately addicted to places like Knowle and deeply regret never having cultivated enough dukes to be a constant guest in such: I have never seen the place beginning with P, and would be interested by any account of it. Of its style, appearance, furniture. How sad it is that nothing in this world ever turns out as it ought to do. If only I had been born a Lord Sackville, or could marry the eldest daughter (no male heir) of a place beginning with P! How I should in a trice set up a printing press of my own, The Knowle Press, and issue 25 guinea editions of you and me and Trevelyan's latest book and on the rarest occasions of just three or four of the selectissimi! I have the whole format in my head, in hand tooled leather, and each of us would have our own colour of cover, though the same pattern. Ah well, it wasn't to be. I must be content with my fleas.

On the whole, after looking through this, it does not seem a very wise letter to send without being certain that your operation is over, I mean with all that about ether & hurting when you move, so I will keep it and write another. I see how mannered and laboured it is, but it is bricks without straw, and all it can do is to cover its paper as best it can, to shew that it is concerned about you, which is what it is for.

Incidentally, this crying business in males has evidently fluctuated. On the whole, I dont think Chaucer's males did it much: Malory's did (or were they his sources?): Shakespeare's didn't (albeit unused to the melting mood): nor did Cervantes—Sancho is always boasting about not crying: the classical age, contrary to what one would expect of that supposedly unsentimental time, did, very much: the Lake poets, again contrary to expectation, on the whole didn't; and so it goes on. If I venture to prophesy I would say that we shall see the House of Commons bathed in tears before we die.

I'll keep this till I know, and write another.   love from TIM

October 1st, 1944   *Doolistown, Trim, Co. Meath, Eire*

Dear Bunny, One good effect of living among illiterates is that you have to read the books you do possess again and again. This week I have been reading Headlong Hall, Nightmare Abbey and Don Quixote. I was amused by your father's last note in the second of these.[1] Also I was astounded to notice what a good plot it had. I always thought that Peacock simply assembled a collection of crotchets, let them argue and

[1 Actually grandfather.—D.G.]

162

married them off in the last chapter epeissodically. But the plot of Night-mare Abbey is water-tight, marches sequently from first to last through plenty of relevant action and is one of the few unique plots extant, since the hero does not marry either of the heroines at the end, but remains poised as a bachelor in his own natural imbecility. No loose ends, except the ghost in the bloody turban, who ought to have been identified with the lady in the secret chamber. And what a mine of quotations Peacock is! I believe an industrious author who liked to head his chapters with quota-tions could do so all his life, without going to anybody but Peacock.

Don Quixote is full of them too. What a darling! So candid, generous, simple and innocently vain. If Cervantes hadn't killed him so utterly at the end I would have half a mind to write a continuation, just for the pleasure of taking him out of the box again and loving him. I began at the beginning of the second part, and was struck by the coherence of the plot there too. It is much less picaresque than the 1st part. All the incidents grow naturally out of the branch, like twigs. Do you remember in Forster's excellent book about aspects of the novel, when he is talking about round and flat characters? The latter just go on behaving according to formula, but the round ones suddenly do things that are just the opposite, and become real. There is an amazing instance in Don Quixote. It is after the don has been lowered down the chasm (Montesino's), where he dreamed about the enchanted Crystal Palace, but Sancho wouldn't believe his stories of it. Then they go for their ride on the magic horse, and when it is over Sancho himself begins romancing about his imaginary adventures with the stars. Quixote knows that he is fibbing, because he had been on the crupper of the horse all the time, with his arms round the don's waist. Instead of resorting to his usual explanation, that all the irreconcilability must have been due to enchantment, he takes Sancho aside and whispers quite calmly: 'Sancho, if thou woulds't have us credit all that thou hast told us just now, I expect thee to believe that I was in Montesino's cave—I say no more.' After this cold-blooded, conspiratorial admission, by implication, that he has been fibbing himself, he steps quietly back into dreamland, as if nothing had happened. In fact, he leans out of the flat page for a second, a solid figure, and cocks a snook at you.

I have read a few pages of another book this week, but too ghastly to go on with it. I get books from a charming and well-informed old book-seller in Dublin, called William Figgis, who claims to have known your father, and every now and then I weakly let him recommend a modern novel, which he is not qualified to do. This last is called Friday's Child by Georgette Heyer. It is supposed to be a 'period' piece, of the Regency. As I have just finished Horry Walpole in nine volumes and Greville in five I am rather well up in the Georges for the time being, which increases the agony. The first, amazing sentence is: '"Do not, I beg of you, my lord, say more!" uttered Miss Milborne, in imploring accents, slightly averting her lovely countenance, and clasping both hands at her bosom.' Now the astonishing thing about this is, that it *does* to some extent capture the Regency idiom. The only thing it doesn't capture is the way the regency thought. All the characters are dukes and earls, slightly P. G. Wodehouse, who fight duels in an insane travesty of some bastard misalliance between Rafael Sabatini and Jane Austen. Do not, Bunny, I implore you, read it, uttered Mr. White, clasping his grubby hands and slightly averting his hirsute countenance, because convalescents are notoriously unbalanced, and you may think it is the best book you ever read.

I wrote you a different letter before this, but I am going to hold it back until I know how well you are going on.

Dont you admire me for being able to cover all this space with nothing to say?　　　　　　　　　　　　　　　　　　　　　love from TIM

October 4th, 1944　　　　　　　　　　　　　　*Room 26, 2nd Floor,*
Private Patients Ward,
University College Hospital,
Gower Street.

Dear Tim, Thank you so much for your very encouraging letter. I'm afraid 2nd sight let you down as I am being operated on tomorrow.

I am very comfortable here & am quite sufficiently in contact with other patients—a man who coughs, spits, or snores like a porpoise is lightly veiled from me by a curtain, but we can see each other in the looking glass.

I am extremely cheerful—get the Times for breakfast & am reading Henry James an author who has improved with time.

Radio is a bit of a curse I admit as light music appears to be audible for 16 hours out of the 24.

I shaved for the first time without a looking glass—& as I use an old-fashioned razor am pleased with myself that I completed the task successfully. That means nothing to you.　　　　　Much love, BUNNY

October 6th, 1944   *Doolistown, Trim, Co. Meath, Eire*

Dear Bunny, I find this among the débris of my desk after a bacchanal week, which I copy out and censor, with a headache:

Dear Bunny, I am tight! Isn't that splendid? From 1st April to last September I drank nothing but bacterial water, but now I can sterilise it with aqua fortis! Hardly able to put one pen before another, I hasten to hail you with three times three, anxious to learn whether you are still face downwards, as if you had been spanked? Dearest Bunny, we are agog to hear the best possible news, and even when tipsy make the greatest efforts to attend to your sufferings, and to the news that they are over. Write, write, or rather tell Angelica to write, and when I have my headache to-morrow it will serve as an antidote for it, to learn that you are a living man. All Doolistown is at the stretch of anxiety. Mrs. McDonagh's Novena has its tongue hanging out: Brownie sleepless: Father What-You-May-Call-It has been fee'd to such an extent that he is thinking of buying a farm in Mayo for his sister's son: poor Tim is acold on his knees, till the skin is as thick as farm boots. Surely all must be over now, and our efforts crowned with success? Admit it, you kippered Bunny, and allow us to stagger off to bed. It is too bad of you to keep us worried. We rack our brains for something to say, and nothing comes, but are determined to be true to our trust, even if we have to send you lists of fat stock prices. Till the sage of Tupp's Mousehole is on his legs once more every three post-men shall carry him a hoarse, half-human cheer, so help us God. N.B. I must keep off God, you say, and the Theory of Art, so to hell with them. Brownie tells me I sent you some swaggering messages when she wrote last. The fact is, it is the booze. Luckily I shall have to stop on monday, as I have no more money to buy it, but I thought I would be tight for one week this October, for the look of the thing. As I dont drink till October, on principle, I thought I had better get drunk then, also on principle. N.B. I must keep off principles. N.B. I have discovered that getting drunk on Irish rum is exactly the same as having ether. You get the sweet, sick, persisting aftermath. N.B. Is rum made of ether? What are all these N.B's anyway? They are N.B.G.   love from TIM

October 11th, 1944   *Doolistown, Trim, Co. Meath, Eire*

Dear Bunny, Just as I posted my last letter about rum there came two excellent ones from you, shewing that you are going into battle with great composure, so we hurry to write again. You will have begun sleeping naturally by the time it arrives, and all will have turned out for the best, and that will be when you will be the pleased to receive congratulations and homage, which this brings.

I am glad you can see the man in the mirror. You will come to love him in spite of his snores. You will think what a jolly nice chap he is, one of the nicest you ever met. You may even visit him once, after they let you out. But it will be only once. You will probably give a little extra money to the hospital, out of gratitude. Your main innate fallacy, due to having been born in a kind and liberal family with similar people always within call throughout your life, that human beings are decent on the whole, will receive immense stimulus from the joys of convalescence. I expect you will already have shed a few sentimental tears, a course of action which I recommended to you in a week-old letter, which I am keeping till sure you are out of pain.

Please may I repeat that I am not expecting you to answer this shower of letters. They are only to egg you on, will cease as soon as I know you are better, and I only want one post card from Richard to tell me that. Use your convalescence for writing a long short story. If you want to fill my cup of joy, you can dedicate it to me. love from TIM

About October 12th, 1944   *Doolistown, Trim, Co. Meath, Eire*
  [*Postmarked* 17.X.44]

Dear Bunny, I see by your letter that you are growing pettish about the Irish, and cannot understand why they should ever again expect to be sent any petrol, after failing to help you to defend them from the Hun. (Sighs, goes over to window and gazes out at muck heap, chewing his whiskers.) Well, well. I wonder if you suppose that petrol is sent here in a stocking by dear old Santy Bull, the big hearted Barnardo? The Irish answer could be put in one sentence, which is: that they expect, not as a right, but as students of human nature, to be sent petrol just so long as they pay for it, and not one minute longer. They think that old Barnardo Claus would do the same for the devil in person. They had an idea that trade was a matter of economics. And about being defended from the Hun, they might add that they didn't ask you to. If they were very naughty, they might even enquire whether you intend to partition Poland, which you are defending from the Hun, in the Ulster way, or in some other?

The trouble is that you sentimental English have not got the faintest idea of the Irish character. You dont know that behind the façade of banshees, Holy Mary's, leprechauns and creatures of that ilk, we are the most materialistic race in Europe. Our age-old cynicism would make you jump in your skins.

Even if you only read the works of Wynwood Reade, you must be aware that human beings have been ranging round Europe for the last 500,000 years at least, and that the eruptions of civilisation in the Nile, Tigris, Indus, etc. valleys were only about one sixtieth of that time ago. These explosions, like volcanoes pouring out lava, drove the preceding races out and out to the sea rims, till they could not go further. Here we are jammed together in inextricable confusion, men of Crô Magnon and of Neanderthal and of all the other failures. The débris is on the rims: Lapps keeping up the stone age in Narvik, early Celts celebrating the mass of St. Sécaire in Brittany, Minoan bull fighters still in full swing in Portugal, and us here. We are not a race. We are a rag-bag of defeated races. We have seen history sixty times longer than you kids have, and always on the other end of a New Weapon.

These volcanoes which spurt out the lava of new races send them forth always with new weapons, bronze hatchets, or iron rapiers, or arquebuses or flying bombs.

They drive the rabble in front of them, away to the devil and the deep blue sea. In the last few centuries they have even hustled us over it, to America.

What I am trying to tell you is that there are no 'Irish' as such. Unlike you English (the newest of the amalgams, except for the scarcely-born Americans) we are the mixed ancientry, who have been kindly defended from Huns, for thousands of years before you were thought of. This is why we are blazé, why cynical, why materialistic. When you have been hunted round Europe since wars began, by an endless succession of people defending you against each other with copper hatchets, you tend to grow alergic to honour and glory. Even to 'civilisation'—which is what I understand you are defending at present, and which is coterminous with warfare.

Do you realise that I am actually living in the house with a Neanderthal man? The Crô Magnon people were able to recognise images on a flat surface, their predecessors not. A few years ago I photographed Paddy McDonagh and his wife and the farm in various aspects, on a reel of film which happened to come out with great definition, and the right way up. They were delighted. They exclaimed what beautiful pictures they were, and said: Mr. White, sure its a credit to your hands, to draw photygraphs like thim! And all the time they admired them, they were holding the photygraphs upside down.

Are these the people you are fussing about, because they dont help you to defend them from the Huns? They dont know which Huns you mean. They dont know where Germany is. They think the moon is a phosphorescent balloon which is regularly blown up and deflated by a gentleman called Ould Moore, thus determining the weather. What is the good of being cross with such people? The one thing they do know, from bitter experience through tens of centuries before you were even dreamed of by William Conk, is that nature is red in tooth and claw. Personally, I confess, I agree with them.

You really must get it out of your head that Ireland is interested in whether Kingstown ought to be called DunLeary or whether there ought to be a border or not (it has existed since prehistoric times anyway) or in speaking the Irish language or even particularly interested in the supposed persecutions of the catholic church. All these matters are only the acrimonies which are flogged up by the vested interests of politicians and priests, to whose advantage it is to stir up a stink. Swine like these have to nourish the delusions of grandeur and persecution manias, to have something to work on. But the real Irishman, who just digs potatoes, is not out of your war for any such reasons. He is out because of an immense ancestral memory of defeat—not necessarily at your hands at all, but always and ever, long before you were there, from everybody—and so he only wants to be left alone. That is the one thing he really does know. They can sometimes agitate him superficially about Borders, Banshees, Saints, Scholars, Shamrocks, English oppressors and all that: but it is only a superficial muddle. Underneath is the prehistoric reason.

Incidentally, it might sober you to reflect that you yourselves will arrive here eventually. We are the cul-de-sac. Here we stand, in a perpetual rain storm, picts and celts and teutons and Scandinavians and normans. A Heidelburg man is holding an umbrella over that intelligent anthropoid lady with opposable finger tips. And we are here because we didn't master the new weapons. And I am here already as your advance refugee. And in a few thousand years there will be standing our poor Bunny beside us, hunted out of England by a death ray or something, with the rain dripping from his spectacles. We are the Piccadilly Circus of the races: they all come here in the end. We are pitiable creatures—I mean it in a kind way—and not creatures to get indignant about, only because they are too tired to go on.   love from TIM

October 12th, 1944   *Room 25, Private Wing, Univ. Coll. Hospital,*
Gower St.

Dear Tim, I am lying flat on my right side which makes it a scrawl. The operation was a success but its a big job & needs a mixture of willpower & toughness to get over. I am doing very well.

Luckily for me the surgeon trusted to his diagnosis & did not confirm it by inflating my spinal chord with air or oil. He extracted an object like half the rim of a brace button from my spinal cord, lopped off part of the damaged nerve & I am rapidly getting better.

I have now been turned over & can write much more easily.

Well I've nothing to tell you about anaesthetics. I had a shot of Ompolin & then gas & oxygen for a 2 hour operation (10–12). My doctor Cyriax described how when he had got down to the bone, & opened the canal, Harvey Jackson probed with a finger felt the object, cut a membrane & the cartilage leapt out like Blake's infant.

My first impressions were about 3 when I saw Angelica distinctly. My other impression was of seeing William: and of astonishment at his deep dark red cheeks & white skin. I was sick a bit at intervals till evening & then someone gave me shot of morphine without my knowing it just when I was needing it.

In the night four nurses gathered round me at intervals & lifted me into the air. Those who clutched my thighs caused me agony & when they accidentally bumped me on the wound I screamed. However they turned me three or four times like that when one of them suggested, next day, turning me over the other way onto my belly.

I began to organise the procedure next day.

I lie in a rubber ring & can stand it precisely 2 hours after which I push my arm through & roll out of the ring onto a pillow which the nurses pull to the other side of the bed.

They then put the ring behind me & I roll into it.

As soon as I could I noted that I could move my legs but that I was afflicted with a partial paralysis from the waist down. My cock was like a frost bitten acorn & I had no power of making water. However I got hold of a bottle and tried every damned trick in heaven & earth—& at last managed to make water—thinking of Falstaffs question to his boy & the doctor's reply.

'The water was good water but the man who made it had more diseases than he knew of.' That was, Jackson tells me, a really big victory. For the first few days this partial paralysis was greater than it is now—but it is fading everywhere & with it the sciatic pain when my thighs were touched clumsily near the nerves.

I have two jobs to achieve now. To regain my lost powers in my left leg—particularly movement in the big toe, & to tone up the flabby muscles.—and to heal the deep hole in my back. I think rather more than another fortnight in bed will be needed for the latter — & a lot of determination for the former.

At present all is well. I have been piling food into me but nothing has come out the other end so far.

Well forgive all this detail but I thought it might interest you. I have planned a long story about a hospital in the manner of Conrad.

Much love, BUNNY

October [*20th*], 1944   *Doolistown, Trim, Co. Meath, Eire*

My dearest Bunny, I am so delighted to hear that the operation was successful and so angry that you wrote so soon and so worried that you will go on wasting your time answering these letters. I think I had better tell you at once that I will write twice more and then stop. Thus, if you will stop answering when you get this, you will be saved from continuing as a monologue, as I have been doing for the past few weeks.

Your description of the operation turned all my blood to water. I think if I ever got half the rim of a braces button jammed into my spine I would prefer to spend the rest of my life in bed, rather than face it. Have you lost much weight? After going through such hell so manfully I am sure you will be rewarded with complete recovery and will be able to wiggle all your big toes like mad and the frozen acorn will blossom like a rose. You must hurry off to Tiddly's Arsehole or Tupp's Intake as soon as possible, for I know you wont come here, and there you must skip with the mountains like young rams.

I can't think why you should want to write a hospital story in Conrad's style. What is wrong with your own?

N.B. The moment I got back from my tonsils I began writing a story about hospitals, so there is evidently a reaction-hysteria in such matters. Beware.

N.B. Your story about the ticking clock when you had gas the other time misses the point. My control was a conversation consisting of different words, so I could tell when it began to repeat. Your ticks were all the same, so you would never have known if they were repeating. As a matter of fact, I also once went off with a clock ticking, now I come to think of it, and I vanished at an *odd* number. The repetition was Tic-Toc-Tic-Toc-Tic ... Tic-Toc-Tic-Toc etc.

It has been very difficult to write all these letters to you, not only because there was no news, but because I had to guess how you would be feeling, without much data to go on, and it was difficult to know whether to be bright or serious or pitying or what. However, now I am going to assume that you are getting well again.

I have managed to scramble back on the water-waggon and am safe again, though it was a close shave. I sort of missed my footing on the tail board, ran madly for several paces to keep up, and hoisted myself on again breathless, just in time.

I have been shooting at a few hares, partridges and fesants lately and am distressed to find that my eyesight is going. It is either that, or lack of practise, but I miss much worse than I used to do. I think it may have something to do with my kidneys, which I upset by giving them far too much M & B, while trying to over-rule my tonsils. Now I am once more trying to lull them into a sense of false security, with abstinence and Doan's Kidney Pills.

Keep on twiddling that toe. love from TIM

October [30th], 1944 Doolistown, Trim, Co. Meath, Eire

Dear Bunny, This is the last of my series, unless you decide to grow worse again, until we resume a normal correspondence at the proper intervals round Christmas time. When you do write at Christmas, please look back and answer some of the questions I have asked by mistake viz:— about Petworth, about whether the D. Grant penguin contained pictures of you & Ray, about whether you are still writing for the New Statesman etc.

If you are not going back to the N.S., do you think it would be any good my applying for the job? I shall have to earn something soon somehow, and work at regular hours for somebody else I wont.

I was delighted to hear that there is to be a new edition in May next year: the more Garnetts the better. I suggest for names: if a boy, Damned Garnett—named after a brother of Praise-God Barebones, whose full name was If-Christ-had-not-come-thou-hadst-been-damned Barebones— if a girl, Cornucopia Volumnia Garnett. Another good idea for a female name would be to name her after the Rabbit Woman of the 18th century— considering your own nickname—but I have most unfortunately forgotten the rabbit woman's name. She convinced a jury of doctors, in the Joanna Southcote style, that she was in the habit of giving birth to Rabbits, and had quite a lot of them. She is in the D.N.B., and is mentioned in passing by Horry Walpole, but not by name. I often wish I had begun keeping a card index about ten years ago, and I would now if I could afford a secretary, for it is most annoying to know things like this without being able to fix the details. When I was reading the D.N.B., I used to dog-ear the page when it was amusing, and my only way of tracing the Rabbit Woman now would be to look back through about 1000 dog-eared pages.

I am at present in a foul temper about censors. For the sake of my Bestiary I have to consult inaccessible 12th century M.S.S., and I have a kind of magic lantern which enlarges microfilms, so, when I want to verify something, I have to send 3d to the library concerned, to get a microfilm of the page. Well, they wont let me have them. It really is too fantastic. If it were me that had written for permission to import, I could just understand the suspicion that some single individual might be a spy, but it was the staff photographer of the Cambridge University Library who wrote for permission to export, and was refused. So we must suppose that these shop assistants of censors suspect the British Museum, the Bodleian, the C.U. Library etc. of being vast espionage organisations! What an inspiration! Dont you remember the fun we used to have in the B.M. Reading Room, pouring champagne on dear old Olga the Bulgar out of her satin slipper and blowing bubbles with her green jade cigarette holder? Eheu fugaces. Yes, and the gat which Sir Arthur Quiller-Couch used to pack under his armpit, and Sir Sydney Cockerill running a roulette wheel in the shadow of the subject index, and Dr. Basil Atkinson tapping out messages to Himmler in monkish latin on the transmitting set we used to keep in the manuscript room! What times we had! Never shall I forget the day when Trevelyan put his Order of Merit down the décolletage of X.13—she was the platinum blonde, you remember—and sold the plans of the mongolfier balloon in exchange for her black lace garters.

Pah! Dear Bunny, would you do me the favour of stopping the cant which goes on in England, just for a month of two? I suppose belligerents become doped and lose all power of recognising cant when they hear it, but you might try. I can remember howls of virtue about how Art at any rate was not to be allowed to suffer and books were not to be rationed and culture would go on. In point of fact, only rot can be published, because the paper rationing makes it pay publishers to issue rot, instead of giving higher percentages to writers of not-rot. Nobody except official war artists and other arse-creepers can paint, because of the shortage of Flake White. And, as for culture, as for scholarship, it is forbidden ipso facto, and the greatest libraries in the world are suspected of being spy-rings!

I see with extreme pleasure that the Archbish of Canterbury is dead. Well for us if they all were. Was it he or some other who declared that one human life was worth more than Monte Cassino? Did you ever go to Cassino? Such a glorious place, pavements unimaginably old, courtyards so graceful, baroque and every other style since the 10th century blending without a murmur, the birthplace of a superb mediaeval script, the home of a bestiary. The truth is, of course, that Monte Cassino, which was irreplaceable, was worth about fourteen army corps of human lives, which are unfortunately all too replaceable. Anyway, thank God we can't replace the halo round old Temple's cock.[1]

How is yours, by the way? I was much concerned about the frozen acorn.*

Until Christmas then, Bunny, this is to wish you the very happiest and most absolute convalescence, because now that I have no microfilms, no flake white, no readable books, and no Cassino, there is practically nothing left but you. I put you at 20 army corps.　　　　love from TIM

[1 In a letter of Feb. 27th, 1943, here omitted, Tim had written: 'I have been listening to the news which informs me that the Archbishop of Cant has been addressing somebody or other on the 'Sacredness of sex.' Do you suppose he has a halo round his cock?'—D.G.]

* Mine, though unhaloed, underwent a joyful resurrection.

Dear Bunny, I have nothing to write about, so I must write about books.
Dont forget this is the last letter but one, if you are better. If you are not
better I shall just go on writing, so you had better get.

I got a letter from that annoying man Basil Blackwell about 2 years ago,
who asked me to write a children's book for him, 'like Arthur Ransome's'.
I said I couldn't write books to order, but I wrote the story which I am
dedicating to Amaryllis, and it wont be published by Blackwell, not if I
know it. Then, about a month ago, I saw an Arthur Ransome book in a
shop window in Dublin, so I bought it to see what I ought to write like.
I tried to get into it, but failed, and gave it up. Then, this week, with
nothing else to read, I had another try, and did get in, and rather liked it.
Have you ever read any of his? I think they might do for Amaryllis at
some future date, as he has grasped the fact that children like to be by
themselves in their adventures, and not bossed about by a lot of amiable
grown-ups as the real heroes. Also he does not write with one eye on the
grown-up, as I do, but seems to be a pleasantly childish man himself. It
was called The Picts and the Martyrs. As a parent I consider it your duty
to read it, if you havn't. Of course it isn't within miles of the great books,
like Treasure Island, but it is a good, simple second ranker. I can't get it
out of my head that I was at school with this Ransome. Anyway, there was
a Ransome in my house at Cheltenham, a woman-skinned, faintly coffee-
coloured person with black hair and brown eyes, who was not much good
at any of the things we considered important. He committed the frightful
solecism of weeping when he was caned once, and was subsequently
removed by his parents. I heard after that he had married a woman much
older than himself, and lived happily ever after. Thinking back, I realise
that he must have been a sensible person, and his parents too, but he
shocked us out of our skins. Personally I know I would rather have died
than cry, and frequently nearly did, partly because I could never have
looked my comrades in the face again and partly because one so loathed
and despised the torturer that one wasn't going to give him the satisfaction
of thinking he had hurt. I used to try fiercely not to limp. I think people
have different degrees of sensitivity to pain. You could beat some of them
like carpets. It used to hurt me like hell. I suppose it hurt this Ransome
person even more. Anyway, I can remember his bottom, which was a
royal purple. We didn't bully him for crying. We were too shocked. He

went at the end of that term. I often wish I could be your angel for a brief giro through the purgatories of the real world, all quite unknown to you, and you my Dante. Ray understood Reality, you not. I suppose Ray was the most impressive woman I ever met. Perhaps we would start in a good English Public School for our first circle, then go on to a cosy little Irish farm, with no literate person handy, where they saw the living horns off bullocks nearly two years old. For our last circle I think we would drop in on the Dail, or the House of Commons. Satan's fundament.

I have had a very bad week for books, apart from Ransome, clearing up stuff which I failed to read before. I have been toying with Mary Shelley's Frankenstein, but it bores me to tears. I never liked the Godwins. I must try again. And I used to have a great wish for C. S. Forester, because of Brown On Resolution, The Gun, and Captain Hornblower R.N. So when I was in Dublin that time I bought 3 more of his books which were in a window, and they are awful beyond belief. They are called Plain Murder, The Shadow of the Hawk, and some other one that I can't be bothered even to remember the name of. It's a funny thing about Forester, but I expect that you, in your wartime atmosphere, think that The Ship is a good book. Wait ten years, and you'll see. It has traces of hysteria which are unpleasant to non-belligerents like myself. It is rather instructive to read it alongside of 'Our Penelope', which was written by the actual ship's company of the ship he thinks he is writing about. The two books are about equally bad, and bear no reference to each other.

I wonder if you still ever review for the New Statesman? When you stopped, I stopped taking it in, and have since assumed that you were not writing. Perhaps wrongly? It will be a bore to have to buy up all back copies.

I still can't get into poor Georgette Heyer. There are some books that one simply can't face without a nose clip. I shall keep on trying, hoping that if I manage to get in it will be like eating a durian—horrid smell, nice taste. At present I still fall back from the smell, half fainting.

I remember reading Hawbuck Grange, which you mention, and not caring for it much. I think it was his shortest book. But, oh, dear, dont talk to me about Surtees. He and all my lovely books that you saw at Stowe Ridings, including the Encyclopaedia Britannica, are still there, and I can't get them out. I am missing the Enc. Brit. twice a day. The people at the Ridings are too stupid to cope with censors, and Pickfords ask £50 for sending them over, which is ridiculous and beyond my means. It kills me to think of them.

I was amused at the idea of Richard buying the Anatomy of Melancholy. I wonder what he will make of it. I hope to be able to enjoy it when I am about 63. That is, of course, if I go on learning till then.

Did I ever tell you that since I have been in Ireland I have read the whole Dictionary of National Biography from cover to cover. It is packed with amusement. One day I am going to publish an anthology based on it, called 'Dry Blood and Distant Thunder'. N.B. If you ever mention this to anybody, they will steal the title, so dont, and dont steal it yourself.

How are those toes wriggling?

Dont answer. love from TIM

P.S. I have just remembered that I wanted to beg a boon of you. Can you make Angelica send me a *small* tube (oil) of *Cadmium* yellow, *if it is on the Select List?* I can't get it in Dublin. I want a very vivid yellow like Crome, which is not permanent, and I have Aureolin or whatever it calls itself, but it is not brilliant enough. I want a fierce, permanent yellow. The tiniest tube would do. A sort of electric yellow. But it must be S.L. I dont know if cadmium is this, but I think it is. It is for my oviparous creeper, which wants to turn into a firework. All the background is Prussian blue. Guests scream when they see it.

November 11th, 1944 *Charleston Firle, Lewes, Sussex*

Dear Tim, This is the last letter till Christmas, written to answer some of your questions & remove some misconceptions which always generate themselves in corresponding with foreign countries.

1. There is no portrait of either me or Ray in the D. Grant penguin. There are two of Angelica.

2. I have never stayed at either Petworth or Penshurst though I have been shown over the latter for 1/–. When I wrote to you about the Septuagint story I was staying in the same house in which I am living now. In default of Petworth you will have to be content with a description of Charleston. It is a farmhouse on Lord Gage's estate with a walled garden, a pond in front of it & various additions in the form of studios, a pottery kiln etc at the back. Angelica was born in it & I lived in during the last 2 years of the last war. Its present inhabitants are Clive Bell, Vanessa Bell, Quentin Bell, Duncan Grant & at the moment Angelica, Amaryllis

& myself. There is also Grace who with her husband & small son lives in what is called High Holborn which has a separate staircase leading out of the kitchen. The farm buildings & land are part of the farm nearest— Tilton—which is leased & run by Lord Keynes who is a very old friend of everyone here. He is the same as the Economic Consequences Keynes & is now in Washington with Lydia his wife. Charleston is illustrated in the penguin by plates 7, 10, 22, 29, 30. Life here follows a very ordered pattern. Clive shoots two days a week or more as a result of which we have lots of pheasants, partridges, hares & rabbits to eat & occasionally a snipe or duck. At other times, he sits in his own rooms & reads—at the moment G. Ferrero's History of Roman Empire in French. He goes off to see friends & gives lunch parties in London pretty often. Quentin who is about 34 is a painter & before the war a potter also. He has recently had his appendix out. He works half the day on the farm & paints in the afternoon. Angelica & he are painting a lovely young cock pheasant hung up against a looking glass. Their time limit is till Monday mid-day as we want to eat it on Monday evening. Quentin also reads a good deal: at the moment Ranke's history of Europe. Both Clive & Quentin are social & genial characters but in Clive's case it has become overlaid by a dogmatic & rather noisy manner. No one sees anybody else in this house except at meals which last a long time. There is very decent draught beer & a tot of either rum or sherry or something in the evening—also a cigar provided by Clive. As I am convalescent I have breakfast in bed. However for the last 3 days I have got out across the cow pasture each morning before lunch. Yesterday I got as far as the nearest wood & put up a cock pheasant. I get tired quickly & am pretty lame but sit down on tree stumps.

Duncan is silent, & has a great many irons in the fire,—goes into Lewes to do lithographs—decorations for churches, conferences with Bishops about which we tease him. The only animals are a fine Tom Cat who lets Amaryllis pull his fur & tail, and a dog which doesn't belong here but to Lord Gage but which Clive always takes out shooting. He is an elderly Black Labrador.

Talking of shooting—William went up to Ridley Stokoe a fortnight ago & shot a cock pheasant, a partridge, 2 grouse, a blackcock & a snipe. —a pretty good mixed bag & very respresentative of the place.

However my description of Charleston has not begun. To begin with every room has been decorated & redecorated several times by Duncan &

Vanessa during the last 28 years. The walls are covered with pictures varying from Cezannes & Matisses to almost anything or anybody. The seats of the chairs are in cross stitch & the curtains also made at home from their own designs. All this is now a half-seen background. Long rooted habits govern behaviour & thought as unconsciously & as rigidly as at the court of Louis XIV. There is therefore a sort of spiritual crystallisation which affects everyone—Duncan much the least. This can be at moments irritating, at other moments extraordinarily restful:—as restful as it would have been to live at Gryll Grange for example. Conversation at meals is more like Peacock than like any other writer.

But all this has remained much the same for a very long time. One is aware therefore that one is present at one of the last Peacocks—taking part in Gryll Grange rather than in Crotchet Castle—that to be sure was when Roger Fry was still one of the party,—or Nightmare Abbey when Julian filled the house with his turbulent vitality & warmth. Julian was killed in Spain & his death has left this house a colder place. His disappearance has frozen much of Vanessa, has without either of them realising it, left Quentin isolated, as Julian was his elder brother & the leader in all their enterprises & absurd projects & amusements—and Clive a figure engaged in unconscious make-believe & bluster—the pretence that he is at all events unchanged. Vanessa has been ill this summer and is still rather tired & exhausted.

Thus we are mostly rather crocks—but you would not guess it when things go well.

I have done nothing since I have been here except read a lot of books—none of them very good but somehow I have been desultory & far more interested in my muscles than in anything else. My daughter is a pretty beast but the last few days she has been a little devil, squealing & lying flattened out on the floor like a partridge when she has been in a temper.

3. Angelica will get you some Cadmium & possibly some Flake White.

4. I have not written anything in the New Statesman since Oct 1939.

I seldom see the paper & intensely dislike almost everything in it. In fact I loathe its whole outlook. The page I used to write is now written by a man called Pritchett. He is a nice chap but has rather run dry. I dont think you would suit the paper or it would suit you. They are all 'planners,' base & ignorant journalists etc. Why dont you write for the Cornhill which has recently been revived & has a lot of life. The address is c/o John Murray Albemarle Street w.1.

Angelica & I are suffering from the usual uncertainty—no girl has been found to look after Amaryllis or do housework—yet one is essential as Angelica's pregnancy advances. Probably we go back to 41 Gordon Square about Nov 23 & I resume work at my office.

But it may turn out to be preferable, if a woman is forthcoming, to go to Scearnbank as soon as I can travel & walk freely. Meanwhile we are suffering like half the inhabitants of Britain from the feeling of dispersal. My waistcoat, coat & trowsers are each in a different county: travel is difficult I am lame, whenever shall I collect them again? Practically everything is like that.   Very much love BUNNY

[? *November 25th*, 1944]   [*Doolistown*]
Dearest Bunny, Brownie died today. In all her 14 years of life I have only been away from her at night for 3 times, once to visit England for 5 days, once to have my appendix out and once for tonsils (2 days), but I did go in to Dublin about twice a year to buy books (9 hours away) and I thought she understood about this. To-day I went at 10, but the bloody devils had managed to kill her somehow when I got back at 7. She was in perfect health. I left her in my bed this morning, as it was an early start. Now I am writing with her dead head in my lap. I will sit up with her tonight, but tomorrow we must bury her. I dont know what to do after that. I am only sitting up because of that thing about perhaps consciousness persisting a bit. She has been to me more perfect than anything else in all my life, and I have failed her at the end, an 180–1 chance. If it had been any other day I might have known that I had done my best. These fools here did not poison her—I will not believe that. But I could have done more. They kept rubbing her, they say. She looks quite alive. She was wife, mother, mistress & child. Please forgive me for writing this distressing stuff, but it is helping me. Her little tired face cannot be helped. Please do not write to me at all about her, for very long time, but tell me if I ought to buy another bitch or not, as I do not know what to think about anything. I *might* live another 30 years, which would be 2 dog's lifetimes at this, but of course they hamper one very much when one loves them so desperately, and it is a problem. I am certain I am not going to kill myself about it, as I thought I might once. However, you will find this all very hysterical, so I may as well stop. I still expect to wake up and find it wasn't. She was all I had.   love from TIM

As a matter of fact, I believe they did poison her. But what does that matter? she was everything, everywhere, for ever, my Brown.

November 28th, 1944   *Doolistown, Trim, Co. Meath, Eire*

Dear Bunny, Please forgive me writing again, but I am so lonely and can't stop crying and it is the shock. I waked her for two nights and buried her this morning in a turf basket, all my eggs in one basket. Now I am to begin a new life and it is important to begin it right, but I find it difficult to think straight. It is about whether I ought to buy another dog or not. I am good to dogs, so from their point of view I suppose I ought. But I might not survive another bereavement like this in 12 years' time, and dread to put myself in the way of it. If your father & mother & both sons had died at the same moment as Ray, unexpectedly, in your absence, you would know what I am talking about. Unfortunately Brownie was barren, like myself, and as I have rather an overbearing character I had made her live through me, as I lived through her. If I got another bitch and the same thing happened I feel it might be the end of me when she died. I shall never be married, and have no friends except you. An alternative might be to bury myself in Museum Libraries for the rest of my life, and to grow dessicated in them, keeping my eggs to my own basket, which, when destroyed, will be unable to regret them. Or I could get two dogs and breed up vast families of puppies, but what would be the good of that? It would only be an occupation. Brownie was my life and I am lonely for just such another reservoir for my love—not for an occupation. But if I did get such a reservoir it would die in about 12 years and at present I feel I couldn't face that. Do people get used to being bereaved? This is my first time. If it was going to ache less when I got it again 12 years hence, I think I might chance it. Or I could get a bitch who wasn't barren, and keep one or two of her puppies about us to help tide over the next time. Perhaps this last is the best idea, unless the Museum Library one is. I would value the advice of somebody in his right mind who was accustomed to bereavements. I am feeling very lucky to have a friend like you that I can write to without being thought dotty to go on like that about mere dogs.

They did not poison her. It was one of her little heart attacks and they did not know how to treat it and killed her by the wrong kindnesses.

If I can learn to eat a little, I will go to Dublin for a week and try the Library dodge. But I will not buy a dog till I hear from you.

You must try to understand that I am and will remain entirely without wife or brother or sister or child and that Brownie supplied more than the place of these to me. We loved each other more and more every year. It actually grew. Even if I got another bitch, it would take 12 years to get back to where I was on saturday. It was because we were both childless that we loved each other so much. If I got one that had children, we would probably never rise to the same love. An unbearable 12 year future comes in again. So I will stop going round and round.   love from TIM

It seems to be insoluble.
The first advice that will spring to your lips will be 'Take a wife'.
That is quite impossible.

November 29th, 1944   *Doolistown, Trim, Co. Meath, Eire*

Dear Bunny, I hope this will be the last of these insane letters, and I do beg you to forgive me for writing them. I know I ought not. It helps to write and I believe you to be sterling enough to bear with me, just for these three times. I couldn't do it to anybody else, and without your help I would have died. I have found out how people 'die of a broken heart'. It just means that they lose interest in being alive. Also, it is not the deceased person that dies (for them) but it is themselves that die: all that they consisted of, for the last 12 years in my case, steps into the past, leaving them to start a new life all over again, for which, if old, they lack the power to re-organise and re-integrate, and consequently they give it up. Brownie has been quartering in front of me for 12 years, while I have plodded behind that dancing sprite, so now it is difficult not to follow her still, into the past.

I am afraid that you are going to advise me to get married. It is physically impossible. I can't go into all this in a letter, but I will explain if I ever see you again, and if you want to know.

Now the whole thing boils down to one conundrum. If you were an orphan and a widower without siblings, would you accept the offer of having an only daughter brought by the stork tomorrow, knowing that she herself was bound to die in 12 more years, probably in your own life-time? The *pro*'s are that you would have those 12 happy years, that you could make her happy, and that she would have lived out her natural life. The *con*'s are, or is, that it would probably be your own death sentence, deferred. I dont think I can go through this again.

I have an affectionate disposition and as I could not take a wife I needed something to lavish it on, which was why, apart from Brownie, I was always fooling about with hawks and badgers and snakes and God knows what else. I know it is difficult to understand old maids like me, except with a kind of pitying contempt, but if anybody can it will be you. (I dont feel at all contemptible.) I loved Brownie more than any man I have ever met has loved his natural wife. We were like cats on hot bricks away from each other, and thought about each other all day, particularly in the last years. It is a queer difference between this kind of thing and getting married, that married people love each other most at first (I understand) and it fades by use & custom, but with dogs you love them most at last. They are meaningless to begin with, and if I bought a bitch puppy tomorrow she would not replace Brownie for a long time to come.

It is perhaps a matter of life or death to me to know whether to re-commence the same long trail with a new puppy, which I feel morally certain would end in both our deaths, because I would be too old to make a fresh start in 12 years time, or whether to have nothing more to do with dogs. In the latter case I might not be able to keep it up (living) and I dont know where I would put my surplus affections.

The whole and single unnaturalness of the position is that dogs and men have incompatible longevities. Everything else is perfectly natural and I would not have it altered in any respect. I regret nothing about Brownie, except the bitter difference of age.

I always tried to hide how much I loved her, for fear of this silly reproach about old maids.

It was because we were both barren that it came to mean so much. If I got a fertile puppy, it would never rise to the same thing (which I want it to) but on the other hand I would probably not die of her death (which I dont want to).

So you see it is quite a nice little problem for you convalescent novel-ists, who write books about ladies who turn into foxes, and I am be-ginning to feel that I am really doing you quite a favour to explain it all so nicely, instead of using you as a weeping post for selfish ends. At least I have not hung on how I cry all day and most of the night, because there is nowhere I can go, neither on long walks nor to bed, where I was not accustomed to go with her. She slept with me, ate my food. The only escape is to write to you, and even that she once shared. I was her com-panion, master, valet, protector, upper servant and physician. She depended on me for everything, and I failed her in the end. Would it have been easier for both of us if she had died in my arms? Could I have saved her? Two things I will never know.

Anyway, there is the problem of the Vita Nuova. Please be tender with it. love from TIM

November 30th, 1944 41 *Gordon Square, London* WCI

Dear Tim, Your letter came today. I wish more than anything that I could come over immediately & take you off for a long walk or some days tour of somewhere in Ireland—I should, apart from anything else, so very much like to be with you & to talk. Unfortunately I am tied by my work, tied by the leg literally, & tied by regulations. I am back at work—very lame still—but slowly growing the necessary muscles. There is one question in your letter: you ask should you buy another bitch. One can only speak for oneself, but I think the best antidote to the numbing obsession of grief is having responsibility to a living creature. So I would say Yes: you should. But not just any bitch. A gun dog preferably as all the job of training will be good for you. Often it will hurt you—but you will realise you cannot dodge the responsibility.

Then I would say the creature should be different in looks—colour or breed—I myself though I have been warned off keeping a dog by you intend to have a pointer when I'm a free man. But you want beauty as well as intelligence: you will know best & you are in a country where there is no lack of beautiful horses, hounds, & women.

Angelica has bought some paints for you & when we can master the customs difficulties we will send them off.

Richard has been with us for a fortnight, & we have been to a couple of plays. *The Circle* by Somerset Maugham was particularly brilliant. I have been slowly reading Don Quixote & am nearly through it. I find the second half very disappointing. It is odd no one has realised that Don Q. is a self portrait. Cervantes had failed completely in life: he had been a soldier a very paladin among the slaves, and then for long years a bad hack poet, befriended & despised by Lope: always struggling to finish a long pastoral: desperately poor.

I read a couple of chapters in a book by Fitzmaurice Kelly but he completely missed the point I thought. Also his chapter on Lope de Vega was irritating as he was a good deal concerned by the impropriety of his sexual life—which shocked him all the more as Lope had a small job in the Inquisition. I read a book by H. E. Bates this week *Fair Stood the Wind for France*. It starts well but he is too much concerned, in the Hemingway method, with describing physical details—and as most of his details are wrong (the book is laid in German occupied France) I wasn't able to appreciate it as much as most. However it is well worth reading as there are good bits here & there.

Richard has been making toys for Amaryllis & got a toy book out of the London Library, the point of which was photographs.

The really interesting thing about toys is that they have remained virtually unchanged through the ages: Toys of 1100 B.C. from Egypt are exactly like wooden toys which are still on the market—anyway in a country like Ireland.

I wish you would write a childs story. I would like to do so myself but dont suppose I shall. If you do write anything & you want me to read it dont hesitate to send it along.   Very much love BUNNY

December 4th, 1944   41 *Gordon Sq., London*, WC1

Dear Tim, Your last two letters crossed mine: I have already told you what I think—however you talk of puppies—or no puppies. I have an idea from Leonard Woolf who has kept 2 bitches in succession that it may depend on her—that if you live on close terms with her, she wont have puppies. But I think in your present mood the greater responsibility you shoulder the more normal & contented you will be. Are there any quarantine regulations as regards dogs coming from Eire to Britain? Because if there are *not*, & if you are ready to take a gamble on the war ending next summer (with Germany) I would ask you to train a gun-dog for me. It is not an easy matter I know. But I think you would do it better than most professionals, & my dog could grow up with yours & your responsibility would be twice as great. I want either a pointer—which at Ridley Stokoe would be particularly useful as one has to walk up the grouse & always will have to. There are quite a lot of birds there but without a dog one has no idea where they are which is a great handicap.

If not a pointer I incline to a poodle which is beautifully intelligent & a good retriever. In France pointers retrieve (also in U.S.A.) but in England people are afraid of their chasing wounded game. But a controllable pointer that will retrieve would be the best all-purposes dog. I would rather have a dog than a bitch—I far prefer bitches—but mongrel puppies are a nuisance & so are crowds of he-dogs.

I hope you dont think this is an attempt to exploit the present position. It isn't. Of course I'll pay cash down for the animal & will go up to 10 or 15 gns. for an animal of hardworking antecedents. You will have to remember the animal would have to live with me & work for me & William—staying sometimes at Ridley Stokoe with Hedley who is a grand man with all kinds of animals. I want a sobersides not an emotional mistress—& shooting must be the business of his or her life.

The animal would also be very useful at Charleston where Clive does a great deal of shooting. At present he has the use of Lord Gage's ancient Labrador—a dull & heavy beast who is getting creaky in the joints but who knows his job.

I had a letter from William & also a parcel enclosing a grouse. He had been up again to Ridley Stokoe but did very badly—was so tired on the Saturday that he fell asleep for the whole afternoon under the high crag. On Sunday he pursued grouse & blackcock, but could never get near them—finally shot a grouse & a rabbit. On the previous visit he got a brace of grouse—a cock pheasant, a snipe, a blackcock & a partridge—also he shot a duck but could not find it—Hedley found it eaten by a fox a few days later. A dog would have saved that duck.

However to turn to your own life—I dont think that you have alternatives open to you. I think you will keep a bitch sooner or later—the fact that she will die by 1960 is really irrelevant. You may very likely die before then yourself. The fact that a rocket may at any moment blow us to bits doesn't prevent Angelica & me from having another baby—all these future events have to be disregarded as you disregard the possibility of a collision when you go by train. Also one does not enrich the past by dwelling on it—one only kills one's own feelings. For nearly two years after Ray's death, I was continually trying to avoid poisoning myself with the past. Doing the things she liked; going to the places she loved was a great help. She told me a few days before she died that it was a great comfort to her that I should make a new life for myself & she hoped it would be what she would have liked herself. And I'm certain Brownie would have told you to fill your life with pheasants & snipe & water-rats. She would not care for the plan of life in a library.

Love from BUNNY

Dear Bunny, I am over the worst, though there is still one thing I can hardly bear to think of. Brownie had immense confidence in me as a doctor and used to come to me for help when she felt an attack coming on. She used to come and look up at me and register being ill. Because I was away, she couldn't do it when she was dying, but she knew she was dying, and went to tell Mrs. McDonagh as a last resource, which failed her. When I think of this my heart is an empty funnel. There is a physical feeling in it. After she was buried I stayed with the grave for one week, so that I could go out twice a day and say 'Good girl: sleepy girl: go to sleep, Brownie.' It was a saying she understood. I said it steadily. I suppose the chance of consciousness persisting for a week is several million to one, but that was the kind of chance I had to provide against. She depended on me too much, and so I had to accept too much responsibility for her. Then I went to Dublin, against my will, and kept myself as drunk as possible for nine days, and came back feeling more alive than dead. She was the only wonderful thing that has happened to me, and presumably the last one. You are wrong that her infertility was due to our relationship. It was the other way round. She adopted me off her own bat, and I took her to the sire at 18 months and several times after, before I cared two straws about her. I also took her to vets, to find out why she flinched at the critical moment, and they said that the passage was malformed. After that, I just used to leave her loose when she was in season. I dont know what I told you before, but I have found out some things. One is that bereaved suicides commit it out of tidyness, not out of grand emotions. Their habits, customs and interests, which means their lives, were bound up with their loved one, so, when that dies, they realise that their own habits etc. are dead. So, as they see that they are dead already, they commit suicide in order to be consistent. Everything is dead except their bodies, so they kill these too, to be tidy, like washing up after a meal or throwing away the empties after a party, and I daresay they find it as tedious. The other thing I have found is that the people who consider too close an affection between men and animals to be 'unnatural' are basing their prejudice on something real. It is the incompatibility of ages. It is in Lucretius. He says that centaurs cannot exist because the horse part would die before the man part.

> Sed neque Centauri fuerunt, neque tempore in ullo
> Esse queat duplici natura, et corpore bino

Ex alienigenis membris compacta potestas, ...
Quae neque florescunt pariter, neque robora sumunt
Corporibus, necque projiciunt aetate senecta.[1]

All I can do now is to remember her dead as I buried her, the cold grey jowl in the basket, and not as my heart's blood, which she was for the last eight years of our twelve. I shall never be more than half a centaur now.

I must thank you very, very much for your two letters, which have left me as amazed at your wisdom as I always was at your kindness and information. I have done what you said I was to do, or at any rate I have bought a puppy bitch. Brownie had taught me so much about setters that it seemed silly to waste the education, so I stuck to them. No setter could ever remind me of her, any more than one woman would remind you of another, except in general terms. The new arrangement looks like the foetus of a rat, but she has a pedigree rather longer than the Emperor of Japan's. She is called Cill Dara Something-or-other of Palmerston, but prefers to be called Killie, for lucidity. She nibbles for fleas in my whiskers. We are to accept the plaudits of the people of Erin next St. Patrick's day at the Kennel Club Shew, where we intend to win the Puppy Class and the Novices: in the Autumn we go to watch the Field Trials, which we win the year after. When we have collected 15 points or green stars and can call ourselves CH. in the stud book we are coming to repeat the

[1 R. C. Trevelyan translated the passage on centaurs that Tim quoted. I give it in its entirety.

> But Centaurs there have never been, nor yet
> Ever can things exist of twofold nature
> And double body moulded into one
> From limbs of alien kind, whose faculties
> And functions cannot be on either side
> Sufficiently alike. That this is so,
> The dullest intellect may be thus convinced.
> Consider that a horse after three years
> Is in his flower of vigour, but a boy
> By no means so: for often in sleep even then
> Will he seek milk still from his mother's breasts.
> Afterwards, when the horse's lusty strength
> Fails him in old age, and his limbs grow languid
> As life ebbs, then first for a boy begins
> The flowering time of youth, and clothes his cheeks
> With soft down. Do not then believe that ever
> From man's and burden-bearing Horse's seed
> Centaurs can be compounded and have being.—D.G.]

process in England. We are to have about 4 litters of puppies. Then it is to be America: the camera men & reporters, the drive up Broadway with typists showering us with tape, the reception at the White House, the spotlights at Hollywood. In short, we are determined to make good.

If you really want a Pointer and were not suggesting him in order to encourage me, I will gladly train one for you ...

Do you think it would be wrong of me to write a book about Brownie, or that I ought to wait seven years before starting? I have a strong feeling that I want to write it now ...

I have joined the Kennel Club as a life member, as I am going to have hundreds and hundreds of setters from now on, to prevent loving one of them too much. When I went to their office about half a dozen dog-like women attended to me so faithfully and gently, and one of them was so exactly like a bull-dog, that I celebrated my entry by crying all over my cheque book. She was solid gold and stood by and gave moral support without speaking. I can't remember whether she barked a bit.

I was very angry when I heard that you were still limping, but on second thoughts I suppose it is only fair to give you about 18 months before you get back to normal. I dont think it is a good idea that you should have gone back to the office. love from TIM

1945

Doolistown, Trim, Co. Meath

Dear Bunny, I agree most gratefully to all your alterations and think it very clever of you to have thought of changing the Holy Ghost into an angel. But can you do this yourself? Please dont despise me too much, but I dont feel quite equal to looking at the book for some time still, because of Brownie. To alter the H.G. will require small changes in the argument about pigeons in the barrels. Also we shall lose the disagreement about its sex in Chapter Two, which I regret. Could you get round that somehow? By slight verbal alterations, or by discussing the sex of angels, or by making it a moot point whether it is the H.G. or an angel? Anyway, the change will tone down the split between natural and supernatural which I mentioned in my last letter, and is a splendid idea if you can manage it.

About libel, I shant let it be published or sold in Ireland. Will this do?[1]

Omit last chapter by all means. Plate Stalin instead of Churchill. Hasten the pace of events from striking the bridge to reaching Dublin if you like, but I dont feel *very* sure of this. You might omit one of the villages which they pass, but not the one with the policeman in it. I dont agree that a corrugated iron ark would be an egg-shell when it was shored inside by two decks and all that 3 × 3 which is shewn in the diagram of the interior. Besides, it only scrapes things before it hits the bridge.

It is very very kind of you to take all this trouble, and your two letters have quite turned my head. I will wire you to hang on to the typescript till you get this letter.

Could you send a covering note to Putnams when you post it, to tell them it is worth publishing? They will inevitably think it isn't.

love from TIM

P.S. We have been thinking about this Ghost on our walk this afternoon. The real objection seems to be that it is too shocking *too soon*. Could you contrive to introduce it as an Archangel, letting some doubts appear later on, whether it might have been the H.G.? Probably this would entail too

[1 Tim was of course unable to do this and a copy reached Mrs McDonagh not long after the book's publication in America. No libel action was brought but her feelings were much hurt and there was no further contact with Tim.—D.G.]

much labour and not be worth the trouble. So, if you do turn it into an angel outright:

(1) Remember it is an *arch*angel and use Michael, not Gabriel, for reasons that will appear.
(2) Retain the argument about its sex in Chapter 2 by adding some such phrase as 'Mr. White, who was orthodox about the nature of angels, said angrily: "It's not a She, its an It." ' (I can't remember how the sentence was originally phrased.)
(3) When the appeal is made to the chimney on the marriage question, alter 'Litany of H.G.' to 'Litany of S. Michael'; for 'Come, Holy Ghost, our souls inspire' substitute some protestant hymn about Angels or Archangels, if you can find any in a prayer book, the only one I can think of is 'Angels in the height adore him', which doesn't seem very apposite; and for the Creed which they say because the H.G. 'comes into it' substitute the *Confiteor*, in which Michael figures.
(4) You will have to find your own way out of the argument about pigeons on the way to Dublin, as I can't remember how it began. The point was that she had known the chimney thing was not the H.G. all along, because it was not a pigeon.
(5) What are you going to do about the descriptions of it as like a mop, having a pair of horns, etc., in Chapter One?
(6) It does seem a shame that you will have to alter the word wherever it appears, which practically means re-reading the book, as I shant see proofs before publication. I can remember it cropping up: when inventing Ark before telling Geraghty, when telling Geraghty, often when arguing with Mrs. O'Callaghan (I do hope we shant have to lose the argument about Infallibility), and after wreck, but there must be many other times. The thought of all this trouble makes me ashamed.

ARE YOU STILL LIMPING?

More P.S.

I reopen to suggest next morning that you might make Michael be *the bearer of a message* from the H.G.

You would mention only Michael in Chapters One & Two. In Chap. Three there is a sentence which begins 'To put it briefly, the Holy Ghost had told them' or something like that. You would alter this to: 'To put it briefly, the Archangel had been the bearer of a message from the Holy Ghost, to tell them etc.'

By this stratagem, you would be able to retain such of the subsequent arguments about the H.G. as seemed best unaltered, without alteration. For instance, when worrying about the fate of battleships, Mr. White could still say 'But we must leave all that to the H.G.' There are several other places where it would be helpful to be able to retain the H.G., though you could alter the chimney-appeal to Michael, as already suggested.

I can't tell you how full of admiration I am, after sleeping on it, for your invention of the angel. It solves the problem of reality-unreality, natural-supernatural, reasonable-shocking, which had been worrying me by its chasm or fissure for months.

April 17th, 1945   41 *Gordon Square, London*, WC1

Dear Tim, I am sorry to be so long but I hope to get the job done next weekend. I would have done it last but we moved up here on Sunday & a hundred bags, prams, cots, & children.

Luckily Richard has been on leave & has made most of the alterations needed. He has also made two others for which your approval is required.

1) He has changed the motto for the sundial to the one mentioned before once.

> I am a sundial & make a botch
> Of what is done far better by a watch [1]

2) He has taken out the reference to Philomena's having a child and the disgraceful behaviour of a dog from the last chapter & inserted it where Philomela first appears—because as he rightly says its much too good to lose. I have only to deal with the pigeon question but I can't do so till Sunday as I work hard all day & when I get back I like to do nothing.

We have been paying our Charwoman full wages for doing nothing while we were in the country. Now we get back & find she has been doing another job too & has left us as Angelica's having a baby might mean rather more work. To my astonishment I found & engaged another charwoman yesterday morning. They are rarer than rubies as most of

[1 See p. 195, and note.—D.G.]

them spend their lives scrubbing the Ministry of Information. Love to
Quince & Killie & to you   BUNNY

P.S. The new charwoman has given up & we have got a female Ancient
Mariner with a white beard.

Easter Sunday   *Scearnbank, Edenbridge, Kent*

Dear Tim, I am afraid I think you are wrong about your two books. The
Elephant & the Kangaroo is great fun. Nothing much needs doing to it,
except what I have already told you & with which minor changes you no
doubt agree (the omission of the last chapter which you suggest is the
biggest.) On the other hand the second book is the devil & all and I have
to write seriously, & be read seriously.

You have stumbled upon a most beautiful subject which you will
never get again & you have the opportunity to write a masterpiece.
Occasionally, for a few pages, you let us know what it will be like. But
you have not stopped to think, & instead of writing a masterpiece you
have filled it up with a lot of twaddle about Miss Pribble & the Vicar,
written in a facetious Meridithean style which honest children will hate.
It is far worse than the bad parts of the Witch in the Wood. And it is a
real tragedy, for you are on the edge of a book which will make you
immortal.

I implore you therefore to withdraw the M.S. from Putnam. To stop
bothering about dogs, or drinking, and to think out the whole thing again.
Miss Pribble & the Vicar are no use whatever to anybody. They are not
in the least amusing: they are inept & they must go. Instead of these
stock clowns you must really face the fact that the Lilliputians are human
beings with characters as intensely strong as yours & mine & Ray's and
I. A. Richards. You must remind yourself of several things. They are
grown-ups & Maria though so powerful is a child & must often exasperate
them.

Then though they have a tough time & a dangerous life, what with
the owls & breaking in young rats to harness, they are a *civilized* people.
They have their traditions. Some are poets & only Shakespeare will help
you there. They are painters & sculptors—they are fond of miniature
painting on lockets etc: they act plays too & there are astronomers
among them. I dont wish to tell you about your own people. I only
mention these things so you should remember & realise your problem.

Maria I feel most strongly must fall in love, or come under the domination of one among them. Though she's only a child, she will feel jealousy and behave like a fool & be made to feel ashamed by a hop o' my thumb—whose poems can be compared with Suckling if not with Keats. Her love makes her want to possess more than ever—her childishness makes her foolish—but all the time she has to restrain her passions and use her brains. And then there are moments of wild delight—For example model aeroplanes ... which the man she loves insists on flying. Of course he puts in real ailerons & controls. There is one other severe thing I must say & that is that this is & should be a child's book. But you spoil it by putting in jokes at the child's expense e.g. quaternions—which the child doesn't understand & which it rightly feels are in bad taste as you would not put them in if you were telling the child the story. Now this book may easily be the big thing of your life so dont be angry & misunderstand me, & dont be lazy. I know I am asking a lot. But I know I am right. Very much love BUNNY

April 1945   *Doolistown, Trim, Co. Meath*

Dear Bunny, Thank you very much for your letter about the Maria book. It is quite right, as usual, except that you under-estimate the sturdiness of the plot. I can do everything you say without upsetting it. I will change the Vicar & Miss Pribble into real people, give Maria more character and remove all farce. Count the pages on which Miss P. and the Vicar appear, and you will find less than 30. I only need to re-write those thirty as serious description, with no dungeons etc. and all will be well. I can substitute some probable form of mean-minded attrition (by the new Governess) for the melodrama. It is easy to cut out the tongue-in-cheek remarks about quaternions etc.* I will put in 2 more chapters about the culture of Lilliput and about a row they are going to have with Maria concerning model aeroplanes. [This will make you angry, I hope, as I, and the People, consider bunjee aeroplanes a childish frivolity. I also hope to annoy you over 'writing like Suckling or Keats'. Of course they didn't. In English they wrote heroic couplets. And as for making Maria fall in love with one of them *seriously*, the idea has shocked me dumb. I

---

* I want to retain the Lord Lieutenant at all costs. Also all descriptions of the Palace, even if grown up. Children like to be offered grown-up jokes *so long as they are not at the child's expense.*

will try to make her have a favourite, like a favourite toy soldier. Perhaps you meant this.] As for giving any of the People real characters, I dont like to give realer ones than any that Swift gave—Flimnap, for instance. I will give them a more grown-up collective outlook, and will make it collide with Maria's childish one, over her foolish aeroplane. I read your letter every morning before setting to work, and have already put things straight so far as Chapter Seven. This was what I was trying to say when I told you that the plot was solid but the tone needed blue-pencil. (Quaternions etc.) I now see that it needed more blue-pencil than I could have asked you to do, because of the re-writing of those 30 pages. It remains true. I suffered agonies trying to swallow your denunciation for 2 days. Now, the third day, I am actually enjoying the alterations. At first I had feared it would mean re-writing the whole thing. Now it is just a rather ingenious piece of carpentry-joinery and almost restful, like jig-saw. I can do it in a fortnight, and you will see that I am right. Please keep the old typescript, in case you want to restore anything from that, to the new one which I will send soon.

Please send the Kangaroo to Putnams, but not Maria. Thank you very much for all. Are you at all pleased with me for being so meek? Please do be. I had half a mind not to answer for a bit, to see if you got uneasy and wrote to calm my insulted feelings, but then I remembered how angry Johnson got when Bozzy played a similar trick, so I write to send best love from   TIM & QUINCE

As his letter shows, Tim tinkered with *Mistress Masham's Repose* but he was unable to make the effort to see his book anew and to take my advice. Had he done so it might have been by far his best. However, lacking the vulgarities, it would not have been chosen as Book of the Month.

Some time in May 1945   *Doolistown, Trim, Co. Meath*
Dear Bunny, Your second letter arrived today. So did the re-typed Lilliput book. After a mental struggle, I have decided not to send you this. You will have to read it eventually to Amaryllis when printed, and three times is too much to ask. Anyway, no power on earth would now persuade me to alter it a third time. I am sending it direct to Stanley Went. I am cross and liverish and this is a business letter ...

PLEASE SEND the Ark typescript to Stanley Went NOW [I MEAN *NO W*] because if you dont I can't devolve my affairs before September and consequently you will have to fetch Quince. I dont agree to either of Richard's alterations. His sundial motto may be funnier, but it would give too cheap and tinny a view of Mr. White's essentially pathetic and hopeful character.[1] If the buried baby story is introduced earlier, it gives away the fact that Philomena is to survive the flood, and if anybody is known to be going to survive it, all suspense is destroyed.

Stanley Went's address is:

G. P. Putnam's Sons
42 Great Russell St.
WC1.

I have writ myself into a good humour, so here are some non-numbered paragraphs. Your invitation to me to come and spend the rest of my life as your bedesman is what I would rather do than anything else in the world. But first I must amass some money because for some insane reason I could not bear to be a Creevey. Also I really must find out where I stand as regards nationality etc. I have a secret plan for going to live in America, or, best of all, near Vancouver Island. Probably I shall be able to visit you in September for a fortnight, but it might not be for more. All depends on money and on what my future life wants to be and the McDonaghs look like selling this farm in July and what with that and moving and God knows what else I dont know where I stand. If I sell my car, it will be something. I could get naturalised as an Irishman next February, if it would help me on my journey to the Americas or in any other way. I really can't bother to think about all this bosh, as I am much enjoying to write a book about Horace Walpole. Really you practical men have reduced the business of life to bosh. Why can't I just fly over to the Stokehole in Sept. and give you your dog? Oh, no. That wouldn't be practical. We must have exit permits, and travel permits, and identity cards, and tickets, and bills of health, and censored letters and Jesus knows what else. And I have to pay for this, as well as your standing army and your arterial roads and your down-and-outs, out of my pittance of an income, when I would much rather let the down-and-outs die in

[1 The rejected motto for the sundial was first published by Hilaire Belloc in 1923. The famous Garnett omniscience failed to spot the plagiarism and Tim did not own up.—D.G.]

Nature's way instead of undermine the breed, and dont use the arterial roads, which kill my dogs, and detest everything to do with armies and am sent half mad by all the forms. Damn you all and God bless Horry.

love from TIM

May 25th, 1945   41 *Gordon Square, London* WCI

Dear Tim, Dont write me silly bad tempered letters identifying me with the inland revenue authorities or anyone else who happens to annoy you. If you are in a bad temper wait until you are in a good one before replying to a letter like my last.

With regard to the Ark: you told me to make any alterations I liked. I did so, telling you what they were, & returned the M.S. months ago to Stanley Went. You had better write to him about the sundial motto & the buried baby. Incidentally I agree with you.

It's not a question of my tailor's measurements but of yours. I am not asking you to have a suit made for me, though if you brought a suit-length I would buy it. But you had better get all the clothes you want before you come.

I am quite pleased to wait till September for Quince.

Angelica had a most charming daughter on May 15th who is called Henrietta Catherine Vanessa. They are both very well & the creature takes enormous meals & is putting on weight. She is not a replica of Amaryllis.

You are such a curmudgeonly badmannered churl suffering from persecution mania that I think you had better become one of Mr D V's subjects. Then they can shut you up for life for writing the Ark!

Love from BUNNY

June 18th, 1945   *Doolistown, Trim, Co. Meath, Eire*

Dear Bunny, I have had your cross letter which tells me not to write when I feel ill, and I have been waiting patiently to feel well, but there is no time to waste. Perhaps you were cross because I did not seem grateful for your offer to support me for the rest of my life. But dont you see that I value your friendship too much to risk losing it by becoming a nuisance? Unless I have money in my pocket so that I can take myself off as soon as you begin to look restive I cannot stay with you. I ought to have written more affectionately, but it is like the little boy I once gave a watch to, who was so over-awed that he only snatched it and ran away without a word, only in this case I had the sense not to snatch the watch. The invitation dithered and bothered me, because I should have liked to accept it so much, but saw it was impossible.

Anyway, I have been struggling through multitudinous seas of incarnadined tape, to find out what the practical position is. I find that I can probably sell my car here for about £200. But in England I might get £400-£500. I am not allowed to sell it in England unless I leave my domicile here, and become domiciled in England—which I could do, because the McDonaghs are selling the farm.

But if I do become domiciled in England, I may become liable to be taken by one of your press-gangs and shipped to conquer Japan, which I dont want to conquer.

Nobody in Dublin can tell me what ages they conscript in England, and they all with one voice tell me to write to an Englishman to find out. The only Englishman I can think of is you. Can you tell for certain?

If it is safe for people of my age to be domiciled in England—these hateful official words—I will try to borrow £100 and will bring the car over to sell in September. Then I shall be a free agent and roaring to get at the pigeon-studio, saw-pit, swimming bath etc.

If not safe, I could sell the car here for £200, be naturalised as an Irishman, and petition for a fortnight's ticket-of-leave to visit you with Quince.

If all fails, I shall have to bribe somebody who is going over anyway, to deliver Quince to you in London.

If you take a paper which advertises cars, will you look in the advertisement pages to see if a 1936, 20 h.p., S.S. Jaguar, re-bored, 50,000 miles, tyres new, battery re-plated, laid up for war, really would fetch £400-£500, as they tell me here?

They steal 33% from me for import duty or purchase tax or something but I would still be coining money.

And do be sure about your facts about press-gangs. I am technically an 'Englishman domiciled in Eire', but if I came over for good would be demoted to a plain Englishman. Here we are just trying two Irish soldiers for desertion, because they went to fight for England and were coaxed back under the idea that there was an amnesty.

I was so glad to hear about the female Garnett. The more the merrier. What experiences you have been through since she was thought of! Do you still limp at all? love from TIM

I am not good at saying I am grateful when I feel it deeply, and in any case I find it difficult to believe that anybody would want to have me as a guest for long.

June 20th, 1945   41 *Gordon Square, London* WC1

Dear Tim, I was so glad to get your letter. I have just sent you a telegram as you dont tell me how old you are & your liability for National Service depends upon that. In point of fact I doubt whether there has ever been any question of calling up anyone who had had T.B., although you might have been put to Farm work in England, much like what you have been doing in Ireland.

I am afraid I was not being as generous as you think. I had no intention of offering to support you for the rest of your life: the standard of living I could offer would be very low: what I did offer was a roof over your head —as I have two roofs—& Butts Intake otherwise Duke Marys is empty. Anyway it only costs me £8 a year.

You can very easily make enough by casual journalism to keep you in a state of independence until you publish another book.

I don't know about cars—you should sell before they start making new cars or importing them from America. I will try & find out soon. You could certainly get more than £200, as Austin 10s are fetching £300. But with a high horse power the prices are not proportionately good.*

Our great excitement here is that we are moving to Hilton next week. There is a fearful lot to do—packing all my books in fruit trays: clearing up accumulations of odds & ends such as Williams paintings & Richard's book binding tools.—not only at 41 Gordon Square but also at my mothers & at Scearnbank, which has been taken by my tenant at Hilton.

I feel rather overcome at the idea of seeing the place again: all the trees grown so big & the past so near in me & already so far away in them & in things like them: but the rooms & furniture unchanged.

Richard will be on leave & will help me to move in: Angelica & the babies will come down when we have got the place habitable.

---

* Probably your car will fetch more in September when the petrol rationing may cease—when the high H.P. of your car will not be such a disadvantage as now.

I have just sent my secretary over to the Labour Exchange at Sardinia Street & the official information is that men over thirty are not called up for any form of military service now.

I shall find out the exact position in regard to other forms of work, but I shall be surprised if they direct you into any. They have several millions to find jobs for, now.

Later. My secretary has inquired at the chief Ministry of Labour bureau who stated that they are not directing any labour except skilled workmen. They advised you to inquire from the British authorities when you apply for an exit permit. [I thought exit permits had already been abolished] However when I get the answer to my inquiry about your age I can let you know more. Nobody over 41 is now directed into certain jobs. Nobody over 30 is required to do military service.

Much love BUNNY

July 19*th*, 1945   *Hilton Hall, Huntingdon*

Dear Tim, I have just got your letter sent to Gordon Square in which you tell me of your difficulties. I will gladly lend you £50. if it will help. I owe you about £15. for Quince's keep and you can repay the rest after you have sold your car. In the mean time I do seriously urge you to consider whether you had not better come to England, bag & baggage, dogs & car, as soon as you can arrange for transport, and for the time being become my tenant, of my Yorkshire cottage. The rent is £8 a year & the rates are about 25/– a year. I will, if you like, charge you 5/– a week rent. For that you will get a roof over your head; a place very cheap to live in, with blankets, sheets, beds, & all household necessaries,— a place which you can leave & lock up without any worry, whenever you want to. It is a good place for writing & an excellent place for the dogs as it is adjacent to a grouse moor. There are even trout in the R. Swale though they are not easy to catch. There is no chance of my going there this summer I am afraid. It is probably rather bleak after the end of November and there is a chance of getting snowed up in January February & March. It is easy to obtain the necessaries of life. Please do not interpret this offer as an attempt to make you into my Bedesman whatever that is. (I thought it was the man who carried the plate round in Church & I haven't a Church.)

Anyone else who has borrowed the place has always borrowed it, though I made one lady who lived there for a month replace the coal she had used.

I can deeply sympathise with you in moving—as I have just moved myself—though I was longing to do so. Fortunately Mrs Sidgwick, my tenant, fell in with my plans for arranging her life to suit my own convenience & took Scearnbank. This saved me paying rent for it & enabled her to move out of Hilton.

The St Ives furniture van went plunging headlong through the wood down the cart track being ripped open by branches & snags & fetching down saplings like a rogue elephant. On the way back it stuck. Next day it loaded up with my stuff at 41 & I drove to Hilton with the men.

Hilton Hall had been used as a furniture warehouse & menagerie for five years; no room had been scrubbed or swept & filth hid the mouldings of the wainscot. I have never seen so much dirt. Dog & cat & tortoise messes in the hall, a jackdaw stuffed with maggots on the hearth (it had fallen down the chimney).

Luckily Richard turned up to help & the village helped too.

Now the whole place has been made habitable—we distempered the dining room on Sunday. I catch a 7.20 train twice a week at Huntingdon (I have got my car back) and either spend a night in London or go to my mother's for the night & return the following evening to Hilton. This is a rather strenuous life.

Angelica is well: the place is very lovely: if only I didn't have to rush up & down to earn my living I should be quite happy. Please let me know when you are coming over & as I said I can advance £50 on the car's security if it will help.   Love from BUNNY

July 1945   *Doolistown, Trim, Co. Meath*

Dear Bunny, Thank you very much indeed for your charming letter and offer to lend me £50. I wont accept it at present, but it is a wonderful feeling to have it behind one as a kind of backing if the worst comes to the worst. I have sent 3 large oils to an exhibition here which they call Living Art, for which I am asking 51 gns. each, so if any of them sell I shall both be able to do without your loan and laugh at you for laughing at me as a painter. I would not have sent them, except that a person called Raymond McGrath begged me to do so. They may not be even accepted. If not, I shall simply have to give them to you, as the frames will be worth a few pounds.

About this cottage. I would far rather accept your offer and live in it, instead of with my mother, but I have an awful feeling that you dont understand the dog side of the thing. Who is the neighbour who owns the adjacent grouse moor, is he nice and is he a friend of yours? For on general principles it is fatal to take gun dogs to live near a stranger's grouse shoot. He is furious with you for coming, regards you as a poacher, warns you off the land, and is your competitor, not friend. He gives you far more trouble than a farmer would, because the farmer would be willing to let you the shooting, but an adjacent Duke merely forbids you to take your dogs *even for walks*. I am not looking for shooting, but fear that taking dogs to live near a shoot would practically confine them to the house.

What about Hedley, who sounds much safer? If there was a village near him, I could board with him when your family was away (if he is nice? or wanted a boarder?) and could retreat to the village when you turned up.

In any case, the one remaining Irish boat has now sprung a leak, and there are 2000 destitute passengers howling on the pier at Kingstown.

I am within 5 chapters of the end of my typing. It looks as if I could stay at Doolistown till September. If so, and if I can sell a picture, I will be off to the West in August, will hand in a good many application forms to various bureaux before I go, and will then face the boat with a cork in the bottom as soon as they give sailing ticket.

Dont forget to make me an editor.   Best love from TIM

August 5th, 1945   *Doolistown, Trim, Co. Meath*

Bunny a mic, You are like one of these new-fangled surgeons who make people walk two days after breaking their legs. I am hobbling, and already beginning to feel grateful for your brutality. I hope to set foot on Hollyhead c. Sept. 17th. One has to chose a remote target like this, to give time for the various permits to hatch, as some of them take six weeks. I find I shall need seven separate permits and one sailing ticket. You would not have got one person in a thousand to do what I have done i.e. to set the whole machinery in motion without having anything to pay for it with. I have written to America for money, which ought also to arrive c. Sept. 17th. I did not want to wire for it, as it seems important to let publishers believe that one is never poor. In any case, if the synchronisation coincides properly, I shall receive my money and all the permits on Sept. 17th, which is the earliest it could possibly be done, and I hope you will be able to wait till then? If very sea-sick, I may not penetrate to Hilton till 18th or even 19th, as the only boat is an afternoon one and seas prostrate me.

I am still at Doolistown, as the highest bid we got was £2,800. Next Monday I take Quince to Mayo, by pawning my fabulous watch. I return here (I hope) on or about August 22nd and shall be packing etc. till Sept. 17th.

I wrote to offer to live with my mother, because she is old and lonely, though frightful, and I am the most dutiful of men. Luckily she replies that I must first destroy Killie, for fear that Killie might bite her dog. I think this lets me out. She once suggested that I should destroy Brownie, for similar reasons, as if I were to ask you to put away Angelica, Richard, William, Amaryllis & the new one, to visit me at Doolistown. I shant bother about her any more. It is not that she is lonely for me in particular, but just anxious for any edible person, having by her own efforts already driven away her husband, paramour & only son. So I would be very glad to borrow your Yorkshire cottage, if you can assure me that the local shooter wont make a dead set at Killie with his keepers. I wrote about this before. When you answer, write to Doolistown.

But would you let me stay with you at Hilton for a fortnight, after Hedley's, before going to the cottage? There are some skills I want to learn from you, notably microscopy and book-binding. I need them both badly. Also I want to plant 2 peregrine peaches at Hilton, or a peregrine & a sea eagle.

My 3 pictures seem to have been accepted by the Living Arts, so you will have to be a bit respectful in future. They were framed by Victor Waddingtons, whose gallery was beseiged by hysterical crowds all the time they were in the building. I am asking 51 guineas each for the 2 large ones, and 11 guineas for a tiny one. If even one of them sells I shall triumph over you most horribly. If they dont, I shall just say that I am painting for posterity—certainly not for antiquity. And if they do sell I am going to indulge myself in painting 6 more at your cottage, and have an exhibition of my own some day.

It is possible that this farm may yet be sold before I get back from Mayo. In that case I will write again, to give you a new address.

Now I must desist, as it is time to send some of my great-grandmother's thumb-prints to the Department of External Affairs in re. permit to breathe.   love from TIM

August 10th, 1945   *Hilton Hall, Hilton, Huntingdon*

Dear Tim, The public news today is that the Japanese have surrendered: the most moving comment is the B.B.C. report from China of crowds weeping with joy after eight years of war. But I don't want to write about public news—privately, for me, the news means that Richard is unlikely to be sent to the Far East & that both he & William will be released earlier. Incidentally William has entered for a Trades Union Scholarship for a year at Oxford writing an essay on the themes (a) 'It would be a tragedy if the workers came to power without a comprehension of our cultural heritage.' (b) 'The workers should have their own culture & be proud of it.'

William took the line that (b) could only be true if they understood (a) our cultural heritage—since culture was a continuous growth.

However today we (William who has been on leave from the coalpit for a week & I) proved how unaware we all are of our cultural heritage in Hilton. Six years ago, or so, I bought the remains of a derelict farm house in order to turn it into a village hall. I may, in 1939, have spoken to you of the Royal Arms painted on its walls upstairs. Well nothing could be done during the war & in five years the greater part of the building fell down in ruins, leaving only one room upstairs with the Royal Arms & one downstairs with a pretty panelled Qn. Anne room. The panelling of the room was worth saving & William & I today went to measure it with a view to transferring it here to line a new room which is planned as a nursery for Amaryllis & Henrietta, to replace the present coal cellar & hat & coat lobby.

We began to work prizing it loose & when we lifted away a whole end of the room saw, behind the 18th century panelling,—paintings—a figure in a ruff.

When the panelling was got away we found 3 female figures & the top half of another, painted frescoes on the plaster behind the panels——I should guess the date to be 1600.

One female figure was playing a lute with a stag looking in at the window—& an inscription below saying 'maydes should be seen not hearde' but that the stag did not listen to her melody. The next was a very over dressed young woman with a wonderful hat & ruff, & an inscription which said that Ye eagle is not so keen to take her prey as I new fashions spie to make me gay.

The Third showed a terribly fast girl one of the Bright Young People of 1600, smoking a clay pipe & blowing out a cloud of smoke & holding a cocktail glass in her hand—with the inscription

> 'Nonsense is Nonsense though it please my mind
> But it is not suited to my sex & kind.'

As you can see they were gay frivolous pictures, but oddly revealing a light hearted *topical* civilization—This little farmhouse had been inhabited by people who liked the sort of culture represented today by Rex Whistler—& I thought of A … B … and F … R … —who are as capable of such civilization as an old magpie & a stud boar: the principal farmers of Hilton today. . . .   Love from BUNNY

[*Undated*]   *Hilton Hall, Hilton, Huntington*
Dearest Tim,
 … Tonight as I was chiselling off the tap roots of a Doyenne du Comice pear which has never borne, it occurred to me that your fears of being committed to me were very nonsensical since you were always free to quarrel with me—even if I didn't quarrel with you. Probably we are both by now such intolerable people that such quarrels are inevitable. However do not let us anticipate trouble: let us rather, at this moment, think of the grouse, woodcock, blackcock & odd pheasants not to speak of rabbits, which you will shoot & I shall miss, of the defeated hopes of finding a fish in the river, of the competing plans for rebuilding a nursery from a coal hole;—of our hesitating explorations of the interior walls which have sprung up during five such different years of experience. There are books, people, so many things to communicate—you will my dear Tim, be welcome & I look forward to Sept. 20 as I used to look forward to V(.J.) day—which is either today or tomorrow.
                              Love from BUNNY

September 3rd, 1945   *Doolistown*

My dearest Bunny, It has just struck me that a phrase in my last letter about borrowing £200 may have frightened you. I wrote it thoughtlessly. Of course I could never need anything like that figure, and more than probably wont need anything at all, not even to cash the Quince cheque which I already have. I can't think why I should have written it. I am quite sound really, with the car to sell and my ever-memorable gold watch, but the delay of the Americans must have upset me.

Well, my Travel Permit actually arrived today! Tomorrow I shall go to Dublin for a sailing ticket and to take any more oaths that may prove necessary. Really, it is almost like running in the National. What with the necessary money hovering in America and the need to synchronise not only money and self but also car, books, luggage, and Killie's season; so that we all reach the same place at the same moment, one's life is neck-and-neck.

I have been burning papers all the morning, and sorting your letters since 1939, and cursing you for sometimes omitting to date them. What a prize they will be one day. They do not date. I mean, you dont always, and they never do. Enclosed are some photographs which I turned up, and which I presume I am now allowed to send through the post. They depict Quince & Killie in last winter's snow, going somewhere in a hurry, as puppies do. No (4) is the spot they went to see.

I sent Angelica a mystic message yesterday. I wonder if it will arrive. No need to answer this, which is only because I am getting excited at the idea of coming.   love from TIM

September 4th, 1945   *Hilton Hall, Hilton, Huntingdon*

Dear Tim, Your [not altogether unexpected] scholarship has thrown a flood of light on the Park Farm paintings. Armed with the Granger catalogue I called today upon my friend Mr Henry Hake, Director of the National Portrait Gallery.

It seems that some enterprising engraver of the reigns of James I & Charles I, persuaded the chief & most fashionable whores to have their portraits engraved as visiting cards with discreet marginal notes in the corner such as *a gn a time* or even *5 gns. a time* or *a bitt of gold ye night.**

* I rather fell in love with the portrait of a girl who had inscribed in the corner '2/6'. But I was always a man of simple tastes.

The astonishing thing is that one of these has been used as an ornament of the living room of a small Huntingdonshire farmhouse. Who were the other two pin-up girls? Mr Hake is excited & I hope will come down to see them.

Meanwhile Leigh Ashton who is curator of the Vict. & Albert Museum is coming down next week with a carpenter to make arrangements for cutting them out. I have presented them to the Vict. & Alb. Museum. as it seemed the only way to save them from destruction. Hake was able to produce the engraving as described in the Granger Catalogue & it is the same. It is apparently an extremely rare one.

Hake was very interested to hear of your article about Horace of which I am sending him a copy.

I am rather doubtful whether the caravan will be repaired & decorated in time for us to live in it, & maybe the weather will be cold by then. So I am going to book rooms at Mrs Nevin's from Friday 28th Sept. until Sat. 6. Oct.

Let me know how things go with you. I don't think, even if the petrol situation allowed, it would be worth the expense of taking your car all the way up there, simply to do 4 miles a day. We can bicycle, I have one bicycle at the Farm up there & one at Hilton we can take up with us.

There is a later engraving of Moll Cutpurse as an old woman, wearing man's clothes, which although in profile, might very easily have been the same face drawn 20 years later. She is profile & not full face, but has the same long & pointed chin.

When I was at the Nat. Portrait Gallery Hake took me to see the Kit Kat portraits—a really marvellous collection all painted by Kneller or his backroom boys of the brains & breeding which made up the Whig party. There was a very striking one of Robt. Walpole, as a young man.

I have as many cartridges as we are likely to want considering the dearth of birds. There are at Ridley Stokoe, my gun & Williams, & at Hilton, a walloping magnum which I will lend you if your gun is not at hand.

I have also bought a couple of nylon light salmon casts in case there should be a flood & rumours of fish.

We have had a pleasant week at Hilton with Richard on leave, and Quentin, Angelica's brother, staying with us, & workmen puttying up cracks in the walls.

Richard also built a new brick wall which had tumbled down—supporting a flower bed—& repaired his canoe. There was thus a pleasant atmosphere of things being done.

We are hoping to see you on the 17th or 18th & shall expect you to stay in bed for a day or two until you have recovered from the sea voyage & the emotion of returning to your native land.

Very much love, BUNNY

September 7th, 1945   *Doolistown, Trim, Co. Meath, Eire*

My dearest Bunny, I'm sorry, but I have failed to get a sailing ticket until the 24th. They simply are not to be got. There is only one boat still in action, and that one, which has worn out its bottom by constantly rubbing it against the Irish Sea, daily carries about fifteen hundred people each way. I went personally to have a jolly day queuing for the ticket on the 4th, and the 24th was the earliest day unbooked, when I eventually waded to the counter. All the clerks adopt the attitude of Well-its-not-my-fault, so I will adopt it too.

When I do reach Hilton Hall on the 25th, will you have done two things for me? (1) I shall have two starving dogs, for whom there ought to be waiting two loaves of bread and as much milk as you can cadge from local farmers, if any. They get a pint each here at least, often two. (2) Will you be able to give me a hot bath? On the way across England I shall buy germicides, antiseptics, suppositories, vomits, purges. Then, when we have boiled myself and dogs for twenty minutes, and burnt our clothes, and fumigated the car, I hope to be able to speak to an English-man, out of doors, with the wind away from him, if he wears his gas-mask.

Love from TIM

September 9th, 1945   *Hilton Hall, Hilton, Huntingdon*

Dear Tim, Your letters, photographs of dogs, mystic message & Granger's catalogue have all arrived.

I send you with this a cheque for £100, because if the American money doesn't turn up you will need it & it will save you missing the boat. You can pay me back when you sell the car.

The Granger Book is very important. I dare say I wrote to you about the Nat. Portrait Gallery where Hake produced the engraving in question.

But it is now clear to me that two of the three paintings are portraits of Moll Cutpurse. She left her money, by the way, to pay for a conduit to run with wine on occasion of the Restoration. Quite likely the violent Royalist, Sparrow was one of her lovers. Its a bit odd nevertheless to find her.

Leigh Ashton, curator of the Albert & Victoria Museum is coming down on Wednesday with a carpenter to arrange the removal of these pictures. Saving them was urgent so I have given them to the V. & A.

You may find the rationing of things here a surprise. Clothes—drink & tobacco are the most tiresome, but you may find the absence of meat & bacon needs getting used to.

I understand you aren't allowed to bring cloth through the Customs— or drink, or food. We have a lot of cider in the house & there will be a little rum & whisky when you arrive.

I am proposing that you settle here until you have recovered & that we go up by train with dogs, guns etc on Friday 28th to Ridley Stokoe. Then we stay there until the end of the following week & then go to the Yorkshire Cottage where you can stay as long as you find it endurable. You can explore the country around there profitably as it is almost the best in England.

I am so glad Quince is growing up into a tolerable character. In the photographs he looks surprisingly solid & beefy with a mastiff's jowl. I do hope we can get on together.

I have today planted out hundreds of wallflowers, pansies, sweet williams, sweet wivelsfields, violas, & cabbage plants and I am tired & my back is breaking. Yesterday I planted hundreds of bulbs which is the most boring occupation on earth as there is nothing to show for it. In the end one shovels the little ones into a common grave.

Much love, BUNNY

September 12th   *Hilton Hall, Hilton, Huntingdon*

Dear Tim, did you get my last letter with enclosure written last Sunday? I have just got your letter to say you will arrive here on 25th. I propose therefore that I give you & the dogs 4 days to recover & go North on 29th or 30th.

How will you get here? Your car wont be licensed or insured or have any petrol. Probably you have thought of that yourself. The fuel officers in this country take 8 weeks to perform their natural functions—like elephants.

There will be something or other for the dogs to eat & hot water flowing plentifully in the bath. I hope if anyone casually says he smells an Irishman you wont imitate Hervey.[1]   Love from BUNNY

September 18th   *Pub in Dublin*

17th Sept. Spend afternoon in queue, to be told by doting doorkeeper at Visa Office—told with pride—'Oh, we *never* answer letters in less then 18–20 days.' Stay night in Dublin.

18th Sept. Same queue from 7 a.m. to 12 p.m., when one of the overlords tells me I can't have a Visa, because I have no employment in England. (Amazed to find on his desk the letters I wrote asking for a permit in 1942.) I throw myself on my knees and plead that I have a widowed, divorced, bedridden mother on death bed, which causes him to relent and give me a *visitor's* visa, which means that I shall have to go through the whole farce again in England. Will have to report to police and you may have to go before a Commissioner for oaths, to swear that you are employing me as a valet. In any case, I *shall* arrive on or about the 25th.

Quince is the only remaining problem—except the car, which still lacks one certificate.

I have hired accomplices to go with me in boat train at 6 a.m. on 24th, and these will patrol the queues at pier, trying to bribe some other passenger to father Quince. If this fails, they will take him straight back to Dublin, where Messrs. Spratts of dog biscuits will export him as cargo on the *evening* boat—the only boat he is allowed to go on—and I shall have to wait at Holyhead until midnight, when I meet him. In that case I may be a day late at Hilton.

And now I'll have another bottle of stout, please, and you might hand me that illustrated catalogue of nice comfortable coffins.   love, TIM

Tim arrived with the two dogs at Hilton Hall. He had driven in his

[1 Someone said to Hervey: 'I smell an Irishman.'
'You won't smell one again,' replied Hervey and bit off his nose.—D.G.]

car from Holyhead and he left it at a local garage when we went North. Quince was as big as a yearling calf and quite as stupid and clumsy in the house. He kept sweeping crockery off the table with his tail.

A few days later Tim and I and the dogs took a train to Peterborough where we changed, and Tim persuaded the guard of The Flying Scotsman to allow us to travel with the dogs in a luggage van at the end of the train. At Newcastle we changed into a train for Falstone and from there got a hired car which took us the two miles to the Crown at Stannersburn where Mrs Nevin made much of us and Quince was shut up in a stable.

Next morning we were met by William at Ridley Stokoe who had come over from the coal mine, where he was working, in Durham. There were a fair number of grouse on the moor to start with. On the first day we went over the moor, William and I as guns, Tim as dog-handler. The dogs made several points at frogs, sheep and bumble bees which was rather a strain. However they eventually made a point and William and I crept forward, one on each side. A grouse rose; we fired simultaneously, and it dropped dead in the heather. This was a definite success and we all rejoiced. Unfortunately it was the only one as far as the dogs were concerned. The trouble was that once we had been all over the moor, we had chased all the birds off it as far as that day was concerned. Tim was disappointed. Next day, after William had gone, he told me that I had brought him up to Northumberland on false pretences. He had been led to suppose that I had a proper grouse moor but my 300 acres was too small to be any use. I apologized for not being rich enough to own a real grouse moor.

Tim had refused the loan of my magnum and it had been left behind at Hilton Hall because he said that he had no interest in shooting, but only in working the dogs. He now wanted a gun, so I lent him William's. It is a beautiful old weapon with an exquisite balance, of which William was rightly fond, and I was horrified, on Quince misbehaving, to see Tim thrust the gun through the loop in Killie's leash, drop it on the ground and run after Quince. Killie, dragging the gun over the rocks and stones of the moor, ran after Tim. I managed to catch the bitch and rescue William's gun. I was angry. It was a miracle that the barrels had not been dented or the stock broken. But I was also deeply shocked that Tim should have done such a thing. He strode off in a rage, refused to come in to the farm for lunch where the Hedleys expected us and abused me.

In the afternoon the dogs were shut up in one of Mr Hedley's hummels and we went shooting, walking through a field of roots where the Hedleys were working. Several pheasants got up and Tim shot one of them.

There are black game at Ridley Stokoe and Tim said next day that he had never shot one and would like to do so. We went round the north side of High Crag. I kept on high ground and Tim went round below. A blackcock rose within shot of him; he fired and yelled to me: 'Mark where it falls.' But the blackcock, flying strongly, and keeping out of range of me, swung round the western side of High Crag and I was able to watch it until it disappeared into the forestry.

'Did you mark where it fell?' demanded Tim, striding up. When I told him that the bird hadn't fallen but had flown away unscathed, he was very angry with me. He asserted that he knew that he had hit it mortally. He had heard the shot strike the bird, and that it was lost because I had not been watching. This was not true. Only one bird had risen, Tim had fired at it and it had flown half a mile with no sign of injury. We were again on bad terms, but worse than before. Because, though Tim thought I was unduly fussy about William's gun, he was on that occasion a little ashamed of himself. But this time he was convinced that I had robbed him of his blackcock.

Fortunately, however, before we left Ridley Stokoe, Tim shot a greyhen which flew out over our heads from the top of High Crag as we were standing under the little cliff on the western side. That made things a lot better.

Apart from these unfortunate quarrels, and the total failure of Quince as a gun-dog, I think Tim enjoyed himself at Ridley Stokoe. He liked the beauty of the place: the crags and the wildwood and the river. William remembers his saying that the air was so wonderful to breathe. And he liked Mrs Nevin and the Hedleys. It was his sort of country and they were his sort of people, though I think that Hedley was a little critical of him. I did not enjoy our visit so much. By the end of it I felt sour and glad to get away.

I don't remember the details of the difficult and tiresome journey from the North Tyne to Upper Swaledale. It must have been most exhausting with changes at Newcastle and Darlington, the dogs and guns and crowded trains. And then a hired car from Richmond to Whitaside. However we reached Duke Mary's: I installed Tim, introduced him to the Appletons and the Sunters and next day took the bus to Richmond and the train to London. Tim came down to the road and saw me off.

Dear Bunnie, When you were gone I surged up the mountain in the mist and began housework—made the beds, swept the rooms, washed up, pumped water, arranged larder, took stock of stores, unpacked, gave Killie two weeks meat ration, which she ate at one gulp, and got everything shipshape & Bristol fashion. I laid the fire in the bedroom, in case I get 'flu unexpectedly, and found a lovely red tablecloth with fans on it, which makes the kitchen table gay. The mist lifted by noon, but not dispersed. It is still hazy. Lunch was pilchards and milk and butter and breadcrumbs and tomato sauce in a casserole, and bread and golden syrup and cheese and coffee left from breakfast. Quince had some bread and milk. Best find of morning: a tremendous thermos flask, so that I can make hot coffee overnight to help me lay fire in morning. The oven door wont shut. I am going to beat it with a hammer.[1] I wish there was a bill-hook to chop wood. Everything is so tidy and so beautiful that I am panting to get home again, and find my red table cloth and the fire burning and bread and jam for tea. I am writing from the fell above Duke Mary's, with 2 maps to spy out the land, a gargoyle brooding over Swaledale. I dont know what turn my Yogi will take yet, but it may be an unpleasant one—perhaps a werewolf living on blackcock, and the farmers will have to come out in bands with shot guns, when I take to lambs. There are some artillery bumps going on, and the inevitable aircraft, and some people are shooting grouse opposite. Their shots re-echo up Arkengarthdale. It sounds like two of them. The fell is on fire on both sides of our valley, but not badly. [burning heather] I suppose you are at Peterborough. There is a cock grouse talking behind me. The dogs are running about. I have found a mushroom, on the way up. The white heaps of lime for fertiliser shew up among the jig-saw fields, and there is still the Japanese print effect towards Ravenseat, because of the haze. I have spotted the pub from the map. I am at lat 54° 23', long 2°, and the Roman camp is on my right and I am near Guy Mine (disused). A Flying Fortress or something has just missed me. I am very, very happy, and when I gurk there is pilchards.

I am sorry about that temper at Ridley Stokoe, and wont mention it again. It was because I had tried hard to make Quince so that you would be pleased with him, and when I saw that he was unsuited to the country it was a disappointment which I blamed on you.

[1 He did, and broke it.—D.G.]

There have been nine gunshots opposite in half an hour, never more than three at a time.

I am writing to Sydney Cockerell to try to get me into the London Library, but if he fails I will fall back on you. Also I am writing for the books and pictures. There is nothing else but two trunks, one of clothes, one of tools. I will go to the Food Office etc. tomorrow morning. I need potatos from the Appletons. I am enclosing cheque for Mrs. Nevin, as it seemed better to post it and prevent argument. You are still much out of pocket for taxis etc.

Please give my love to Angelica and tell her my heart bleeds for her attempts to provision you up this crag when ill.

What do you think? Killie & Quince have just caught me a rabbit! I looked up and saw her chase it out of some bracken straight into his mouth! It is very naughty of them, as I told them, but since I was greedily paunching it for tomorrow's dinner they seemed to doubt my sincerity. Anyway, now that you dont need Quince I dont care what they do. I must go home and skin it.

Now it is night and we are beside a fine fire in the golden paraffin light, the two dogs snoring on the loopy mat after an extra dinner for the house-warming, and Killie's arms round Quince's neck. I have been reading Pukka Lil's book about Lawrence—evidently a hoax made up by Beachcomber.[1] She could not have existed. I had a long talk with Mrs. Appleton when fetching the evening milk. She tells me the Fuel Controller is at Grinton. The keeper's daughter has become a postmistress and is no longer available for washing at Duke Mary's. I have a great list of things to do and order tomorrow, and a sack or bag for carrying things, but I can't find a needle to convert it into a rucksack with. It seems that I shall find it fairly easy to feed us, by getting lots of vegetables for myself and giving the meat and milk to the dogs. Tom has promised us a weekly rabbit. I must get some curry powder or something to make it taste of something else.

Monday.

The excitement in Reeth on Saturday was that a middle-aged farm labourer with all his relations dead had gone mad and was walking about in nothing but a boiler suit. He has been removed. The house at the bottom of this hill with the chinese dragon-cloud for a wind vane belongs

[1 *The Golden Reign* by Claire Sydney Smith.—D.G.]

to some colonel or other and is up for sale, asking £2000. His son missed Tommy Appleton and me with a ·22 on saturday by inches. He is a 15 year old red-head. In Reeth there is a literary publican at a pub called the Buck (I think) who has two or three hundred books of the Everyman type, which will be useful to me till my own come. He is called McLoughlin, poses as an Irishman, has been a schoolmaster or something, and is rather a crook. Mrs. Appleton is being a darling. As I could get no rations on saturday, she sent up an ounce or two of butter. On Sunday she gave me a dozen home-made cheese buscuits, and tried to give me a Yorkshire pud, but I wouldn't have it, as it was obviously for their own dinner. I am turning out a splendid cook and had for my Sunday dinner: pea soup, roast beef and baked potatoes, bread and cheese, coffee, square of milk chocolate. I sweep the house every day, make my bed, wash up and keep all decent. I have a time table worked out, which will allow me to write 4 hours a day, apart from housework and shopping. I met the wife, daughter & grandchild of keeper Alderson yesterday on the fell, and they were rather uncivil, disapproving of Quince and Killie, who were rushing about madly under clouds of grouse. I have never seen so many birds, although such a bad year. You trip over them. I suppose the overlord kills 200 brace a day for ten or twelve days. I never saw stone butts before.

I locked my door the first night, but not since. I have to drag innumerable loaves of bread and other rations up the hill in a sack on Mondays & Thursdays. I must stop, as this is my (time-table) writing hour, and I have to write to Quaritch, Cockerell, furniture removers etc. The fuel controller at Grinton is a swine, they say. I wrote to him for the coal, as he was away at market on Saturday. *Do you mind if I strip all the wallpapers before colour washing?* They are coming off anyway.

love from TIM

October 23rd, 1945   *Duke Mary's Low Row*

Dear Bunny, Your vegetables were a rip roaring success.[1] I have just eaten an epoch-making salad containing two lettuces, grated carrot, half beetroot, one small onion, grated cheese, one egg, quarter apple, two potatoes and some stuff out of a bottle tasting of walnut pickled. It has no label, and may be furniture polish, but if so it only shews how right

[1 I had sent a hamper from Hilton Hall.—D.G.]

one is to eat furniture polish. I ate the whole lot and am living like a fighting cock and even managing to put aside a tin of something every now and then, for when the snow comes. You can't think how successful Shackleton is being, and how happy. I cook and house work every morning—and so far I have made my bed every day, like dressing for dinner on the Congo, and kept all fit for visitors—and walk dogs in afternoon and read or write in the evening. Monday and Thursday I shop. Everybody is being charming to me, particularly the new publican's wife at the Punch Bowl, who helps me in getting fish etc. All my cooking has been dashing, ambitious and successful, except once when there was a lack of dripping and a dull red glow appeared in the frying pan, and once when the same pan burst into flames, with all the bacon ration. But I am not a frying panner really and have conquered the oven with a hammer. I carried coals all this morning from the 3 Sisters, had lunch at the P. Bowl and won 3 games of darts, shopped and met your pal the Vicar coming home, who insisted on giving a fifty yard grand lift in his silly motor car. He exasperated me into telling him I was not a Christian of any sort whatever, and this within 15 minutes of meeting him, and I am not usually so horrid. So now he has been insulted by two people from Duke Mary's, poor fellow. Since then I have been continuously munching salad.

The tragic side of the picture is that Killie has been served by Quince, as was feared, through a muddle of the Calvert girl's, who washed my floor on Saturdays. If you don't want Quince do you think you could send me his pedigrees etc, so that I can sell him and cut my losses?

I have made friends with Alderson who has given permission to take dogs discreetly on moor. I may be taking a small moor next year, a tiny one. They kill 200 brace a day for 12 days on this one, and have Halifax, Blandford, Eden etc as guests. I am invited to shoot rabbits next Friday. I have fixed the London Library through Sydney. Could you drop my gold watch at that shop to be mended? Don't drop the chain or they will cunningly file pieces off to swindle me. I have been reading—nearly finished—all your books. The Twilight of the Gods is 100% better than I thought it was when I was too ignorant to appreciate its scholarship. So is Lady Into Fox much better than I remembered. Aldrovandus is arriving in deep cargoes—folios weighing fifteen pounds apiece. There is £50 worth of paper in him, let alone print. I am very happy and beginning to forgive you for losing my temper.   Love from TIM

How's Angelica? I am getting to understand her more through Julian Bell's book.[1] Give her my love and I mean this.

273 feet of bookshelves ordered. Start colour washing tomorrow, and putting putty in cracks of doors. Tommy Appleton has gone mad on archery. I love him very much. Everybody and everything is perfect except the vicar. When you turn me out I shall just move across the valley, high up, to get the South sun. The Calvert girl is 17 and exquisite. Shall I explain to her about Quince?

November 13th, 1945   *From Duke Mary's*

Dear Bunny, Your welcome news of the comfits from Fortnums[2] arrived today—welcome because I have woken up with a feverish chill or mild dose of flu. I shall certainly have to get a small Valor Perfection stove, as it is really too bad having to light a fire for a hot drink when shivering and the Primus is not really efficient—it is too small, takes too long to boil things and does not warm the room. With that, I shall be able to say I have every luxury. The cottage is now quite repainted, the floors scrubbed, the candlesticks polished and I have done my first baking day & first washing (Rinso) and ironing day. The Calvert girl has not been near me for 3 weeks. The new colour scheme is the same as the one you had, except the tiny bedroom, which is different but not unpleasant. If you dont write to the contrary I shall paint the in- or beige-side of the doors (whose cracks I have filled with putty) GREY. The black sides shall still be black. I am buying a new padded small armchair. The shelving should arrive next week, but I dont know when the books will. I shall have to change things round from room to room a little to accomodate the books, but all can be changed back again when wanted. The tiles are not yet mended.

I have had no time to explore the neighbourhood, beyond walking across into Wensleydale one day, as I have been too busy. The village has taken me to its heart and invited me to all concerts, Home Guard dinners etc. At the latter I sang—you know what my voice is. It was so as not to seem stand-offish and gave great pleasure.

I have ingratiated self with the new publican at the Punchbowl, and

[1 Julian Bell, *Essays, Poems and Letters*, with contributions by J. M. Keynes, David Garnett, Charles Mauron, C. Day Lewis and E. M. Forster.—D.G.]
[2 A hamper of unrationed delicacies which I had sent him.—D.G.]

216

drink there one day a week. It is worth it, as his wife sells me sugar, butter etc. to keep me going.

Talking of keeping going, have you any news of the car? I shall need money soon, and you told me 3 months ago that they were a dwindling asset. If the garage man shews no signs of action, shall I write to my old garage in Buckingham to collect it?

My head is going round like a top, so I shall back to bed. I have fetched the milk & told Mrs. Appleton to send up Tommy with a coffin if I dont appear by dusk tomorrow.

Thanks for 2nd dose of vegetables.   love from TIM

1946

January 16th, 1946   *Hilton Hall, Hilton, Huntingdon*

Dear Tim, I suppose Achilles' tent was not as cold as Duke Mary's must be this week—but do some time or other answer my letters, if your fingers will hold a pen. Let me know how you are, & how your affairs go. Have you got Quince still, or have you disposed of him? I understand that the cross between Pointers & Setters was once valued & was called a *Dropper*. I cannot imagine where I got that information but I have not invented it.

I have been having a hellish cold, but am better.

I gather your car has gone from Knights.

I suppose you know that 36,000 acres of N. Swaledale are for sale for £60,000.

Richard & William were here over New Year.

As Angelica said in her letter we are ready to brace ourselves to putting up with a puppy visitor for the sake of seeing you.

No doubt your visit will be unwelcome to our cat (particularly if she is kittening) but we must firmly override her in this case. Have you read *Animal Farm* by the way? I will send you a copy. I believe I am writing about your work for the French.   Love from BUNNY

January 17th, 1946   *Duke Mary's, Low Row, Richmond, Yorks.*

Dear Bunny, Yes, it is cool at Duke Mary's in the snow, particularly as candles will blow out in the bedroom with door and window shut. How am I? Not very well. I have had 3 feverish chills, once a little delirious, and now have a permanent sore throat. Yes, I have Quince still, and he is the bane of my life. The hell of feeding him and his bastard on the top of this alp is breaking my heart. You probably learned about Droppers from some letters in the Field between Croxton Smith and another, or else from a book by him called British Dogs. Yes, I managed to get the car away from Huntingdon. It has now missed the market. I can get no offer for it whatever. So I shall have to keep it. I am trying to arrange some way of selling the watch, without your help, as my finances are again serious after the débacle about the car. The acres of Swaledale which are

for sale presumably belong to Ld. Rochdale. The old lord died last year
and the new lord does not shoot. If I were to stay here I would try to get
Crack Pot moor to rent. It is a small bit of only a thousand acres or so
and was once let separately. One could kill 50 brace on it. It has a little
shooting hut with an oven, and one would live there in August. While
you were entertaining Richard & William, I was entertaining Timothy
Bagenal. He arrived on a 12-hour walk and I gave him dinner. He was
carrying six buns, 2 tea cakes, 2 tins condensed milk, 2 lbs of sandwiches
1 lb dates, apples, bars of chocolate, meat pies, 1 overcoat, 1 macintosh,
1 waterproof cape, 1 pr. cyclists trousers, spare pair of socks, compass,
torch and 2 hats, one for if it was cold and the other for if it was wet. I
gave him a pound of fudge for fear he should starve. He had no umbrella.
Even if you and Angelica and the cat are willing to put up with your
dog's puppy, I am not willing to put up with transporting it 200 miles to
St. Ives, presumably in a perambulator. No, I have not read Animal
Farm, though several reviews of it. I have read all the books you left here.
My own books have not come from Ireland, so I am stranded for literature. I can't read the last sentence in your letter, which seems to state that
you are writing about my work for the French. There is little news from
Swaledale. A mosquito crashed last week above Angrim, killing its 2
occupants. The snow is not deep yet. I have persuaded Margaret Calvert
to come and do me for a couple of hours every morning, while I am
seedy.   love from TIM
I have emptied the tap as instructed, but the rain tank itself is frozen.

January 22nd, 1946   *Hilton Hall, Hilton, Huntingdon*
Dear Tim, I am sorry you are ill & the dogs are such a curse. I gather
from an indistinct phone call from London that Putnam's want to see you
urgently—they wanted the telephone number at Duke Mary's. This is to
say that we should be delighted if you could come for at least a fortnight
from the 30th, if it is in any way convenient.

Angelica is going to Charleston for a week with the babies, but
Margie will be able to look after us.

Angelica says she very much hopes you'll stay for at least a week after
she gets back & sends her love.

There will be hot water (occasionally) & warm rooms always & you will be able to get better, & then, if we must quarrel we can do it on equal terms. But I dont feel like quarrelling & I want to see you & I send my love.

BUNNY

January 22nd, 1946   *Duke Mary's, Low Row, Richmond, Yorks.*

Dear Bunny, Thank you very much for your repeated invitations to Hilton, but really I dont think I can face it till the spring. The puppy is enormous, a sort of Hound of the Baskervilles, but only in the wobbly stage of walking. I couldnt possibly carry it and my own suitcase and lead Quince and Killie, without having enough money for porters and taxis, in these awful post-war trains and the dead of winter. It still pees on the floor. I dont trust your dog-feeding arrangements. I am terrified of being brow-beaten and contradicted whenever I open my mouth. I dont feel well. Altogether it would be far nicer for me if you would let me propose myself some time in April, when the car will have been done up, the puppy & Quince I hope eliminated, and myself richer. Far richer—the message from Putnam's was of terrific import.[1]

Please thank Angelica for her kind message. The letter she wrote me was a very nice one indeed and when I do come in April I hope to gossip with her for hours about soufflés and layettes for puppies and all the thousand little things which we housewives find so absorbing. Persil or Rinso? The soft-ball stage in sweet-making without a thermometer? Should puppy be allowed to suck her thumb?

The postman on the opposite side fell dead on his round last week like a sparrow in the snow. Tommy Appleton has applied to become a policeman. Margaret Calvert who is working for me is a darling, but is inclined to screw screws with your chisel etc. I have got some clogs, which are beautifully warm and comfortable, except that they ball badly in snow. I am being persecuted by the woman at the Punch Bowl who has fallen in love with me. They called her baby doll about thirty years ago. The rain water tank is frozen solid. I got drunk on Xmas eve and bought a goose which was being raffled to be murdered. It looked so noble in the bar parlour, surrounded by its loud and boozing assassins. But it was not grateful and has wandered off to live with somebody else.

love from TIM

[1 *Mistress Masham's Repose* had been chosen by the Book of the Month Club. —D.G.]

April 18*th*, 1946   *at Woodlands, Stowe Ridings, Buckingham*

Dear Bunny, Thank you very much for sending the watch, which arrived safely. You will be astonished to hear that I have sort of become engaged to a brat not yet 21, and I want to bring her to Hilton for you to see, when I come. May I? She has met you (aet. 14) when you came here before the war, and says you were a big, silver-haired man who looked very kind. I assure her that you are not kind but cantankerous. She is afraid you will disapprove of her. I hope you may not ... I must not tell you about her, as she will probably read this. Anyway, may we come soon?

I am leaving here tomorrow, to see how long I can keep away from her and will be staying for a day or two at

The Shellswell Arms
Finmere
Bucks.

If you will write to me there, I will come back to fetch her and bring her if allowed. It is a little difficult to kidnap farmer's daughters who are half one's age, because farmers are so conservative. I am sort of on trial for being engaged and they are taking it reasonably well considering. Nobody has actually *created*. It was her Ma who took my breath away this morning by suggesting that I should carry her off to see my 'father confessor', as she calls you, so I am jumping at the chance.

Dear Bunny, pray dont congratulate nor scold me. If I dont marry her I will never marry anybody and I am sick of the pale cast of thought. I forgot to tell you that the book about Malplaquet was about [her]—she is Maria—and that it is a Book of the Month Club thing in America this summer, which seems a good augurio. I am trying to escape with her to America before the money falls due, as it will save about £2000 to do that.

I feel quite mad.   love from TIM

P.S. No, dont write to Finmere. They can't take me. Write to Woodlands.

As the reader will have gathered, *Mistress Masham's Repose* had been chosen for the American Book of the Month club. The £15,000, or whatever it was that Tim would receive from this windfall, would be liable for income tax and supertax as one year's earnings if he continued to reside in this country. I therefore urged him to go abroad and suggested New Mexico, or even Mexico itself. Tim however refused, as it would mean that if he ever returned Killie would have to spend six months in quarantine for rabies. I then suggested that he should live in the Channel Islands, which he thought was a good idea.

May 5th, 1946   Punch Bowl Inn,
Feetham, Low Row,
Richmond, Yorks.

Dear Bunny, Perhaps its best not to arrive and terrify Amaryllis, so you wont be sorry at my tale of woe. I have caught a hideous cold from sleeping in the damp cottage, and xxxx[1] has gone home by train, but not in dudgeon, and I will be staying at this pub until things clear up a bit. Among other nuisances, the car has bust. I hope to come south in say a fortnight, in which case I shall just call at Hilton, with precautions, possibly in a mask. The £10,000 which I told you the B.M.C. is to give me turns out to be £15,000. They have got more numerous. It is important to get out of this communist country before September, when the money is to fall due. I wish you could think of somebody who would help me out. Anyway, I shall have to go to American Consulates or whatever they call themselves when the car is repaired.

When we got here, I found that Mrs. Appleton had had an accident—sprained ankle—which developed into blood poisoning, and she was expected to die. I took John & a sister to see her in Darlington hospital. Now she is better. Tommy has got something wrong with his eye, so I am taking him to a doctor tomorrow. You see we are all ill.

xxxx says she wont marry me now, but I am hoping this is a fad.

love from TIM

June ?26th, 1946   Duke Mary's

Dear Bunny, Thank you for your letter. To be written about by you in the B.O.M. publication will be the crown of my literary career, however horrid you are. How surprised I would have been to be told this ten years ago.

I dont think I shall be able to get to America in time to save my money, but I'll still go, if its only to save on the next book. I couldn't

[1 The girl he had hoped to marry.—D.G.]

go via Spain, because of quarantine for Killie. It seems a bit odd to sacrifice about £8000 to save a dog 6 months in quarantine, I fear you'll think.

xxxx appears to have jilted me completely, you'll be glad to hear. I am much distressed and still hoping against hope. Not one single person that we have met in any walk of life has approved of our marriage, so I am sure I am right in wanting to marry her. But God, its hell to be a Troilus at 39. She is now in the arms of Diomed, ... Its too ridiculous. I dont mean the county cricketer, whom she had far better marry, but having to go trapzing about at my age. What a nemesis! ...

The rats have become a positive plague. They hold parties and sing vulgar songs all night and break the crockery and run over this letter as I try to write. I am now going to put poison down and go to bed.

love from TIM

Picture for Amaryllis

?November 30th, 1946   *Grouville Hall Hotel, Grouville, Jersey, C.I.*

Dear Bunny, This is where the winds of history have blown me to. I will buy you some postcards of it tomorrow, if I can get any, but they are misleading. They are photographs taken either at dawn, when nobody is up, or else in the winter, when the trippers have withdrawn. You must imagine them either in a fine winter solitude, or else with organised tripper campers laid on the cliffs and beaches like seals basking in myriads. In this particular (small) hotel there are no less than four Colonels. Each one is more ghastly than the next. They lie, bully and are fools. That is the winter population—of toffs—who play goff. The summer population is of shop-keepers, who bask in scanties.

Can you imagine England put in a hot bath, so that everything shrivells up? Like the creases on one's fingers. But more so, more shrivelling, so that London becomes Brighton, Brighton Huntingdon, Huntingdon a village, the village a house, and the house merely a back garden? Such is

Jersey.* In the middle parts of the island—what they call the *country* parts—
there is not a farm house more than 100 yards from its neighbour. The
cows are actually tethered, because the value of their grass is so great, like
goats. They are on grass rations. The biggest farm in the whole island
may be 30 acres: the average one, about three or two.

There is a sense of crowded minuscule. This is in the winter. In the
summer, God knows what the misery is. But the odd thing about these
horrors is that they seem to be qualified by quite a lot of goodness.

Laws and so on, here, are kind to the verge of madness. The last
murder in Jersey was about 60 years ago. When you are had up, the
justices say, 'Dear me, the poor fellow, what can we do for him?'

The climate is equally obscured. The island has the sunshine record for
the British Isles. It never really rains, far less snows or freezes, and the
sunlight is there all the time. But it is a humid island. Apparently you can
be sunny (bright light) and wet (merely a damp air without rain) at the
same time.

Factual comparisons are strange. For instance, we have no butter,
milk or egg rations. Cigarettes cost 1/2 for 20 and I can get as many
double brandies as I want for 3/–, if this means anything to you. The rest
is on rations more or less like England and real estate costs the same.
One of the startling things is that tradesmen treat you with courtesy.
They dont say, 'Bugger off and stand at the back of the queue, till we
close at 12 noon.'

On the whole, although it is terribly enclosed and pressed together, I
think one might do worse than settle here, if one could. Perhaps I will
settle down and build, on Book-of-the-Month-Club money. At least it
would be no worse than spending it on gin. In the winter there is not a
single tripper-seal on all the beaches. Perhaps I will buy a Martello
Tower or German Fort ...

Will you and your tribe come to stay with me if I do? How is Angelica?

I can't tell you how frightful the colonels are. They say, 'Well, the
STATES are all right, but they are a lot of old fogies. They wont make
any decision without expert opinion. [The States are their parliament.]
Now I,' say the colonels, 'as a SOLDIER, dont agree with all that rot. *I*
think that all that is needed is COMMON SENSE.'

No doubt you will agree with these colonels, my dear Bunny, after
your wartime experience, and after your statement to me in Northumber-

* An island of allotments.

land that education was perfectly useless, but all the same I have a sneaking idea that perhaps dumb idiocy is not a virtue. If not, why dont you OR RICHARD come to these climates for a spell? The sailing is horribly dangerous and vomitorious. From here to France there is not 20 ft. of water, and I am agog to smuggle. The ship I came on was a day late.* For discomfort, danger or profit I can't think of any better sailing water. What does Richard say?   love from TIM

P.S. (Next day) In spite of my drunken insults to your worship when I was writing last night, and I am as drunk again tonight, I think I will dare to post it. I drive round and round the island like a fly in a bottle for 3 hours every morning. There really is a good deal to be said for it. Although the horrid Sheenies have pushed up apparent prices of houses to insane levels, I may, if I am very quick, get a decent house at more or less English cost. There is one house in particular which would be glorious to have. It is of the island's pink granite, standing on a pro-montory which gets the sun all day and has a tiny harbour below it, like this:

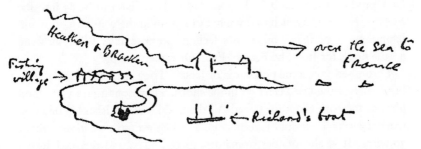

If I can't get it—its owner is some relation of Hector Bolitho—I shall buy a few *verges* (1/3 of an acre) on some similar headland and build.

In the next fortnight I hope to charter an aircraft and fly round Guernsey etc., just to make sure.

The Bolitho house was built in 1936 or so by some professor or other, who made one big room for his library. It is *not* of such horrible archi-tecture as is common on Jersey, but it is of the local granite, which they fit together more beautifully than any jig-saw.

Jersey-French, which is Norman, is splendid. It is just such a French as my grandmother used to speak when she went to France in Victoria's golden day. If you can't think of the french word, you use an English one.

* From the gale.

e.g. 'Si vous ne pouvez pas penser du mot français, vous usez un English one.' Perhaps this is an exaggeration.

But you know, dear Bunny, that I never exaggerate.

love from TIM

December 24th, 1946   *Grouville Hall Hotel, Grouville,*
Jersey, Channel Islands

Dear Bunny, I have only just seen in a rather old copy of the New Statesman that your mother is already dead. After you first introduced me to Tolstoi in 1938 or '39, I read every book she had translated ... and all the Russian novels translated by anybody else—and it was always with irritation at the other translators, who seemed to miss her Russian sense of compassion. Thinking it over now, I daresay she may have been the most important of all the Garnetts, and may have had more influence, in a nobly anonymous way, on the impact of two colossal cultures, than anybody either of us will ever meet. To have accomplished this, and to have produced the family at Hilton, and to have lived to be 85 into the bargain, is about as much as my mind can grasp in the way of success and happiness, so perhaps you are not feeling too miserable. Will you write a little book for her, like Beaney Eye? Or rather, for us?

I promised you some post cards of Jersey. They are a little hard to get, but I enclose the few I can find in the shops. They dont give a very good idea, as they are taken for effect. All the middle of the island is one vast market garden or series of allotments. The biggest farm we have is about 30 acres. It is all potatoes, tomatoes, glass houses and tethered Jersey cows. They save the trouble of making fences or hedges by tethering the animal. It gives quite a strange effect to find big (and ugly—they have a horrid architecture) farm houses, with enormous outhouses in which they house all their implements, all sitting in each other's pockets. From one farm house to the next is 50 yards, not $\frac{1}{2}$ mile as in England, which makes you think the whole place has shrunk in the wash.

But there are two other distinct cultures. Mainly on the south-west coast of the island are the vast beaches of fine sand like St. Aubin's in the postcards I send (unfortunately taken at high tide) on which myriads of Jews, trippers and the like bask and scream during the summer months. On the North coast (see picture of Bonne Nuit Bay) is a rugged terrain of cliffs, heather, bracken, not yet conquered by the tripper.

My hotel, by pure chance, happens to be at the junction of these two cultures, so I get good sand and not too many trippers.

I nearly died of the D.T's when I got here, as the pubs are open all day and there is no shortage of anything whatever. Luckily some horsey people made friends with me and asked me to exercise a steeple-chaser for them, which is in for the great point-to-point in January, and needed work. So I hoisted my poor old bones into his slippery little racing saddle and trotted off, about ten days ago, with my pack of pink elephants feathering away between his legs, and since then I have got soberer and soberer, and now I groom him and feed him and have reverted to riding breeches, which is better than the Horrors anyhow. Killie thinks it is the best idea in the world, as she can charge about the sands for a couple of hours every day, chasing the wild geese, of which there are about 400, probably Brents and Lesser (?) White Fronts. They are hoarse and silent.

Would it amuse you if I sent you a copy of a book called The German Occupation of Jersey? It is a secret diary kept in duplicate by a reporter of the Jersey evening paper. It is factual and unexaggerated. It is deeply touching, as the Channel Islanders did *and have* preserved the together feeling of the days of your blitz in England. They didn't get bombed (much) but they did practically starve to death, living mainly on potatoes when they could get them and paying £60 *a pound* for tobacco or £20 a pound for tea. They lived by barter. The Germans behaved with perfect docility and complete lack of imagination. They raped or robbed practically nobody, but issued ten thousand new regulations per diem. The patriotism of Jersey still makes one want to cry. I thought that if I sent you a copy—it is printed on rotten paper by the newspaper's own press and looks altogether awful—you might be moved to give it a terrific boost in Books In General. You know what I mean. I am, say, England, and Jersey is Killie. Yet Killie loves and is loyal to me and thinks I am the cat's whiskers, while I, knowing what I really am, am overwhelmed with guilt and love and gratitude and determination to be better.

Let me send it you.

This hotel is ... crammed with Anglo-Indian Colonels of unknown age, bickering about Poona and their sugar ration .... They quarrel with their moribund wives about how to spell COLOSSAL in the cross-word puzzle. Luckily I have the horse, and books from the London Library, which the horsey people let me read in their house, so I only need eat and sleep in here. Also there are the ever-open pubs. On the whole it is a fine island. England is spoiling it just now, with preferential treatment to make up for the occupation—it was the only part of the British Emp. that was occupied (?)—what about Singapore?—and the shops are bursting with everything you can think of.

Happy Xmas (tomorrow) love from TIM

1947

Les Pieux, Cobo Bay, Guernsey, C.I.

Dear Bunny, It must be about time I reported progress. I'm not really in Guernsey at all, but by the time you answer I probably shall be. Well, my latest vagary is that I have become an *old salt*. All that about being sea-sick turns out to have been just a fad, and ever since I last wrote I have been ranting and roaring all o'er the wide Channel Islands in a succession of hurricanes and horrid little boats. Probably I shall settle down in Alderney where I now am, and buy a yacht. *Dont* send Richard by return of post. He would want to advise me on the kind of boat I am to buy, or even build it, and I am determined not to take any but local advice. These are horribly dangerous coasts, packed with jagged pinnacles of granite rock and raving with currents. Alderney is quite the worst. North-west we have a race called the Swinge which runs at a maximum of nine knots and south-east we have a kind of Edgar Allen Poe maelstrom called the Race which also goes at nine knots. They say that seven tides meet there, and you can actually see seven waves whacking together from different directions. We got here in the sort of steamer the woman used for beating her husband to death in the bath with. Its best rate was seven knots and it took us nearly six hours to cover the 21 miles from Guernsey. We were 3½ hours overdue on this short trip. They told us in shame that she had been totally disappearing for a minute at a time. If you looked over the blunt end when on the crest of a wave you felt that if you fell overboard you would not be drowned but would break your neck by the fall. Gannets, eagles etc. could be descried flying far below. Everybody was sick, including a naval gentleman from destroyers. So was I. But the wonderful thing is that this is the first time since leaving Ireland, and that I find I dont mind being sick at all. The great thing is to have something to be sick with, it appears. Also its a pleasure to reply 'Yes, it was a bit choppy' when they have been thinking of sending out the life boat for you.

I am getting to be quite an authority on the islands. Jersey is the most continental, the most luxurious, the most polite. Everybody in Jersey says Yes if he can. The culture and architecture are approximate to France. In Guernsey everybody says No if he can. The culture and architecture are nearer to England. There are more rules and ration books. (Pubs in the country in Jersey are open from 9 a.m. continuously till 10 p.m, but in Guernsey they keep opening and shutting unpredictably, like oysters, or English pubs.) Alderney calls itself the Cinderella of the Channel Islands, and, though a cliché, it is a fairly good description. It is the poorest, least visited. It is wind-swept and treeless. The streets are cobbled. The architecture is a cross between Cornish fishing village and Horry Walpole Gothick—*very* attractive. It is only about 3 miles long. The pubs are like English country pubs, with old salts playing Nap or Eucre. The most glorious of all the islands is Herm. It is only about a mile long, but in that mile it includes a lovely sand beach, dunes, heathery uplands, a little forest, rich arable fields and fine cliffs. It has been leased by some charming ex-RAF people who really want only to live there themselves but can't afford to do so unless they run a hotel. So they are organising a luxury hotel, *not* a Butlin, with a golf course etc., the main idea being that they hope all the guests will go away in the winter and leave them to enjoy the island. Nobody lives on the island except the guests and employees. There are 2 cottages besides the hotel, and these can be rented by family parties. WHY DONT THE GARNETTS RENT ONE? Sea-fishing, wonderful bathing, yachting and a little microcosm of a world with everything from plains to mountains and deserts to jungles, all in one mile. Also, though not yet put to rights or occupied, there is a superbly funny manor house in late Horry Gothick, with a chapel out of the Castle of Otranto. Sark is the only island I havn't and can't visit. It has a mediaeval law that bitches may not land, so this cuts out Killie and me. On the other hand, it has a gaol of one room standing by itself which has not been occupied since 1870. I am thinking of landing with Killie defiantly, for the pleasure of being locked up in it. They give you the key.

There are some lovely laws in these waters. If you stand in the main square in Jersey and shout 'Haroo, mon prince, on me fait tort!' you practically bring the island to a standstill. Everything has to be stopped until your grievance has been attended to.

Bunny, what am I to do? I have an awful feeling that I am going to buy an enormous castle or fortress in Alderney, which covers about an acre. It is totally inconvenient, but so gloriously situated, half in the sea, and so dramatic and sun-drenched and lonely, and still in working order as a fortress because the Germans used it—

The other thing is to buy some tiny Walpole cottage in one of the cobbled squares of the town—

And then there's the yacht—Oh, dear!

The Huns have pasted Alderney worst. They used it as a concentration camp. It is all concrete and barbed wire and buried Russians. Pre-war population was 4,000—now 700.

If I buy my castle, will you bring all the little Garnetts to run about in it sometimes? It is so sunny and healthy and hungry-making. And you can eat ORMERS!

I hope to send you the Ark book soon.   love from TIM

June 6th, 1947   *Gros Nez House, Victoria St., Alderney C.I.*

Dear Bunny, I have bought, but solely as an investment, for about £800, a delicious little Frenchified house in the main *place* of Alderney. I still really mean to get one of the fortresses I was telling you about in the end, but for the mean time we live in this house. It has an annexe for my chaplain, and if I spend £1000 on bathrooms etc it will be almost as nice as Hilton, in a humbler sort of way. I would date it about 1850, but of course fashions took longer to reach these outposts: consequently it is of a better and (then) old-fashioned period. Say, 1790. It has two immense greenhouses (broken) but with the vines in them. Also orchard, garage space, main drain, cobbled square—almost everything the heart could desire. I shall put it in order and re-sell for about £4000. Come, come quickly, to see that we do nothing wrong.   love from TIM

June 15th, 1947   *Gros Nez House, Alderney*

Terrific Bunny, Then your room is booked from July 10th for a week. Before I post this I'll get flying timetables, also boat, if any. There's a rumour that boats will come direct from Weymouth in July, if you care for such. One good thing on Alderney is that they put out the electric supply at midnight. We can't drink all night as well as all day without using candles. Dont forget to send me John's and Tommy's surname.

                                        love from TIM

Its no good bringing clothing coupons etc. *here*, unless you mean to fly over to Guernsey or Jersey one day, for about 7 hours, which is possible.

This place is just a cobbled Cornish fishing village, much wrecked by Huns. We merely have the village shop.

All here are much agog to see you, as I have been boasting as usual of the most famous man I know.

I bet the salmon that you pulled the fly out of the mouth of was directly down stream.

Bring a ration book, but we'll principally eat lobsters. She can do soufflés. Good!

1948

February 24th, 1948   3, *Connaught Square, Alderney, C.I.*

Dear Bunny, I am sending you a couple of dozen ORMERS. A gourmet like yourself will know all about them, but in case you dont I had better give you some information. To add a relish to the feast, may I say that they are *supposed* only to exist in the Channel Islands, in Mexico and in Japan. I dont swear to this. I do swear to the fact that they are unobtainable except at lowest Spring tides, which means for about three days twice a year. They taste of meat rather than fish (a bit like sweetbreads) and it is well known that archangels live on them almost exclusively.

The way to cook them, which is inexpressibly tedious but well worth doing, is on the other pages.   love from TIM

During the summer and autumn of 1948 I planned to visit Tim's new establishment in Alderney, but I did not actually go until October 21st, and then made the mistake of going by sea, from Weymouth. There was a full gale and we were unable to enter the harbour for several hours. I was extremely seasick and on arrival went to bed and stayed there for the rest of the day.

During the rest of my visit I spent the time walking round the island, talking with Tim and drinking large quantities of Jameson's Irish Whiskey.

A good many of Tim's acquaintances came in for drinks and to relate the latest doings of their friends on the island.

We also climbed up the lighthouse, talked to the lighthouse keeper, visited the rock gallery hospital made by the Germans. From Tim's New Year's day letter of 1949, I suppose I told him that he must stop drinking himself to death.

November 11th, 1948   3 *Connaught Square*

Dear Bunny, You will think, if I guess right, that I have not written to you because I have been tipsy. The fact is surprisingly to the contrary. Your visit stimulated me so much that I accepted the two days hell of sobering up, and I have been too busy re-writing the final Arthur book to write letters! It is now with the typist!

You know I was telling you about my life of co-incidences? Three days after you left, the newest Strand Magazine arrived. In it was the enclosed statement.[1]

This puts paid to what we were talking about. If it is *not* a coincidence, then my agent has been gabbling. I wrote to him last year about the project, since I had to enquire about Stevenson's copyrights.

Except to him and to you, I had not mentioned the idea to a soul, and I doubt whether a person of even your celerity could have got back to England quick enough to get into print what was certainly printed long before you came.

I am sending you in a separate package the copies of the Kings speech on the Channel Islands. Personally I shall do no more in the matter.

I have yet another shock for your rooted belief that I am helplessly drinking self to death. My theory, and our rigid sailor's here, is that nobody ever drank themselves to death. Well, as you know, he has had pneumonia 3 times this last month—continuing to drink 2 bottles of spirits a day. On Monday he fell screaming upon his back, was hauled into an aircraft on a stretcher, flown to Salisbury, and operated upon instantly for a strangulated femoral hernia. He has survived it! Really, the man is a Nelson. With all his arms and legs shot away, and now most of his intestines, he still stands ramrodly upon his quarter deck, and claps the whisky bottle to his blind eye.

I am always asking favours of you; but now I dont know what the etiquette is for the present one. I dont know whether I ought to ask you, or the editors of Horizon & New Statesman. So I will ask you first, and then you can advise me.

I have discovered in my heart a fanatical desire to write the critique of your Peacock, either in your old page of the N.S & N or else in a full-length article for Horizon. But it strikes me that the N.S & N (which I should prefer) is a pretty good *selling* vehicle, and therefore it would be wiser to get Desmond Macarthy or E. M. Forster or Walter de la Mare to do it there.

Anyway, (a) have you any influence to get either of these jobs for me, (b) if not, and if you approve, and if so you must say which, then *what*

[1 That Mr John Connell was writing a sequel to *Treasure Island*. Tim had discussed doing this with me during my visit.—D.G.]

234

are the names of the editors in question (supposing that it is the correct etiquette for me to write to them directly)?

The Customs Officer who made you pay 21/6 on your bottle of gin exceeded his duty, and should be reported. If you like, I will do so from here.

I thought of sending you my diaries as a present now *en bloc*, to save this codicil, but then, suppose I want to use bits of them during my own life time for chaff? So I will write the codicil. In fact, just for fun, I think I will write an entire new will. I shall leave everything to the R.S.P.C.A, my books to my college (Aldrovandi etc) and my literary remains to you. Supposing you pre-decease me, dear Bunny, which I firmly intend that you shall, and indeed you flatter yourself on this boozing theory in respect of longevity, then I shall have to find somebody else for the diaries.

I have gotten a housekeeper plus husband to look after me. They will be in the cottage by Xmas.

I have netted 2 more clients for the painter, who is boring me to tears, but apparently here forever.

Killie has caught her first mouse—a suckling one about this size

—but she is proud of it none the less. Even at that, I had to help her.

On the whole, I'll enclose all this in the King's speeches.

love from TIM

1949

In the following letter Tim is wrong, or irrelevant, about all the notes in my edition of Peacock to which he refers, with the possible exception of attributing 'I'll be a butterfly' to Beau Brummell for which he gives no proof. It was typical of Tim that, without looking it up, he should have challenged my attribution of a quotation from Shakespeare. A moment's reflection would have told him that I had looked it up.

January 1st, 1949   3, *Connaught Square, Alderney, C.I.*
Dear Bunny, This is New Year's Day, so I really must have one good resolution. It is to write and thank you for Peacock. Little as you will believe it, I am still stone cold sober—the deplorable result of your moralisations—if you only knew how slavishly I follow your dictates you would be a little more careful what you say—and the reason for not writing before has been confused, turgid, hastened, busy, if not wild-eyed. I think I have bought the island of Jethou—which I dont really want—and this has meant a good deal of seafaring. Also there has been the garden to set to rights, and I have bought another garden, and what with one thing and another it has not been possible to write. One just falls into bed, asleep.

Well now, about Peacock. It is a *splendid* job. It is the only job I know of which really lives up to a cliché. It really does 'fulfill a long-felt want.' Nearly all the identifications were news to me, and one or two of the notes positively Gibbonian. Incidentally, I couldnt agree with you more about the badness of Melincourt. I positively believe that miserable little shrimp Shelley wrote half of it. But it needed somebody like you to say so.

Now I am going to exasperate you with a few notes.

Page 186, note. I thought 'men have died etc.' was from Hamlet, but I am too lazy to go upstairs and verify.

Page 229 'as the sun at noonday'. Are you missing a quotation here? Peacock makes the same quote elsewhere. The full is 'as the sun at noon, to verify (illustrate?) all shadows.' It is from Bacon, Donne or Sir Thomas Browne.

Page 617 'butterfly'. I query Thomas Haynes Bayly. The song has

236

been attributed to no less a person than Beau Brummell, who is said to have published it under the initial B. The last verse ran:

I would be a butterfly
Born in a bower
Christened in a tea-pot
And dead in an hour.

If you are interested, I could give you another verse and more details.*

Page 817 Which St. Catharine is he talking about? I think he has two of them muddled.

Page 945. Now here I really get on my hind legs. 'Sesto'. I can't give you *any* reason at all, but in my inmost heart, as a person who once spoke Italian fluently and read Dante for fun, I am telling you, de haut en bas, that 'sesto' is probably the only Italian word which Peacock *didn't* misquote. I am still too lazy to go upstairs, and anyway I have no Italian dictionary there, but I am telling you that my SUBCONSCIOUS tells me that 'sesto' is short for 'se stesso'. I further guess that 'sesto' was the actual word used by Dante—I am calligraphy } sure it is a quotation from orthography Dante—in his time, dialect and orthography. The quotation means: 'Nobody likes to be the only one to apologise.' Or: 'In a quarrel nobody likes to apologise of his own accord.'

Il pertirsi da se stesso nulla giova.

There, that's all the torture I have to put you to. And honestly I didn't know the name of the Victorian lamp.   love from TIM

Il pertirsi da se 'sso nulla giova.

P.S. You are most unfair to my dearest Monboddo. Even Johnson thawed to him, as he did to Wilkes.

P.P.S. He wrote Darwin half a century before Darwin wrote himself.

January 16th, 1949   3, *Connaught Square, Alderney, C.I.*

Dear Bunny, You simply can't do this to your friends. Why should you be allowed to lope off to some bloody Bevan hospital, while all of us are almost sick with anxiety?[1] Particularly if you have promised to outlive us? It is most unequitable and if I wasn't certain that you had broken out already I would be seriously cross. Please pull yourself together and stop taking advantage of the National Health Scheme.

* But it means going upstairs.
[1 I was in Huntingdon hospital with a virus pneumonia.—D.G.]

237

My own little things in this island are going on beautifully. I even have a pussy cat aged about six weeks. It occasionally crawls out of the bottom of my bed, a tiny black atom, to my great surprise.

As for ——, presumably I told you when you were here that I was paying him five (FIF) guineas a week to keep alive.

He is unbelievably a sniveller and idiot, but he poses a problem.

Suppose you found a maniac called the douanier Rousseau, who could paint and was a maniac, would'nt you feel frightful if you didn't help the fellow?

I am not saying at all that he is in the same class as Rousseau, nor even that he is rational.

But there he is, a rogue, swindeller and idiot, and it seems to me that it is up to me to keep the wretched fool alive. (? ? ?)

February 14th, 1949   3, *Connaught Square, Alderney, C.I.*

Dearest Bunny, So far as I can see, your next visit to the Channel Islands is going to be to the island of Jethou. It once belonged to Compton McKenzie, but we can't help that. *Since* him, it has belonged to an American millionairess and, as you know, all Americans insist on central heating, tooth paste and the germ war. Consequently it is fitted with 3 tiled bathrooms with showers, radiators and everything else I can think of, except a hair waving machine. It will be absolutely my own—not a soul there except my own retainers—and there is an 18th century cannon which I shall solemnly blow off to salute your arrival. This time you will be able to bring your whole family.

I plan to live a life of feudal ceremony. I shall drink whisky out of a horn at stated intervals, and when I am drunk or in my rouse the cannon shall be discharged upon my battlements. And in your cup an onion shall be thrown, every evening after dinner.

Since you were here, I have got back to my old form. That is to say, I have alternated bouts of the wildest sobriety with other bouts which were rather Evelyn Waugh. In the former, I have sent 2 books to Cape and managed the desperate intrigue for Jethou (I have the owner humbled now, but nothing signed) while in the latter I have done so many things that I dont know how to begin telling you about them.

Item: I have been challenged to break a glass in my bare hand in a pub by pressing it. It was a round glass like a balloon but smaller, and it fitted beautifully into my hand, and the obvious thing was to squeeze it. So I did, but then all stood agast, for a perfect *fountain* of blood gushed out— so much so that I have had to throw away the trousers and shoes that I was wearing. It was my right hand, and hence this handwriting.

Item: I have proposed marriage to a perfectly frightful female aged 50, but stinkingly rich, and am now trying to wriggle out of it.

Item: On flying to Guernsey on one occasion, I observed to my fellow passengers: 'If we tumbled down on that, what a tinkle we should make!'

Item: I have been driven round and round Guernsey by the unhappy but subservient Bailiff, with a flag on the radiator.

Item: Stayed in a Guernsey hotel with 3 of my guests, when the bill for one week came to over £100. (This is good for one, if one does it two or three times in a lifetime.)

Item: had a row with the B.E.A. (nationalised) about Killie, and told a pilot with the A.F.C. and bar that he was a stinking little puppy and that I learned to fly before he was born –which was quite untrue.

Item: Been to church, where the Vicar, who fits his pulpit like a cork in a popgun, ranted away about Communism, which he had unhappily confused with theosophy, with a far-away look in his eye. He has become my best friend in Alderney, drops in uninvited every other night, and bursts into the most fearsome blasphemies, mingled with reproaches to the Income Tax authorities or the ecclesiastical commissioners or stories about how he fell off the pier at Blackpool or (last night) how they shoved some kind of instrument up his penis in order to disarrange a stone. One is always afraid that these stories are going to creep into his sermon un-awares. He is a pet. With his enormous Roman nose and mottled complexion he bawls away about the last time he caught syphillis, occasionally remembering to throw in some pious remark about Boys' Clubs or the 39 Articles. I am thinking of getting ordained myself. He is certainly my favourite vicar and probably the only living excuse for Xtianity. By the way, did you know his name was St. John, and that he is a nephew or younger son of some peer—not Bolingbroke, but something like Bledsloe, I suspect?

Although I date this the 14th, it is really Sunday. I must now hurry off, put on my funeral bakemeats and totter off to church.   love from TIM

Did you ever get the letter I wrote you when I heard you were ill, or was I too drunk to post it?

239

April 2nd, 1949   *3, Connaught Square, Alderney, C.I.*

Dear Bunny, Will you just humour me by reaching up to your book-shelves, taking down your Nonesuch Donne, and reading page 378? It begins with the formidable reflexion that Cardinals are infertile and consequently cannot propagate their species, and goes on, with rising indignation, to relate how a Pope once ravished a manly, reverend and *bearded* Bishop. You will have read this often before—as I have done—but one ought to draw each other's attention to this kind of page about once a year.   love from TIM

Yes, and in a *mitre*—which makes it much worse.

1950

Dear Bunny, Oddly enough I was inventing an endless letter to you on the very day you wrote to me, and it began by asking what I had done to offend you? It is very tiresome of you to suspect me of being annoyed with you, as *I* am the only one who is allowed to suspect *you* of being annoyed with *me*. You should know by now that I have always been devoted to you and always will be.

Well, there is plenty of Channel Island news. You know Princess Elizabeth came to see us. She came in a battleship with two cruisers and lots of M.T.B's—a prodigious sight. For they came head-on at us, in a bee line, like this.

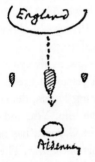

It was a most *marked* thing, if you see what I mean. They didn't sort of drop in, in passing, but came like an arrow to the gold—tremendous— particularly as they all moved together as if supported beneath the sea on a turntable. I dont quite seem to get this feeling across. Our usual sea lane, on which we see the great liners, goes *past* us, thus ⎯⎯⎯⎯⎯⎯⟶ But our princess came forth to Normandy with pride and might of chivalry *at* us, thus ↓   (i.e. from an unusual point of the compass. Was this what impressed me?) She had really said she was going to Alderney from the moment she left Portsmouth, and my God they came at us as if they were going to run us down. We were transported. She was *exquisitely* beautiful, and so nice. The fun of the day, however, was that an unlucky cadet from Dartmouth chose that very season to steal an Admiral's Barge from there, and make a bid for freedom. He ran out of fuel before he could get to Cherbourg, so put in to Alderney almost simultaneously with the British Navy, and was instantly clapped in irons. Poor boy, it will give him a confused idea of Sea Power in after life, as he can but suppose that there is an Admiral in every port. To the eternal credit of the R N, they did not shoot him on the quarter deck or expel him from Dartmouth. They took him back and caned him, to make some sort of a demonstration, and I am told they secretly say that anybody with enough initiative to steal an Admiral's barge will probably make an excellent admiral himself, later on.

Did I tell you that I had had the stone or gravel in the kidneys like Pepys since I last wrote? It is an excellent thing to have, as it is not particularly dangerous, but hurts like hell. I always thought it was pompous and bogus of Dr. Arnold to say on his death bed, 'Thank God for giving me this pain', but frankly that's just about what I did feel. When one has lived on rose leaves for a long time it is quite good for one to have a pain—a change, like a week at Brighton.

Your friend the Vicar has gone off to live at the best hotel in Guernsey, where he finds it more cosy. Presumably he will look us up occasionally, if only to collect the Easter offerings.

And my friend —— —— has, as always expected, started to gnaw the hand that fed him. He is in Jersey at present, and writes me wild, denunciatory, abusive, threatening letters, demanding £75 which for some reason or other he says I owe him. Yes, and you figure in one of them. 'Your so-called friend, David Garnett, has *warned* me against you.' He was in a looney bin during part of the war. The trouble is, he will probably turn up some day to dot me on the nose. There is nothing I can do about it except always open the front door very gingerly, and wish it was on a chain. I hope he doesn't bring any firearms. These demonstrations of affection are tiresome.

Now here are two things you can tell me—if they are not top secret. (1) Didn't Lawrence say the Mint was to be published in 1950, and is anything being done about it? (2) Didn't Lawrence have an unupsettable motor boat doing 25 knots which only cost him £185, and why can't I have one for Alderney?

I had 370 bunches of grapes last year, but there was a glut at Covent Garden and they were a dead loss. I am just getting the garden & fruit trees into shape for next season—rather late.

My friend Cheshire the V.C. has been writing to me, and I am a little worried about him. On reflection, I suppose he has killed more humans

than any other living being. He not only bombed all through the war &
invented path-finding, but went to Nagasaki with the atomic bomb.
Well, anybody else would have just left it at that, but as Cheese is one of
the loveliest people who ever were, he has been trying to purge himself
ever since by doing good deeds. He has got himself £20,000 in debt trying
to help ex-service men, and now runs a free hospital for 60 incurables out
of his own efforts & pocket. This is fine, but he also turned R.C. (I
suppose to sort of confess it off himself) began sitting up all night and
eating too little. I *itch* to try and cure him of the R.C. stuff, but dare not
interfere, in case he really needs something of that sort to rely on. Tell me
I am right not to blunder in?

The noblest thing that has happened in Alderney since your visit, is
that we have got a library. Some old hens decided to try and collect one
and I sternly refused to have anything to do with it, expecting it to be a
tattered collection of Ruby M. Ayres. But they were *not* old hens, and
how wrong I was. By begging in the right places, principally America,
they have got together 2500 books, and the astounding thing is that they
are quite good books. The fiction section has plenty of Bates, Shute,
Garnett etc., and there are History, Biography, Art, Travel, Children's,
Belles Lettres, even Reference sections! The ladies sit-in on a rota from
10 to 4.30 unpaid: the books are housed free in the Militia Arsenal, and no
money goes out at all, except for light & fuel. We pay 3d. to take out a
book, and this goes to buying new ones. By the way, do you feel like
sending them some of your throw outs? Wren Howard did. (One of the
books from your publishing house is in—the Stevenson letters.) Needless
to say, I have become their bedesman.

(Oh, bugger, I've just knocked off my cigarette ash into the ink
pot.)

Of all things, I am writing a *film* at present. I got sick of having my
books wrecked by the script writers, so I thought I'd try doing the finished
article myself. Then nobody can re-write. Its about Queen Caroline
Matilda of Denmark. Never having been to Denmark I keep astonishing
myself by the vividness of my local colour. You'll see.

I'm on the water waggon at present. Its just one of my passing phases
and I hope it wont last long.   love from TIM

Dear Tim, We have been up here for a week with two children. Today there is a keen north wind, which brought the snow last night & the hills are white in the spring sunshine.

This letter is really to ask you about those possessions which remain of yours: a tigerskin, rather a pale one, two idealisations of xxxx,[1] & two other pictures, a book of drawings, a pair of waders & wading brogues. Some things have been destroyed which were yours—a moth eaten ancient pair of riding breeches, a broken & cracked pair of shoes—the legs of a pair of waders with the feet cut off.

You ask about the Appletons—Well you know Mrs Appleton was lamed & crippled by falling downstairs & that they moved & went to Low Row two or three years ago. Then came the bitter winter: Appleton lost about half his sheep & had to give up his milking cows.

Last autumn they had to give up the Low Row cottage as it was wanted & have moved back. Appleton is very happy to be back, but his health is very bad. He has no 'wind' he says & can only climb up hill very slowly. His eye glitters, his frame is emaciated. I think he has T.B. & is probably wildly happy & optimistic. The nearer barn in which he used to milk has the roof fallen in. I think they are pretty short of money & everything.

Meanwhile both sons are married & each has a son & a daughter—Tommy now works for the I.C.I.

I read Peter Freuchen when it was published here. Do you know about the Pacific Coast Indians & their system of exchanging gifts? My memory is failing but I believe the word for it is Potlatch unless thats a whisky.

Anyway one can't consume anything except gifts. So I come with a bottle of sherry to Alderney & say 'we'll have a party.' You then have to improve on it—with a case of whisky—I retort with 2 cases of champagne—everyone joins in, always raising the anti until there is no fish, flesh, or firewater left. After that we live very soberly & ungenerously for another year.

It worked all right until white men arrived & offered to buy capital goods & offered consumable bottles of whisky in exchange. Then the Potlatch orgy ended in there not being a tent, or sledge, or dog, or fishhook in the damned community & they could only keep alive by working for the whites who owned everything of that sort.

Henry Ford would probably say he gave away a million motorcars in

[1 The girl he had intended to marry.—D.G.]

his lifetime if he were an Eskimaux. By the way the Potlatch people lived on Vancouver Island & had wonderful totem poles.

I will try & write about the more interesting subject of greenhouses, green fly & green fingers when I return to warmer climes. Up here there are only celandines & primroses with which by the way Wordsworth's grave was festooned yesterday by his dozen great great great grand-children—while the Archbishop of York preached that Wordsworths poems were the best cure for Atheism.   Very much love BUNNY

June 12th, 1950   3, *Connaught Square, Alderney, C.I.*

Dear Bunny, Here is this thing, which I post with more than a lot of misgiving. If you will look on the back of the dust-jacket, you will see that it is the first of two volumes. For some reason which I don't fathom—it is something like whirling things round in a centrifuge—all the cruel and sadistic bits have settled in vol. i., while the kind bits about country life, parson Woodforde, palladian architecture, General Ponsonby etc. etc. have all been put off to vol. ii. Anyway, dont be cross about all the birching and head-chopping—all of which they *did* do—until you have seen the sequel. My plot is that when this and its second volume and my other thing about 12th century bestiaries have been properly published, I will send in the three books for a D.Litt or Litt.D or whatever they call it at Cambridge.

I dont mean for an honoris causa one, but for an earned one. You have to put in three works. If that happens, you will ever after have to address me as 'doctor', and I shall sleep in scarlet silk pyjamas with a black velvet night-cap.

Please at least reserve judgment about this one, Bunny, because it makes me feel uncomfortable—like having a son condemned by the magistrates for being a delinquent.   love from TIM

In November 1950 I went by invitation to see my friend Charles Chapman Mortimer at his flat in Sloane Street and was introduced to a tall handsome blonde Belgian lady, the famous animal photographer, Ylla. I discovered that Charles had hatched a plot to get me to write an intro-duction of five thousand words to a book of her photographs. Although I thought the photographs, particularly those of cats, were lovely, I did not want to do this. I therefore immediately recommended Tim, saying that he knew far more about animals than I did and that he was the perfect person to write it. I succeeded in convincing Charles that this was so, and also that much the best plan was for Ylla to fly out to Alderney immediately and see him.

I sent off the following telegram to Tim:

PRIORITY. WILL YOU CONSIDER WRITING FIVE THOUSAND WORDS FOR MOST WONDERFUL ANIMAL PHOTOGRAPHS EVER KNOWN STOP IF YES SENDING YLLA BY SATURDAY PLANE REPLY IMMEDIATELY DAVID GARNETT.

My hopes that Tim had never heard of Ylla were gratified and he met the plane without knowing what to expect, but surmising it was an animal of some sort.

November 22nd, 1950   3, *Connaught Square, Alderney, C.I.*

Dear Bunny, Your telegram took 2 hrs to reach here and I did reply immediately. Also I tried ringing Sloane 6989 at 5.10, but there was no answer. I would adore to write 5000 words for you on any topic whatever, particularly as I happen to be in one of my sober fits at present. But what is an YLLA? That's what the telegram said it was going to be. I hope it is not bigger than a yak or emu, as I have 2 dogs staying at present and a pekinese expected next week. Fortunately I have just built a new greenhouse, so it can go in that for the time being, if it can get through the door.

The reason why I am sober is that last friday the 1st lieutenant of our local submarine threw me out of a window while we were amiably conversing about ju-jitsu. He did not mean any harm, and in fact has done nothing but good, as I fell on my head. It has altered something inside. I was unconscious for hours.

I very much doubt whether my telegram will have reached you soon enough to put the YLLA on an aeroplane tomorrow, but I will keep meeting what planes there are. Also the weather does not look too good and there may be no planes.   love from TIM

November 25th, 1950   3, *Connaught Square, Alderney, C.I.*

Dear Bunny, Well, you old bastard, I have written it for her as best I can. She is a pet. But on your side it was half and half a joke or a shrugging off of your own responsibilities. What next? When a refugee murderer next claims sanctuary with me, I shall send him straight to you, with a covering telegram stating that he is a Guernsey cow.   love from TIM

1951

April 11th, 1951   3, *Connaught Square, Alderney, C.I.*

Dear Bunny, Do please snap out of your Roman seclusion and stop milking the cows and answer one of my letters sometimes?

In writing my notes to the Bestiary, I had to consult the melancholy Burton. I *think* I had pinched my copy from my mother's shelves. You know that my mother and father had spent all their lives hating each other, and that my mother, the only survivor, will tell me nothing and insists on referring to my father—how it hurts me—as Mr. White.

Well, the Burton book has two signatures in it. One is HILL WILSON WHITE (Dec\ʳ. 19th 1872) and the other is NEWPORT WHITE (address indeciferable) 1853.

I loaned this book, which has a book-plate, to a friend in Alderney, who instantly retaliated with these words: 'I was educated at St. John's College in Oxford, which was founded by Sir Thomas White, and our crest is the same as the first quarter in the book-plate of the book which you have loaned to me.'

Now whom am I to write to, in order to establish a relationship with this old lord mayor? (Probably Dick Whittington) You once sent me a letter about going to see Garter-King-Of-Arms, and finding him hunched over a paraffin stove with a wool muffler tied round his neck.

I cannot afford to fee the Garter King.

As I rely on you to advise me on every difficult subject, will you kindly tell me how to start to find out about this? Do I write to Somerset House? Does it cost much? Where do I start?   love from TIM

There must be somebody at Somerset House, who will undertake this kind of research for a small fee? Say one guinea per ancestor?

The point of all this is that if I can establish descent from the gent in question I can probably get a free fellowship or scholarship or something from St. Johns. They always put that sort of thing in their founder's charters.

No doubt I replied to this letter telling him what to do and also identifying the coat of arms in my copy of Edmondson's Heraldry as: White, Hampshire and Fyfield in Berkshire. Gules a bordure sable, charged with etoiles or; on a canton ermine a lion rampant of the second. Crest an ostrich beaked and legged or.

Under Tim's drawing is written in my hand: White of Fyfield Berkshire. The chief interest of all this is that it disposes of Tim's wartime claim that the Whites were an Irish family.

White of Fyfield Berkshire

1952

March 1st, 1952   *3 Connaught Square, Alderney, C.I.*

Dearest Bunny, There is yet another article in this week's Time (March 3)
about flying saucers. Will you be a dear fellow and read it? Because if you
do not forward the following narrative to some hush-hush friend of yours
in the English Air Ministry, or somewhere, I shall really have to send it to
Dr. Walther Riedel in America.

Last summer—if anybody is interested, I could trace the date—I was at
a barbecue picnic at the south west end of Soye Bay in Alderney. It was
dusk. I was sulking, as I always do at picnics when I have to collect firewood and do without liquor. So I was sitting slightly behind the party
who were gathered round the fire. There were several in the party, but at
present I can only remember the names of 3 others beside myself. There
was Mrs. Packe, her husband (an ex-airborne colonel with D.S.O.,
member of Hawk's club, ex-captain of Leicestershire at cricket: in short,
you might think a dependable person) and Lady Sherwill, the Bailiff's
wife of Guernsey, who was staying with me.

While the others talked, I gloomily gazed out to sea, through a
hundred yard gap between the Beacon Rock and Bibette Head. So I was
the first to notice the phenomenon, though everybody else saw it after a
moment or two, without my drawing their attention to it.

A very bright red light came slowly north-east into the part of the
horizon framed by the gap. It was at about the height of a mast-head light
on a small steamer, but it was about 20 times brighter than a mast-head
light. It was travelling at about steamer speed, straight and level. Count
on your fingers, or whatever you have to do when you try to remember
the difference between the starboard and the port colours. This was a
strontium *red*, though it was moving with its right-hand-side facing us.

It paused soon after the others began to exclaim about it. It hung
motionless for five or ten seconds. Then it turned back along its previous
course, *still shewing red*, and accelerated, still at the same level, until it
disappeared once more behind Bibette head, whence it had come. But its
acceleration was tremendous. What had sauntered across from left to
right at steamship speed, now vanished from right to left at a speed which

I will doubtfully estimate at 150 m.p.h. It came with a saunter and went with a zoom.

A. Everybody said at once: 'A flying saucer!'
B. Everybody discussed it for a long time.
C. Everybody agreed to give the story to our local news reporter, and that Lady Sherwill, as the most respectable member of the party, should tell it.
D. Everybody was sober. Even I was, and that was why I was sulking.

For some reason, though we did send a message to the reporter by telephone, Lady Sherwill never did get interviewed. The reporter is rather a silly woman.

I have done nothing about the matter from that day to this. In fact, I thought Lady Sherwill had dealt with it. However, she was staying with me again last month, and told me that she had not been interviewed. Then, today, I read the article in Time.

So I am sending you this, dear Bunny, from an obscure sense of duty.

love from TIM

On second thoughts, I must explain that it is difficult to estimate the course of a moving object when viewed from the side. My marks on the post card are very approximate.

It may not have been coming *out* of the harbour and then back *into* it. It may have been coming *past* the harbour and then back *past* it i.e. in the return direction of Burhou, the Caskets or even Guernsey.

I believe there was afterwards a rumour that some light had been seen from Guernsey.

About six weeks before this happened, there had been a flying saucer rumour from our own airport in Alderney. I took the trouble to ask the fellow who said he had seen it, but he was quite untrained as an observer of things, bad at expressing himself, and afraid of being made fun of. As I did not want to put answers into his head, I could ask no leading questions. From what I could gather from his already confused ideas of what he *had* seen, his was 'a thing like a barrage balloon near the Caskets (Casquettes) in daylight.' But because there had already been a few wild surmises in the air, please dont suppose that a titled gentlewoman, a D.S.O. paratrooper, and an author who is also an artist and therefore an eagle-eyed observer of the passing scene, can have been hallucinated about the facts which I have narrated above.

For the sake of deadly accuracy, I must explain that Soye Bay is also called Soya and also Saye: it depends on the map, or the person you are talking to.

To everything I have told you I could swear on my bible oath, even if a man's life in the dock depended on it.

If anybody in the Air Ministry was interested in the apparition, he should write to (1) Michael Packe Esq. Alderney, and to (2) Lady Sherwill, Guernsey, for independant narratives. I have not and shall not shew my own story to either of these. As a matter of fact, if there are any contradictions, you can rely on your old dead-eye pupil to be the most accurate of the observers.   love from TIM

March 14th, 1952   3, *Connaught Square, Alderney, C.I.*
Dearest Bunny, You have obviously become so absorbed in the udders of cows that you are no longer rational. How *can* you say that these were guided missiles? Nothing that sauntered across the horizon at less than 10 m.p.h. could have been air-borne. The whole point is that it wandered in at ten knots and went away at about one hundred & fifty. However, I have purged my own conscience, and shall do no more about it. If you loftily and sulkily persist in not passing on this information to any of your high-up friends, I can only implore you to keep my letter, if you have kept it, and later we shall see what we shall see.

Your memoirs. Dear Bunny, this is evidently going to be the best book that ever was written, so for Christ's sake dont flag or get depressed about them. In the first place, you must have quite a bragging and even taunting chapter about your ancestors. You could begin with that visit to Garter-King as he crouched over his oil stove in two or three mufflers, but this is not really the important part. The unique thing about you is that you belong to that rarest of all things, a *literary dynasty*. The real excitement begins with the Twilight of the Gods and it goes on, without flagging, through you, to what? I only hope and pray that one of your two sons may carry on this tremendous line, but surely, by now, they ought to have started? Never mind. Perhaps we can safely leave it to the daughters.

It will be thronged with all the great people in the world, and the only difficulty will be to know who to leave out.

It is a *splendid* scheme, and it is timed just right. Your grandfather would not have wished to write it: your father was too close to the facts to write it: and you are just there. If you dont let go of that cow's tit and write it, I shall never speak to you again.

My own news, which you complain about, is as usual *nil*. I am becoming more and more of a recluse, and liking it. In the three summer months this house is full of people, usually with squalling children of whom the parents are proud. I could gladly knife any one of these children, who spend their Al-Capone time bashing each other on the head with shrimping nets, were it not for the fact that I am afraid of being hanged. The rest of the year, the house is empty. I drink one bottle of port each night by myself, which a presbyter like yourself will probably say is too much: I cook for myself! last night I pounded up a mixture of onions, dates and green peppers, wound the mixture up in bacon, tied the cylinders with string, and grilled: tonight I have a roast: and thus the day-by-day goes on.

The garden has been a great pleasure. At the agricultural shew last year, I won three first prizes, to the rage and despair of other competitors. I have three greenhouses now.

For the rest, I have discovered and exploited a new vice.

Bunny, I hate to admit this, but I READ.

So, as I now dont live in your real world any longer, you must forgive me if I now go back to David Balfour. I left him at the very moment when he was walking with Alan on the sea-shore in Catriona, and we see a red-headed ghillie popping his poll over a distant whin—FAREWELL I GO BACK INTO THAT REAL WORLD.   TIM

April 2nd, 1952   [*Alderney*]

Dearest Bunny, Now that business is over, may I send you a rather tipsy letter, with few hopes that you will reply in kind?

You tell me that you are sixty years of age. If you go on ploughing and milking and picking apples, you will certainly die at the biblical age of 70, and serve you right.

Now I am not yet fifty. But I have the whole thing planned. When I am ninety—you will then have been buried for thirty years,—when I am 90, I repeat, I intend to be dragged along the promenade at Bournemouth in a Bath chair. On the right side there will be a wicker-work container holding a brandy bottle: on the left, there will be my binoculars (for observing the bathing belles), my parasol, my dog-whip for hitting

253

pettishly at some dreadful old Setter with snow-white hair, and my bottle of whatever pills I may be taking at the moment. All these will be in plaited containers, together with perhaps a box of cigars. I shall wear a twa-snooted bonnet, a plaid cloak, a tartan over my knees, a gun-metal hot-water-bottle with handles, and an ear-trumpet.

I shall also have written your biography.

Is not this better than tugging at the dugs of cows?

love from TIM

... I note that you no longer write personal letters to people who drink one bottle of port a day. You ought to join the Plymouth Bretheren, damn you.

April 4th, 1952   *Hilton Hall, Hilton, Huntingdon*

Dear Tim, I dont know what your reference to drinking port refers to. I have been writing quite a lot of letters to you lately and my only objection to your drinking a bottle of port is that I'm not there to reduce your share to two thirds of a bottle of port. Personally, if you insist on my criticising I should drink (were I able to afford it) champagne for lunch and a bottle of burgundy to myself in the evening & sherry before dinner & Armagnac or Calvados after it.

However the note on the manticora[1] might read:

'Mr Garnett informs me that a friend of his, Mr Richard Strachey, was mistaken for a mantichora circa 1930, by foolish villagers in the neighbourhood of Ugijar Andalusia.'

It is possible that Little Dick, as the victim of this mistake is known, may regard this as libellous. If so we shall have to omit his name. I put *foolish* villagers to placate him.

Gerald Brenan with whom Little Dick was staying at the time has just gone back to Spain. But I suppose I had better write to him for full details. He can probably remember the date.

I feel sure that D. H. Lawrence who had a mediaeval mind in some ways, has things on the phoenix. But I can't find them. I am feeling a bit exhausted as we had two little girls here to stay with our four & gave them all donkey rides yesterday & the whole six of them were up & rushing about the house at six o'clock this morning.

[1 A note for *The Book of Beasts*, a translation of a 12th-Century Bestiary by Tim.—D.G.]

I am going for Easter week to stay with an old friend in Paris in a flat on the island.

There is still snow lying in the hedges where it was blown by the gale. We had 3 inches of it a week ago.   Love from BUNNY

The information which I sent Tim is incorrect in certain particulars. For 'foolish villagers' I should have written 'sedentary gipsies living near Ugijar'. However, the note in the bestiary on page 52 has led to further evidence of the Mantichora in Spain. In September 1964 I received a letter from a lady who in 1950 was travelling in Spain with three friends. They stopped in Granada up towards the Alhambra in a little inn with a long garden in which they had meals. However, next day their hostess came and said: 'My servants are all leaving today because of the dark bearded gentleman. They will not serve him. They say he is a Mantiquera and will steal their babies at night and cut them up and eat them.' My correspondent cried out in horror that her friend was the kindest of men and would not eat babies. 'Yes I'm sure, but our peasants from the hills still believe the Mantiquera exist and nothing I can say about you will help.'

'We were of course very disturbed at this news. I went to our hostess and said: "Please let us dine in the garden tonight. Tell all the servants to hide in the bushes. They need not come near us. You give us the food and I will show them that our bearded friend is quite harmless." In the evening all was arranged. I sat near Caurino and when we knew the garden to be full of well-hidden peasants (but the babies put away safely in the town) I got up went and put my arms round Caurino and kissed him very lovingly, petted him and said how gentle he was. It really worked and we were left to enjoy our stay and their fears seemed to be banished for the time being at any rate.'

It says a great deal for my correspondent (who is an old friend of a mutual acquaintance) that her demonstration proved so convincing.

April 5th, 1952   *Alderney*

Dearest Bunny, Thank you for your clear note on the Manticore, which I will reproduce verbatim.

Will you please tell your daughter A. V. Garnett that her full names were carefully read out in an Oxford accent on the Home Service of the

B.B.C. at one minute to four o'clock on Sunday the 5th of April 1952. This I hope is the first time she has been on the air, but far from the last.

love from TIM

June 21st, 1952   *Hilton Hall, Hilton, Huntingdon*
Dear Tim, I don't know if I ever told you about Longthorpe Tower—a 13th century peel Tower on the outskirts of Peterborough. It was lent to the Home Guard who made the walls dirty & the owner started to scrape them with a hoe. The features and halo of Jesus soon appeared and he desisted & the Soc. of Antiquaries took over & flaked away with pen-knives. It is a most lovely painted room—upstairs—with all sorts of Kings & Queens & birds & beasts, including a bustard & a bittern. But the point which concerns you is that there is a figure of Reason holding a wheel with five spokes & at the end of each spoke is an animal or bird signifying one of the five senses. A spider for touch, a boar, an eagle, a cock and a monkey.

Angelica encloses a sketch of it. I dont know if this interests you but it might.   Very much love, BUNNY

Wednesday, July 30th, 1952   *Alderney*
Dearest Bunny, I have just been cheering the Duke of Gloucester, so I simply have to tell somebody about my exciting week.

In the first place, I joined this News Chronicle crusade about fair income tax for authors, together with your pal McKenzie, Linklater, Bates, Balchin, Weatly (Wheatley?), R. Graves etc. Against all expectation, we seem to have succeeded to some extent, or at any rate the Treasury is thinking it over, and that we heard last Friday.

Then, on Saturday, a Blood-&-Thunder which I wrote 20 years ago was done for an hour and a half in the B.B.C. home Service. It was full of shrieks and yells and ticking clocks and hideous howls. While it was on a *real murder* took place at Seven Kings in England and nobody paid any attention to the screams of the victim because they thought it was all in the play! And finally, today, the Gloucesters flew over to shew the flag in Alderney, and this pleased me more than all. Really, the Royal Family is a first rate institution. There we stood in our rags and tatters, about a dozen of us, by the horse-trough opposite the Marais Hall Hotel, while he drove by at 4 m.p.h., looking like an anxious porker which had escaped from the Cavalry Club. The chauffeur we had provided for him had a greasy cloth cap on. We raised a faint half-human cheer. I waived my spectacles. And the Duke was doing his royal best to make the party go. He leaned forward, he industriously saluted us, he threw himself with intent, worried, workmanlike concentration into acknowledging our horse trough as if it were Trafalgar Square. He looked rather like a weight lifter who had found that his half ton dumbell was made of papier maché after all. He was putting too much work into it. Yet how nice, how good of them, how splendid to receive and return love, whether one is a porker or not. I wont believe he is dull, ever again, whatever anybody says. And the second time I saw him, he was being driven to luncheon after kissing the schoolchildren, and I was the only person in Connaught Square except Mrs. Carey, so we loyally cried out Hooray! He had relaxed by then and gave us quite a giggle. My whiskers are now six inches long, but it was not a haughty giggle. Give him my love when you go for your order. He is a kind, good Englishman, and a King's son to boot. So Yah! to the Americans and all such riff-raff, say we in the oldest possession of the Dukes of Normandy. love from TIM

1953

April 21st, 1953   *Hilton Hall, Hilton, Huntingdon*

Dearest Tim, ... I heard a moving account of a reconciliation in the Garrick Club when Peary and Cook fell into each others arms—not having spoken to each other since they parted at the North Pole.[1] I wish I had been there to shed tears of joy in the 18th Century manner. Talking of which, my boy, I have just written a pageant—It was great fun & I am not out of the wood yet. It is to be produced outside the walls of Hinchingbrooke. The words are to be spoken by heralds mounted on the wall & grasping scrolls which conceal microphones.

We start with the Man with Seven Wives & cats escaping & running across the stage to put people in a good temper.

I Then St Ivo converting the Saxons & dying at St Ives.

II King John granting a Charter in 1207 to Huntingdon.

III Qn. Elizabeth visiting Hinchingbrooke & knighting Sir Henry Cromwell. She makes a genuine speech.

IV Charles I visiting Little Gidding & being paternal—schoolchildren dancing round the Maypole.

V Charles I visiting Huntingdon in the Civil Wars. His army sacks the town on Sunday afternoon, ladies are chased & raped in the wings.

VI Refugees arrive at St Ives as puritans are going to Church. Cromwell makes a speech (His own words compounded from letters etc). raising recruits.

VII Restoration. Charles II brought over to Dover by Edward Montagu & Samuel Pepys.

VIII The lovely Miss Gunnings at Hemingford are visited by grand gentleman & are later robbed on their way to town by Dick Turpin.

IX Edward Prince of Wales & Alexandra in 1864 go on a shooting party while staying at Kimbolton. The gentlemen with their backs to the audience, with keepers, & loaders, fire at pheasants coming over the wall. After the drive the ladies join them in crinolines—The Duchess of Manchester & Lord Montagu sing The last Rose of

[1 Ian Parsons and Tim White had made a strenuous expedition to Lapland in 1926 when they were at Cambridge together.—D.G.].

Summer. They sit down to an alfresco luncheon—lobster & champagne when the FitzWilliam Pack chase a fox across the stage & kill in the wings. All the music is accurately of the period except for the Saxons & I'm told: 'Plainsong will have to do for them.'
We all flourish & grow in beauty   Much love from BUNNY
Pretty girls are always telling me they adore T. H. White. Why?

In the following letter I have omitted passages about the manuscript of a friend of Tim's which I was ready to accept for Hart-Davis, but which was placed elsewhere while I was reading it.

May 7th, 1953   3, *Connaught Square, Alderney, C.I.*
Dearest Bunny, ... Your pageant sounds a honey. What Milton did for Ludlow, Garnett will do for Hinchinbrooke. Pity you can't put in the purpler bits—Miss Reay, the Hell Fire Club, betrayal of Wilkes etc. How nice it would be to write a pageant which was all purple bits. The Scamperdale family, for instance. The first Earl being buggered by James I in exchange for his peerage—the second Earl destroying the title deeds of his elder brother—the fifth Earl selling his juvenile daughter to George the First in exchange for the Garter—the seventh being hanged for forgery –the tenth crowned with a pisspot by Edward VII for making a pass at Lilly Langtry—the eleventh eating his heart out at Boulogne after the baccarat scandal—the fourteenth voting for Urinal Bevan in the hopes of evading income tax, and finally, through Sidney Whats-his-name, presenting Scamperdale to the nation as a hostel for afflicted lavatory attendants.

Which pretty girls are these who are always telling you that they adore T. H. White? I only have two on hand at the moment. One of them is 21 last month and stayed here for 6 weeks in January. She says she is coming back in September. Meanwhile she is being presented etc. I adore her. The other is about 30, a divorced, blonde, beautiful actress, very nice, but too much of a match for me. She is coming next week. Why does one have to mate with one's equals in age? Women are so much tougher, crookeder, more grown-up, more unscrupulous and wickeder than men that the only hope for our sex that I can see is to marry them when they are about 12. Then there is some faint hope of equality.

... I am on the water waggon till November 1st, weigh 204 lbs, am in good health and am painting lots of fifth rate pictures, mainly of Alderney. I shall have about £100 worth of peaches this year and the same value of grapes. WHY DONT MY GREENGAGES FRUIT? They only produce about half a dozen blossoms each, though eight years old. I give them lime. Do you know what could be the matter?

The reconciliation with Ian Parsons was a formal one. We can now bow on meeting.

... Please do not giggle at my latest folly. I was feeling so old in relation to my debutante that I asked a parachuting cousin of mine who is a colonel to smuggle me in on a jumping course. I suppose it was an effort to be younger, like that horrible old physical culture expert in America who keeps jumping into the Seine. Fortunately, the colonel was much against it. I read his refusal with much relief, only to find that I was disappointed. Now I am trying the only other way of getting on the course, which is to go disguised as a spy. Do you know anything about this? I shall be 47 this month. Love to all   from TIM

June 10th, 1953   3, *Connaught Square, Alderney, C.I.*

Dearest Bunny, Do you remember that I wrote you a letter about catching a salmon on the Mayfly about ten years ago? I suppose you would not have preserved this letter by any possible wonderful chance? I am v. poor at present, and believe that I could turn an honest penny by changing the letter into a 20 minute broadcast, if you had it and would lend it to me.

Also, I might finally be able to polish up some sort of book about Eire, by tacking that letter on to the Letter From a Goose Shooter, which you got published for me by Horizon, and four or five bits from my diary—about a cannibal I met in Belmullet and about being mistaken for St. Patrick by the Archbishop of Tuam while on a pilgrimage and about actually seeing the Will o' the Wisp etc.

At the moment I am commissioned to do no less than 7 broadcasts and 2 televisions, so these sort of things come in handy.

Have you got over your pageant yet, or is it still being done?

(Do try to answer above query about letter, even if busy with pageant, as it is a matter of keeping my wolf from door.)

... I enclose a copy of my latest rarity,[1] signed for your collection!

[1 With this letter was included T. H. W.'s verses in aid of a public subscription towards the restoration of the church bells at St Anne's, Alderney.—D.G.]

DONT send any money. I can't let my friends do so. I am responsible for all the writing on the back, including the bogus request for prayers. If one does things, one must do them to the utmost, and one may as well be hung for a sheep as a lamb. We have already collected £100 on this effusion. Incidentally, if you know of anybody that I could profitably send signed copies to, please tell me of them.

My weight has now gone down to 13 stone 5. I dont know whether it is because I am a lunatic, a lover or a poet. love from TIM

June 20th, 1953 *Hilton Hall, Hilton, Huntingdon*

Dearest Tim, I searched amid a mass of correspondence &—like De Quincy[1]—drew forth a winner.

But I can't trust you with the holy relic—the frayed gut—& so send you a typescript of the letter.[2]

I am going to Ireland—the land of miracles—on July 14.—to Donega & am taking a fishing rod & I daresay about July 21st you will receive news of my having drawn forth a fish wearing a mitre which addressed me in Aramaic, Hebrew, & Latin & which turned out to be St Peter.

—With mayonnaise I suppose he would rank as a sacrament?

Thank you for your poem. I think it is what I mean by poetry. It was very very good. But you were drunk when you signed your name.

I send you a leaflet & perhaps will follow it up with a programme. Angelica, painted up to the eyes—& almost as lovely as she is when washing up—has gone off to a dress rehearsal tonight.

Did you ever hear of Prof. Percy Gardner? An Oxford Archaeologist. He said one good thing. A lady had bored the company with a disquisition upon morals. When she had left, Percy Gardner remarked very gently:

'We must always remember in favour of Mrs Strong that her ideas are not her own.'

This story told to Quentin Bell produced the anecdote of the French

[1 A reference to the anecdote of the young editor who called upon De Quincey who was living in lodgings in Edinburgh and asked him for a contribution. De Quincey led him into a room full of scattered papers, containing a hip bath which overflowed with manuscript. He stirred it gently, plucked out a paper at random and said: 'I wonder if this would do?'

It was the MS. of *Revolt of the Tartars*, which is almost the best thing he ever wrote.—D.G.]

[2 With this letter I enclosed T. H. W.'s letter dated May 27th, 1944. See *supra*. —D.G.]

Academician who had never done anything, or made a witty remark in his life but who attended the funeral of President Felix Faure.

When the body of Academicians in full uniform appeared in the procession, a party of ribald Parisian working men shouted out: Voilà les Coçus (Here come the cuckolds). The unknown Academician suddenly shouted back: Nous sommes seulement une délégation.

Well, well—its bedtime.   Very much love, BUNNY

August 8th, 1953   3, *Connaught Square, Alderney*

Dearest Bunny, I havnt answered your letters because I have been in the midst of emotional and physical storms which have almost destroyed me. I feel like some frightful old character in Molière, or perhaps a Mozart opera. Last January & February I had a girl to stay with me who was just 21. After a lot of half-hearted hugging and stuff I fell in love with her with a resounding crash the day after she left. She floated off for her London season, to be presented and all the whirl of childhood, and I was insane enough to let her go. I think I thought it would be good for her to get the débutante thing off her chest, and also that it would be selfish to deny her these menus plaisirs. She was to come back in September. By July, her letters getting fewer and more stilted, I thought it was about time I went over to see what was happening. Of course she had been growing up meanwhile, and had grown no longer in my direction, but in that of the Eton & Harrow Match—to see which, incidentally, she ditched me. We had the usual scenes of defiance and despair. It ended with me leaping into an aeroplane and flying back to Alderney, where, since I had been on the water waggon since February, the oceans of whisky into which I plunged, like taking gas for the agony at the dentists, resulted in Wagnerian chords of stunning proportions. I had a fight with a sailor in a pub (nobody won: we kept missing each other) and did my best to destroy myself with liquor. Then the little men in my unconscious mind had a committee meeting and, being averse to being destroyed by their raving chairman, decided to immobilise me. I woke up at 4 a.m. in a mysterious agony of cramp which lasted for eight hours solid and was kept in bed by the doctor for three weeks. We never decided what it was. One of my legs had seized up. I am back on the water waggon again now, walking, having discovered that broken hearts can be seated in the calf of the leg. The baggage about whom all this dotage is, is quite a nice creature, just like everybody else of 21. Most of her qualities are negative i.e. she is evasive, deceitful, lazy, selfish etc. Perhaps all women are? She has one positive quality, on which I relied. She is tremendously imitative. She becomes the kind of person she is with, not mimics it, becomes it, and of course while she was with me it was absolute bliss. Letting her go, I had not realised that she would become the Eton & Harrow match. At the moment, she is behaving like the Servants Hall. Its hell to be in love with a lazy, deceitful, selfish, evasive skivvy. I always used to think that Anthony was a clot to lose the battle of Actium—was it Actium—for Cleopatra, and only got just what he deserved, and perhaps he was and did. But he was not responsible for his actions. Its a cloud in one's brain, just behind the forehead, between the eyes.

An astonishing feature of this business is that in 1930, under the name of James Aston, I wrote a book about a middle-aged gentleman—to me then surely incomprehensible?—of exactly 47 (my present age) who had a tragic love affair with a girl of 21! It was called First Lesson. I read it again last week, having forgotten the plot, & I was astounded at James's insight into Tim. Really, he was a very clever boy.

Well, that's my excuse for not answering your letters.

The pageant sounded splendid. I shall keep the programme in a safe.

I'm glad you had your row with Hart-Davies before the publication of the first volume of your memoirs. It would have caused a frightful nuisance afterwards. Do tell me when and with whom they are to come out, as I long to read them. What enormous money prize I wonder will they win, only to have it all taken away from you in taxes, to be redistributed among the lavatory attendants.

Ireland sounds as if it still stood where it did. What magpies and penguins they are—pinching each other's eggs all the time.

Bunny, I took up this large sheet of paper, hoping to cover all 4 sides, but I just can't concentrate. Forgive the egoism. I must be off back to Actium. love from TIM

November 20th, 1953   *Alderney*

Dearest Bunny, Thank you very much indeed for this most valued present of the first volume, which you seem to have pulled off in the face of frightful odds. I have been doing something of the sort myself lately i.e. writing about experiences with real people in Ireland, and I know what agony it is to be threatened with libel on the one side and broken friend-ships on the other. Far the best of your character pictures are of course the safely dead: Lawrence and the charming Ford. Your father & mother are not quite so good—due to the ties of blood I suppose. The Oliviers did not get across to me. If you slept with all or some of them, how could you say so? If you did not, what was so important about them? However, the artificial restraint of having to be nice to living people does help to bring out the niceness of your own character, and probably its always worth working in a difficult medium. I was not pleased with the illustra-tions. (a) There ought to have been one of your mother. (b) I could have spared one or two views of Oliviers in exchange for a picture of the Scearn and perhaps of the house in Brighton. Because you have an acute visual memory for places you are overlooking the fact that the reader has not seen them. If there is a chance in the next volume, do give us some more of Ford's relative truths. What a kinship I feel for him! All my truths are relative. He surely must have had his tongue partly in his cheek?

Do you remember old Sir Sydney Cockerell? He wrote to ask if he might include some of my letters in his next collection and I gave him carte blanche—only to find that he had chosen a vast quantity—something between ten and thirty thousand words! At least half were wildly in-discreet—remarks about the character of Compton MacKenzie etc. or the personal attractions of lovely ladies at the B.B.C. I had to insist on violent cutting. I dont mind being a comic Boswell when dead, but really, while alive, its much too dangerous.

In the Irish book which I am now on, I have made no reference to anybody I value or am ever likely to meet again: it seems the only way to be safe. My very best anecdote, about how I was mistaken for St. Patrick on the pilgrimage up Croagh Patrick by the Bishop of Galway and the Archbishop of Tuam, and fed by them on cold chicken behind the altar, is still terribly awkward. I adored Tuam, and dont want to hurt his feelings: I feared Galway, who will certainly sue for libel at the drop of a biretta. How very difficult it is to write for anything but posterity.

You are of course writing for your own children: the public is in-cidental. Well, you'll have to do some additional volumes, so that you can dedicate one to each. Can you manage to think up some unpleasant characters—who are safely dead—and make one or two ruthless attacks on them? You must not like everybody. It will be interesting to hear more of Rupert Brooke and why you began to dislike him. I am sure you can manage this without becoming pettish. The book arrived in the afternoon, whereupon I went to bed and finished it about three in the morning— slow reading, but then I am getting old.

Couldn't you have one almost entirely cross volume with digs at Sitwells and Sassoons? I long to hear the rumpus.   love from TIM

December 29th, 1953   3 *Connaught Square, Alderney. C.I.*

Dearest Bunny, I woke up this Tuesday morning, the 29th of December 1953, clearly reciting the following memorable phrases:

'Did you ever hear the story, narrated by Squire Waterton, of a certain famed pheasant which was preserved stuffed, not because of any peculiarity in the bird, but because it had fought a duel, a pistol in either foot, with a dishonest keeper near Banbury, and thereafter had fired upon the fellow seven nights together—until being itself taken in ambush by a porter, that is to say a wine porter, near St Stephens?'

What can all this mean? Do you think it is a portent, or merely rivals Kubla Khan?

I have not read Waterton for fifteen years and am certain there is no such story. Notice the prose style—which I place about 1850 (?) Happy New Year   Love from TIM

The style may be earlier in date. Defoe? But then, how could he have heard of Waterton? Can they have met in Heaven? What are they trying to convey to me?

1954

Dearest Tim, Your letter has just come about the pheasant.

The style is certainly not Defoe. Defoe would have made it more circumstantial—he would never have started off by admitting it was a story—nor used the phrase 'a certain famed pheasant.' He would have started off:

'That night we lay at Walton Hall the housekeeper came to us and told us of how dishonest the gamekeepers were in Yorkshire and that the villainy of the last fellow had been brought to light by a strange event which caused him to repent and to confess all.

It seems that about roosting time when the pheasants fly up into plantations an old cock got up suddenly & fired at him twice as it flew overhead, for it was armed with pistols. The fellow was so hardened and steeped in sin that it was not until this same cock pheasant had fired upon him for seven nights together and happening to hit him in the side of the neck that he fell upon his knees crying out:

I confess. Send no more of thy angels against me Almighty God. For even in his repentance he would blaspheme. The cock pheasant was shot the same night by a wine porter of St Stephens and is now stuffed and an object of curiosity to visitors at Walton Hall. The pistols could not be found, but some of the leg feathers are scorched as though by the priming.'

I dont say that's real Defoe—but it is nearer. Defoe would I think have used it in his History of Apparitions & not needed the stuffed bird. Was the visitation purely verbal? Or were there any visual images or intimations of how the deed was done? I suppose it shot the keeper flying? A pheasant is a very sporting bird & could scarcely do less.

I think it may be a case of Kubla Khan—but have you read The Road to Xanadu? Possibly the wine porter may provide a clue. Do you think St Stephens Green is meant, or the Palace of Parliament or is there a church near Walton Hall dedicated to St Stephen?

Did you read Struwelpeter as a child? It is only a short step from hares to pheasants (both game.)

Well—a Happy New Year.

I am buried in the years 1915–1918 & am unlikely to emerge from them until the early summer.

We flourish. At least I hope so.   Much love BUNNY

January 3rd, 1954   *Hilton Hall, Hilton, Huntingdon*

Dear Tim, Which of your friends is Atticus of *The Sunday Times*? Not I, I hasten to assure you. Moreover he could not have got it through me.

I must say I much prefer pistols.

Dont please start a campaign about telepathy on the strength of this occurence.   Love from BUNNY

Shall I send your letter to The Sunday Times & demand an explanation?

[*Enclosure*]

Nature Note[1]

Bad pheasant shoots would be tolerable only if the birds could be persuaded to carry small bombs in their talons and be trained to drop them on the guns. In fact, I would like all semi-tame fauna to develop some offensive mechanism, not because I am anti-blood-sports, but because the odds on the hunter have altered too much in his favour since our ancestors used to hunt sabre-toothed tigers through the Home Counties with bows and arrows.

A baboon in the Mikushi forests of Northern Rhodesia has just shown the way. When a native hunter called Kasenga aimed his gun at him he jumped down from his tree, overpowered the man, took his gun away from him and, using his tail to pull the trigger, shot Kasenga through the thigh and made off.

December 2nd, 1954   *Hilton Hall, Huntingdon*

Dear Tim, Thank you very much for The Book of Beasts which I think is a triumph. The direct terre-à-terre language has brought it alive and makes it seem much more convincing. Instead of having the feeling we are being given a relic out of a museum we feel that a very peculiar person, now alive, is telling us a lot of odd information.

Much of it, of course, is only a little odder than the kind of thing psychologists are always telling us. Thank you for recording the Strachey mantichora.

[[1] *Sunday Times*, January 3rd, 1954.—D.G.]

267

How are you? Do you develop, and in what direction? or have you become an Ormer, unchanged since the palaeozoic & unchangeable till doomsday? What do you read, think, drink? Are you in love?

... I went for a wonderfully idle holiday with a very wealthy old friend for three weeks in France—stayed with Baron Rothschild at Ch. Mouton who gave me 1881 claret—& went on through Aquitaine which I now know better than Yorkshire—its cities, cathedrals, picture galleries, three starred hotels & restaurants where the specialités are trout with almonds, truffled turkey & wild strawberries—There are the most wonderful towns: Cordes which is largely 12th & 14th century—Conques where the ashes of Ste. Foi, grilled when she was thirteen, are preserved in a tenth century golden bust of her ornamented all over with Roman Cameos—with the heads of the Caesars & the rape of Europa bedizening the golden virgin saint who looks like an Inca God.

All that & unlimited red wine was very restful. We were driven by a hired chauffeur in an immense Buick. I then stayed for a week in Paris with a poor Sicilian musician. I have finished my second volume—infinitely better than the first—which will be out in the spring. Directly I have that off my hands I shall do some real work.

After all this boasting & gush please write me a long letter, telling me that you have turned Mohometan, abhorr dogs and fermented liquors and are importing some Circassian girls to serve you with sherbet. My family flourish—Richard is married to a granddaughter of old Sir Herbert Grierson & I have furbished up the cottage next door for him & his bride. My cows flourish but I lose money on pigs.

Much love BUNNY

1955

The first half of this letter asking me to assist a friend of Tim's is omitted.

September 12th, 1955   *3, Connaught Square, Alderney, C.I.*

Dearest Bunny, ... Well, Bunny, I have been having a hectic year. Apart from boozing and writing my best book to date (to be called The Master) I did have one adventure, presumably my last strenuous one, as I am practically 50.

I went down in one of the old fashioned diving suits of the R.N. It seemed worth doing before they became obsolete because of free diving, but it is a crushing occupation for elderly amateurs. The lead on the suit weighs 180 lbs! Imagine wandering about on deck in this and crawling up iron ladders. Even to step over a rope or breathing tube is like climbing a wall. I slightly popped my eardrums and got a nosebleed at about 6 fathoms so have concluded I am now too old for such larks. Also this year I have fractured most of my face bones in a drunken orgy, painted an excellent self portrait (also one of Wyllie), done a lot of schnorkel swimming (an enchanting rock fish of about 2 pounds *lay on its side* one day beneath me, to look up, on the sandy bottom, just like one of those cheery people on an Etruscan tomb—I dont try to kill or catch the creatures, merely to consort with them) and begun trying to take coloured cinema films with self as scripter, director, photographer and everything else—I want to do a sort of Alderney thing like Dylan Thomas's Milk Wood.

Do you know this interesting little leg-pull about Milk Wood? The hill in it was called Llareggyb. Put U for Y and read backwards.

Tell me how you are?   love from TIM

September 14th, 1955   *Hilton Hall, Hilton, Huntingdon*

Dear Tim, ... I also have recently written my best book—a short novel which will be published at the end of October—it is called Aspects of Love. It was a wonderful feeling to be writing seriously again:—and writing very differently. It is a good deal in conversation & it is

incredibly economical—in fact too concentrated I fear for most readers—
not ten lines of padding or repetition in the book. The effect—(on those
on whom it has an effect) is like a very dramatic short play.

I have also coming out at the beginning of October, the second volume
of my autobiography which is called Flowers of the Forest & is chiefly
about the 1914–1918 war years. It is much better than the first volume—
but that's all I can say about it.

Richard knows all about free diving—but hasn't done much this year—
went down & found the wreck of a battleship (18th century) in Devon—
& attended an Archaeological Congress on Under-water Archaeology at
Cannes & looked at the Roman ship near Marseilles. He is married, by
the way, to a grand-daughter of Sir Herbert Grierson & the daughter of
the Cambridge Professor of Anglo-Saxon ...

I send you my very warm love & will send my books.

Affectionately BUNNY

September 17th, 1955   3, *Connaught Square, Alderney, C.I.*

Dearest Bunny, Thank you for your exciting letter. I shall look forward
to the two books *madly*. Dont go and forget to send them. You are one
of the very very few writers whose books I browse about in every year
or two. This summer I have skipped through Pocahontas and read the
whole of the Grasshoppers, which wears as well as ever. Very strange that
this now quite out of date flying should still be as exciting as when it was
first published. It is a lovely book. I think I will try No Love again this
afternoon.

Old Sydney Cockerell has a lot of my letters to him coming out in
October, rather to my disgust. They make almost a quarter of his book
(unpaid—I mean I am) and I couldn't refuse him as he is 88 and bedridden. I dont like my used letters, as I am still growing up all the time
and it is like seeing photographs of oneself naked on a cushion aged six
months.

Richard Aldington's ex- or separated wife was here this Summer, who
says he is now off full tilt to debunk somebody else—poor old Norman
Douglas of all people!

Your 23 Jerseys stun me with admiration. How do you do this and
drink claret too? My 3 small greenhouses of grapes, peaches, nectarines &
tomatoes keep me from ever getting really properly drunk, as the toma-

toes die at once if I dont water them at least once a day in Summer weather. I won the first prize for fruit in our agricultural shew this year, for the 2nd time. Killie is still alive and happy. This is a silly scrappy letter as my housekeeper is talking to me about the sweep and the radiogram is playing Beethoven's 5th Concerto so I will stop

love from TIM

How nice it would be to see the twins.

Would they still howl at sight of my whiskers?

Yes, I knew Richard was a famous free diver. I heard him on the wireless.

November 14th, 1955   *Hilton Hall, Hilton, Huntingdon*

Dear Tim, You have been much in my mind lately: any uneasy twitchings you have experienced as though you were being watched from behind a hedge, bristling at the back of the neck or sudden blushing can be laid at my door. First there was your wonderful review[1] in which you picked out for special praise passages which other reviewers had quoted to explain the nausea with which my character afflicted them—then there has been a correspondence between me & old Sir Sydney Cockerell about you. He thinks you are by far the best letter writer of modern times. I agree. (He sent me a proof copy of the collection of letters he is publishing to prove it. And he wants me to collect all your letters & publish them when you are dead. I pointed out that you are certain to survive me by 25 years at least, & that the task might be better left to an unborn generation … but in any case the old creature is so anxious to read more of your letters that he is obviously prepared to have you bumped off in order to gratify his curiosity. So be careful.

However he has persuaded me to put your letters to me in order. If I complete such a task, I propose to have them typed & if you give your permission would allow the old collector to read them. Would you allow it? If he is a poisoner it might save your life. If not it might prolong his. It would be graceful to say yes as it is fairly certain that he will die long before I have arranged the letters & had them typed.

Nerissa, aged nine, has started on The Sword in the Stone—an inscribed & hand-coloured copy you gave me. She is only allowed to read

[1 Tim's review of the second volume of my memoirs, *Flowers of the Forest*.—D.G.]

it when sitting in a chair with the book on a table & not when lying in a hayloft eating ice-cream.

She is completely absorbed & has not ventured a single remark or criticism but merely looks annoyed when I ask if she likes it. She obviously thinks that only a bloody fool would talk about it instead of reading, re-reading & re-re-reading. I re-re-re-re-read the description of Master Twyti & the boar hunt & King P. & the Questing Beast. It has a wonderful quality: fresh as my walk across a paddock this morning & yet more like a tapestry than a chapter in a book. As a matter of fact there is a tapestry in the Uffizi of a boarhunt which is almost indistinguishable from it—Sir Grummore going head over heels—the Wart couching his spear which has the crosspiece you describe.

That letter of yours to old Sir S.C. asking about armour explains why you are so good. Well, dear Tim, I can't start on yet another sheet of paper merely to praise you.

But do write me a line & let know how you are.

I spent a month in Italy recently.　　　　　Very much love BUNNY

November 18th, 1955　　　　*Hilton Hall, Hilton, Huntingdon*

Dearest Tim, ... These old men are dreadful creatures: if I hang on another fifteen years I shall be worse than any I suppose—but though old age offers the pleasures of unmitigated selfishness and bad manners, I don't really look forward to it!

When I was in Venice last month I was taken to call on a figure called B.B. Mr Bernard Berenson is 90, he is immensely rich, tiny, with a clipped white beard and looks exactly like a spider and lives in a jewelled web which he is leaving to Harvard. He was married to the mother of Adrian Stephen's wife Karin and Oliver Strachey's wife, so I talked about his step-grandchildren (Angelica's cousins) and so on. B.B. was an expert on Italian pictures and supplied the identifications to the pictures which Duveen the dealer sold to Pierpoint Morgan. Roger Fry and Vanessa etc were always extremely critical (to use a mild word) of B.B. and when Vanessa's name was mentioned the spider sitting by me on the sofa burst into vituperation. There was nothing I could do except smile sweetly and reflect on how wonderfully immune time makes people.—The old creature had never forgiven an injury or a slight: the longing for revenge is what keeps him going ... However B.B. did tell me one interesting thing: that my grandfather was the first person he knew when he came to London and that he introduced him to Oscar Wilde ...

My little novel has had beastly reviews ... If people appreciate one in one's life, they drop you like a stone when you die. If they don't appreciate you alive, they dig you up and make a frightful song and dance 20 years later. I only hope I am proclaimed the greatest English imaginative writer before the copyrights run out so that my children have a year or two of easy money. The public taste goes up and down like a stormy sea ... The main body of the ocean—the twilight depths never stirs and the Gilbert and Sullivan operas, the Peter Pans, the Black Beauties and Lorna Doones go on for ever and ever. Which reminds me that I have just read The Prisoner of Zenda. It is horribly badly written, but the plot is real genius. If only it had been available for Shakespeare, my God, what a play we should have had! It's just his style: a double of the king, who wins the heart of the Princess and plenty of swordplay and a subsidiary pair of lovers and a loyal friend like Kent.

Going and coming back from Italy I travelled by the Orient Express first class wagon lits. It was a wonderful period piece: the luxury train of the Prisoner Of Zenda period with imitation stamped leather and velvet— and a little hook to hang one's gold watch on beside the bunk—all faded worn-out, creaking, and yet with a luxury forgotten in this stream-lined age. Someone ought to save one of the coaches for an ethnological museum.

Well, do get better, rouse, rouse, shake out the great pinions and laugh. I am sending you my little novel. You won't care much for it I think, but I like it myself. Yours with love BUNNY

?November 24th, 1955[1] *3, Connaught Square, Alderney, C.I.*

Dearest Bunny, This is a hateful and stupid letter, but I must face it and write it, otherwise I will never be able to look you in the face again. First of all, the letter which you sent *with* Aspects of Love filled me with such pride and pleasure that I could hardly sleep all night, I was so happy. But second, as you predicted, I *dont* like Aspects of Love. I kept fidgetting about and putting it down and starting again, but it was only at the bottom of page 144 that light suddenly dawned on me like an atomic flash. You like cats and I loathe them. This is not a *rational*

[1 This letter was posted with the next dated January 4th, 1956.—D.G.]

273

criticism, and God knows I dont claim to be *right* in loathing cats or that you a *wrong* in loving them. It is just an allergy or a misfortune or a numb place in my mind. You must not forget that you were really beautifully educated by loving, intelligent, unconventional geniuses, who were accustomed to move in the highest ranks, while I was brought up by middle-class, conventional people who had been in the Indian Civil Service since time immemorial. I was being caned all the time and made to roll about in the mud with a leather ball, and this, by now, is *ingrained*. The heritage of this is—you will think it quite dotty—but I can't help it— that I believe human beings ought to be monogamous, like those glorious creatures, ravens, swans, eagles etc.—that if they consciously take a solemn vow in public they should stick to it—or not take it—and that women ought not to behave like headstrong babies. Consequently, to begin at the wrong end first, I see no reason at all why Alexis should not (at 34) have married Jenny (at 14–15)—provided he meant to marry her and nobody else. As a historian, you know quite well that almost every genius noted by man has, at the age of 99, married a girl of 9 or 10, and made her very happy. Try Napoleon. Then start at the other end. I hate Rose, like a cat, for going to bed with Alexis first, then tossing him over for Sir George, and then taking him and other lovers. Surely women are dependable people as well as men? My adored grandfather on my mother's side was a judge, but not a hanging judge like ——. He would have simply (like old Sir Sydney) have answered your various dilemmas in two ways. He would have said. Number One (a Victorian One): It is unfair to ask one male to spend the money to educate the children of a different male.//Number Two: If a woman cannot behave herself accord- ing to the laws which I have given all my carreer to, as an Indian Civil Servant—the laws of honour—then take down her crenellated, lace, Victorian pants, and give her one resounding blow with the flat of the hand on the buttocks. In short, I think your Rose is a selfish, short- sighted, self-admirer and a bore. Obviously you dont think so, and neither of us is right. It is the dog and the cat.

Before I end this letter—which is bound to wound you—I must make one other confession. I was truly delighted a week or two ago to learn that Princess Margaret had decided *not* to marry Group Captain Towns- hend. Mr. Townshend had made a solemn, voluntary oath, in public, to marry Mrs. Townshend till death did them part. If the princess had afterwards married him, she would have been an accessory to the fact of a public lie. Surely it is a dreadful insult to regard women as being dishonourable, childish and allowed to break their potties?

The only sensible person in your book was Jenny—who really meant what she said—and Alexis ought to have married her—I repeat 'married'—and he should have been faithful to her as she to him.

All this Sex is boring me to death.

It is not 'sex'—it is 'honour'—what Sir George was interested in.

love from TIM

1956

Dearest Bunny, For the last two months I have been in a kind of trance—paying no bills, answering no letters, sending no Xmas cards or presents and not even thanking people for theirs. It was a mental log-jam, with all my projects at cross purposes, thwarting each other. Perhaps it was due to some illness. I can only say how ashamed I am, and that even now it is an almost intolerable effort to write. Please forgive me.

One of the first logs in the jam was how to thank you for Aspects of Love while admitting that I did not enjoy it as much as Flowers of the Forest. If Love is the lineaments of gratified desire, where do you fit in the fact that for the last 24 years I have loved 2 setters without gratifying any desires or feeling any? Yet I have been faithful to them, often at inconvenience to myself, and it has been a satisfactory relationship of importance to all 3 of us. You see, I am old-fashioned. I was brought up in a different background from yours. My childhood was spent with Indian Civil Servants who had a tremendous sense of duty and fidelity, and it was also poisoned by my mother divorcing my father with every circumstance of squalor and ferocity. The result is that my reaction to your heroine is that she was simply a willful (wilfull?), selfish, promiscuous, empty-headed bitch. No, not bitch. Cow. Bitches are faithful creatures like Killie & Brownie.

Aspects of Love must have been a good book, or it would not have made me feel so strongly antipathetic to it as to create an 8 week log-jam. I have not even written to thank dear old Sydney Cockerell for his Best of Friends, nor to thank you.

Now I have to begin pushing the logs apart and trying to get people to forgive me.

Among other minor troubles, I have had a miserable Xmas. Killie nearly died of enteritis or something, so I had to spend the time feeding her at 2 hour intervals with all the house doors locked and millions of revellers, carollers, boozers and cracker-pullers in paper hats battering on the doors and howling for me to stop being silly and come out and have a jolly, jolly drink. This with a dying dog, aged 12, whom I love. However, she is better for now.   love from TIM

Dear Tim, There is indeed a profound difference between us. Your letter reveals a mediaeval monkish attitude. I, as I think you know, believe in love and the tenderness and understanding which reciprocated happy love brings with it. I believe that the sexual instinct in normal people is good: possibly the highest good. You can find out what I think about fidelity in several of my books. It is a large part of the subject of Lady Into Fox and of The Sailor's Return. The exclusiveness of love and its secret private nature is the underlying subject of A Man In The Zoo. My experience is that an exclusive passion as a first love is extremely unusual: most young people are more likely to mate well if they experiment a good deal. Naturally this was impossible at a time when a different standard of sexual morals was expected from women than from men, and when a high value was set upon virginity and when honour (in women only) was considered synonymous with chastity. This was almost inevitable (except in certain fortunate islands) until the discovery of birth-control. That discovery has liberated women and made them the equal partners of men. It has made love a matter of delight and not of terror. It has also incidentally made the existence of a special class of women prostitutes unnecessary except for men who are unable to find any woman willing to copulate with them except for cash.

Rose is in my opinion a healthy normal and delightful woman. She is exceptionally sincere and truthful and follows her excellent instincts. Unlike you I do not believe in marriage vows and have never made any. I intensely dislike the whole Christian attitude to sex and marriage. If the first mating is a success as often happens all is well. But if the partners fall out of love they are penalised by the Church and, in the case of Royalty, by Society and if they accept the religious bunkum, they torture themselves and each other. Your remarks about taking down a woman's drawers and beating her smack of flagellation—a perversion, which as you know, is frequent among those who were much caned as small boys, among schoolmasters and judges who have been able to inflict corporal punishment with impunity. But the corporal punishment of women though pleasant for its addicts will not make them live with men they dislike, or give up the lovers whom they do. That is over thanks to the married women's property act.

When you talk of 'the laws of honour' in connection with sexual life I wonder if you mean what you say? The laws of a country are continually changing and being changed. So are our ideas of justice and codes of social behaviour, all of which depend upon the climate of opinion. And the views you express are as dead as the dodo. If you want to understand the relativity of morals read Malinovsky, or that wonderful book by Bateson (the son of the geneticist.) I have replied to your letter because you might have misinterpreted silence. But I don't intend to discuss the subject further. I have been twice married, have had six children and been the lover of an enormous number of other women, so that my views are founded on a great variety of experience which you have avoided. Your experience with one human and two canine bitches does not lead me to treat your views seriously. This is not written in ill-temper. Indeed I wish I could come and see you. I would like to convert you to drinking claret, a more important matter than dragging you out of the middle ages and the company of the Fathers of the Church.   Love from BUNNY

?September 19*th*, 1956   3, *Connaught Square, Alderney, C.I.*

Dearest Bunny, I'm sorry this letter has taken quite a time to get written, but I have been mixed up in one of my usual crazes. It is one which I shall have to not drop if I get tired of it, as it involves other people. Some time last winter I began to think about people who were stone deaf and stone blind, as I suppose most people have occasionally thought, but most people dismiss the thought quickly, on the grounds that they have enough on their own plates already. There is room on my plate, so I went on thinking, and came to the conclusion that the vilest criminal, if he found himself in the next cell to somebody who had been sent to solitary confinement in the silent dark forever, could not but try to tap out some sort of message on the wall sometimes. So I found out the address of an assossiation which tries to help such people and wrote offering to entertain four d/bs per annum on a week's holiday each, paying their fares and expenses and those of their guides, as of course they can't travel alone. The first one, guided by the charming woman who runs the association, arrived about the same time as your letter. She is an enchanting little sparrow of a distressed gentlewoman, living on an annuity of £50 plus her blind pension, and twice as intelligent as an ordinary woman, as she has to be—as brave as a lioness, five feet high. Her remarks from the noiseless cave in which she lives are more *considered* than other people's remarks. She lives and sometimes quarrels with another impoverished spinster, of whom she said to me: 'I generally give in to Mary. After all, giving in is a kind of present.' An epigram! All her observations are like this, and her sensibilities too, just one degree profounder than an unafflicted person's. Well, the whole week was a roaring success. I had learned to speak on my fingers before she came, and had interested John Arlott's very nice children in it, so she was not met at the airport by one boring old novelist but by him and *five* children aged between 12 and 5, who seized her hands instantaneously and began writing messages on them to see if they could! Forty years of silent blindness have resulted in her developing a *loose* action of her feet—which must be ready to give to uneven surfaces in a ju-jitsu kind of way—and she holds her face upwards, as she can just tell if the sun is shining. This, with her half open, faded eyes, and her differentness, and the voice which she has not heard since she was a little girl makes her a bit frightening to children, and ours was the first time she had ever been met and unselfconsciously adopted by children, who continued to behave superbly all the time she was here. When she left, they arrived running to kiss her goodbye, and had bought her a little silver bird-brooch. But *everything* was like this. She was avid for experience ('This must last me for the rest of my life') and we to give it her. She had never been in a boat, or seen a live fish. We hauled her into a fishing boat in a storm, and she caught four herself! We taught her to swim on her back! We helped her to *run* on the sands! She climbed to the very top of the lighthouse, went to a cocktail party, had tea at Government house, and all the time everybody brought her things to feel and smell and in the evenings she poured out her life story and her philosophy. She went d/b at the age of about 12 ... and is now in her fifties. She is self-educated and wont believe in a dear, kind God who afflicts little girls like this—but is some sort of a deist. All this without benefit of Darwin etc. She gets the Black Dog sometimes of course, poor lamb, but is superbly courageous, and gave me quite as much pleasure as I gave her, and we prattled on our fingers day and night, like two babies in a bath tub. Of course I have asked her again for next year and am to keep up a correspondence with her and can write Braille, for which I have a board, and the children comandeered the board the moment she left, to write her a letter each too. I want to teach her to do lino cuts of things as she remembers them out of her head—then we will sell them for vast sums, assuring everybody that they are much more interesting than the infantile pictures of that old humbug Grandma

Moses. (What an Age of Infantilism—the Ba-Ba we do live in. Everybody has to try to write—G. Stein—and paint or make music like the kindergarten. But I must stop about all this, or it will bore you. It has been a rea heart medecine for me and once or twice I could not help weeping bitterly as she talked away of the glorious colours and music which she has remembered all these years and tried to sing in the voice she never hears, some Irish rubbish about colleens. I could have howled aloud for all she heard or saw, but something made me cry silently, still holding her hands without a tremor.

I have had several other crazes since we last wrote. In February I broke my neck, slipping on some granite steps in the frozen garden, which made me consider that there were one or two things I still had to do before I died. While still in hospital I bought a 14 ft. sailing dinghy, which is now the apple of my eye. I put its hair in pigtails with blue ribbons every night. I have also bought myself a superb cinema camera and am making 3 serious films. The one nearest completion is called Birds and Boats, in which we handle eggs, young and adults of all the wonderful seabirds here—puffins, razorbills, guillemots, shags, gannets— sailing round the rocky islands to get them. These, and writing front page articles for the Times Lit. Sup., have been my main occupations—apart from having eleven people to stay this frightful summer, and underwater swimming when I could—did you know I went diving last year with the famous Commander Crabbe? Oh yes, and I also got let in for starting one of these homes for incurables in Alderney for my ex-pupil Cheshire, the V.C., but after oceans of trouble and paper work it turned out that this was not the place to start it in. We lack the necessary facilities. I write once a fortnight to my old crony Sydney Cockerell, and sent Cheshire to call on him, where, in bed, he found Sydney holding a levee for 2 dukes and a marchioness. The latter* incidentally is livid with me and accuses me of being a hothead—of all things for *not* starting the Cheshire home in an island which is not on National Health, not provided with any therapies, not acceptable to Jersey, Guernsey, S.W. Region, or SAAFA, not possible to be visited by relations except expensively by air, and not even cheap to live in. There are a lot of other nots.

Talking of Sydney, I hope you will not be cross if I ask you not to use my letters in your next book. I couldnt refuse Sydney, who is bed-

* The marchioness.

ridden and in his 90th year, but I have hated the book ever since it was published—views of self's bottom laid on cushion in family album, revolting—and it makes me feel awkward about writing letters now, if I think they might be printed in my lifetime. I took a vow then and there not to let it happen again. I want to have what so few authors are allowed, a private life.

Turning to your letter, who is the father of your grandson, William or Richard? Tell Amaryllis, who seems very undutiful not to cultivate my acquaintance after I have dedicated a book to her, that my dinghy is called Popsie too. It should definitely be written with an IE, say I. Tell Henrietta that my dog Killie is 13 years 4 months old, and has gone deaf, but is otherwise as beautiful and sprightly as she ever was. She and I sometimes think of Quince, to whom I sent a visitor 4 years ago, when he was alive and happy. Your Rolls Royce sounds just the thing for Alderney, if only it could have been diverted here on its way back from Italy—but no, you say you are not taking it. Anyway, I suppose this letter wont catch you till you get back. You and it would have made an addition to my visitors book. I keep one *in film*. It begins with me opening the front door and bowing the guests in. Then everybody who comes to stay has to write their names on half a sheet of this note paper, which is photographed for a caption, after which they are photographed for a minute or two, doing something. Wren Howard's grandchildren made a splendid sequence, burying Killie on the beach.

I must stop, as I have all the letters to answer since my blind friend came. Her nickname is Puck—poor, good, bright spirit.

love from TIM

My next book is an adventure story called THE MASTER, dedicated to R. L. Stevenson.

September 26th, [1956]   *Poste Restante Florence*
Dearest Tim, Your letter, forwarded by William, was the first I received in Italy. I have read it twice, once to myself & the second time aloud to Angelica. You are one of the most astonishing, original & extraordinary, men.

Your action in regard to Puck shows such imagination & sensitiveness —such a delightful understanding & so free of saintliness. I love you for every word of it & Angelica was more moved, astonished & delighted even than I. Indeed I think it made her realise your quality for almost the first time. She said something like: 'Such a man so completely able to be original while alone ought to be always happy.' Every word in your letter moved & charmed her.

While you give up your money & time to create new profound joyfull experiences for others—your enlisting the children—your idea of fishing were strokes of genius—I am living the life of an elderly sensualist. This summer has been so tiring & for other reasons horribly exhausting—that the conception of a holiday was irresistible. I had fallen in love with Angelica for a second time, something unusual I believe in husbands who live with their wives—but not unknown among the divorced. Moreover the endless rain; the corn sprouting in the stooks as they stood in the fields; the continual strain of farm accounts, overdrafts, income tax, P.A.Y.E. insurance (I have to pay 8/5d. a week in order to exist) so got me down that I have felt like emigrating to France or Italy. It would be wonderful to have no responsibility, no real property (i.e. land & houses) no duties except to bring up one's children & write one's books. There are moreover several books I feel bubbling inside me.

We drove here in a big Lea-Francis shooting brake which I own 50/50 with William. It took us 3 days to get to Forli beyond Bologna—over the little St Bernard Pass—nearly 900 miles from Dover. We stayed with an Italian family whose daughter is a fascinating intelligent friend of ours. The evening we arrived she took us for a long walk to avoid the home circle—lost her way & we found ourselves scrambling over newly ploughed fields on a slope of 1 in 10—fierce watchdogs barking at us as we approached buildings. Finally I took over leadership saying 'Where there is a farm on the mountain there is a path leading down to the road.' We had just found it when a stream of abuse came from the farm window 50 yards away & then crack! a rifle shot & the whine of a bullet within a few yards of us. The only time I have been fired at in time of peace. But in spite of some savagery, Italy is lovely country & its people are sweet & gentle.

Much love, dearest Tim. I look forward to your next book with excitement.   BUNNY

1957

After reading a review in *The Times Literary Supplement*, I cut it out and posted it to Tim with the words: 'By T. H. White' written on it.

May 13th, 1957   *3, Connaught Square, Alderney, C.I.*

Dearest Bunny, This smells of witchcraft. You ought to be a computer yourself and if so would knock Audrey & Seae into a cocked hat, when it came to detection. But I suspect that you may have known that a previous attack on poor old Julian Huxley in the T.L.S. was by me, and it also mentioned Archbishop Usher. As a matter of fact, I think I will try to mention the holy man every time I go for the biologists, as a sort of signature tune. Can you tell me any facts about him worth reference?

How are all your pigs and cows getting on? I have for the first time in my life gone genuinely mad on gardening—I mean mad enough to go down on my own knees and grub about among the weeds, instead of telling other people to do so. I have developed a reckless craving for geraniums, of which I have about forty varieties, and am up every morning even before the slugs go to bed, mooning about in the dew and paying house-surgeon visits to all the patients. I put these hormone powders on everything in sight and take slips at the wrong time of year. I suppose as a farmer you will have a proper contempt for us ornamentalists, but farmers dont know everything. It is all a matter of making things—pigs or geraniums, it comes to much the same.

Why dont you come over, either now or in the late autumn when your harvest is over, *and bring several of your wives and children?* I am almost full up in July and August, with deaf-and-blind, families of children etc. but the house is roomy the rest of the time and I have become a much better host than I used to be. I dont make plans for the guests.

H. E. Bates suddenly sent me his last book as a present out of the blue, much to my delight. I did not know he knew of my existence. He said you liked it.

Seriously, why dont you bring some young Garnetts here almost at once? May is often our best month—though terribly cold for bathing—and Alderney is a kid's paradise. You ought to begin struggling with aeroplane tickets this moment—they are hard to get. My actual bookings this year are:—

July 9th to 23rd
July 30th to end of August.

There are masses of things to do, as I have a sailing dinghy and a film camera as well as a snorkel and a trowel for the aged. If you came *now* you could go out and sleep some nights on the desert island of Burhou with several thousand puffins etc. It has a hut and a cooking stove. I couldnt come myself, because of Killie. Try.   love from TIM

May 15*th*, 1957   *Hilton Hall, Hilton, Huntingdon*
Dearest Tim, I thought I was right. No doubt Audrey can be trained to tell Bacon from Shakespeare but I used to be rather good at attributions— I once spotted Emerson though I had never read him, but just knew what he would be like.

The chessplaying at Manchester is the work of a very bright young friend of mine—Christopher Strachey. His father Oliver, invented the cipher decoding grid.

No I didn't know about any previous attack by you—or anyhow can't remember it.

I have abolished pigs—but my cows increase & about 2/3rds of them get Certificates of Merit which are hung up in the milking parlour. One has the O.M. but she isn't snobbish about it. My man Harry has been in hospital & then off work for about a month & I have had to do a lot of work rather against the grain—heaving milk churns onto the roadside table before 7.30 a.m. & sitting on the tractor in the afternoons.

I rather sympathise with your geranium madness. I grow vegetables & am a prey to new kinds—this year I am growing Pe Tsai and Vegetable Spaggheti as well as my usual Zucchini & Sweet Peppers. But the garden is in an awful mess.

I can't bring my family to see you as they attend school daily—the 2 elder at Huntingdon Grammar School & the 2 younger at the Primary school. On July 24 we cross the channel & the whole boiling of us drives to a village called Asolo, N.W. of Venice, where we spend a month. By the way did I inform you that I am a grandfather?—My grandson Oliver Grierson Garnett is just over a year old.

It is an awfully nice day: blackcaps singing in the orchard, horse chestnut in bloom, lilac not quite over, tulips out—as I drove back from taking the girls to school I saw sudden glimpses at the corner of a lane of England as unconsciously lovely as it was fifty years ago. Angelica & I went to Italy for 6 weeks last October–Nov. The cars whizz on the autostrada & they plough with yoked white bullocks slow & peaceful & then eat garlic & drink wine. They are a delightful people—though one of them shot at us in the Appenines. But the worlds of the Georgics & The Scientific American co-exist. I should love to visit you in September or October. H. E. Bates is a delightful man: a very old friend of mine.

Much love, BUNNY

1958

October 6th, 1958   3, *Connaught Square, Alderney, C.I.*

Dearest Bunny, Thank you very much indeed for William's new book.[1]
I enjoyed it a great deal and thought it somehow more mature than the
one before—if that is the right word. Anyway, it is oddly individual, not
any sort of imitation of anything I have read. I was in bed with a bilious
attack when it turned up, but enjoyed every story.

For the last six months and more I have been struggling to make a
16 m.m. colour film about Puffins—with sound—in the hopes of being
able to sell it to T.V. Do you or William know anything about marketing
these things? I dont want to start by offering it to Peter Scott, as I have
a vague idea that Independent T.V. pays better than the B.B.C. does. It
is a reasonably professional film taken from the tripod, not a jerky view
of Auntie Flo's backside, and I have not got the faintest idea of who to
offer it to or how to set about getting a fair price. Do you or William
know what the market price per hundred feet of sound film ought to be?

If this weather grows less stormy I shall probably be coming over to
England to go to a party at Jonathan Capes somewhere round about the
14th. It is in honour of some Chinese authoress, but I am really going
there to meet my American publisher. How nice it would be if you had
happened to be invited too!

I had a full house all these summer holidays, with enormous fun and
the excitement of children, so at present I am feeling rather flat. Unless its
the bile.

There is a vague theory on foot that I may be going with Michael
Howard (Capes) to learn to glide at Lasham. It scares me.

How is your own news?   love from TIM

October 15th, 1958   *Alderney*

Dearest Bunny, I was coming to England last Saturday and had just
begun to pack my traps on Friday about lunch time, with the tickets and
everything arranged, when I noticed that I was getting my stone-in-the-
kidney pain again. I had it about eight years ago. Its an unmistakable pain,

[* *Morals from the Beastly World* by William Garnett (Hart-Davis, 1958).—D.G.]

286

not stabbing or gnawing or even acute, but a massive, unvarying, leaden ache, which fills your whole body to the finger tips, so that after a bit you can't sit down or stand up or lie or be still or move or even think. I hoped perhaps it would pass over and rang up the doctor to see if he could give me morphia or something to tide me over the aeroplane trip, because I couldn't have sat still in an aeroplane and would have howled all the way like a wolf. But he insisted on whisking me off to our cottage hospital here, where I soon got the morphia and some atropine, and now all is well. I am just malingering now, as it is nice to be looked after and fussed over by kind women in a warm, clean, organised building. I could come out any time I wanted to, and probably will tomorrow or the day after. Anyway, it has totally bitched all the appointments I had booked for myself this week—one of which was to have a course of learning to glide at Lasham! (Looking out of the window here, I dont seem to have missed much gliding weather.) One of the other important things I had to do was to get the sound commentary onto my puffin film and for various reasons too boring to bother you with I now can't get that done till about the 1st November. I shall probably fly over round about then. I am at present waiting to hear from Michael Howard of Capes—who I was going to stay with—to know whether it will still be convenient for them to have me in November. Everything is in a total muddle. Why do people use the phrase 'people of that kidney'? I am a person of a very exasperated kidney at present.

I must stop as my only means of posting this is via the Night Nurse, who at this moment goes off duty. You must have had a terrific time in Italy.   Best love from TIM

October 18th, 1958   *Hilton Hall, Hilton, Huntingdon*
Dearest Tim, I am so very sorry to hear of your sudden illness. I do beg you to take care of yourself. I am very sorry we could not meet—& I hope that when you come to London we shan't miss each other.

I am going to Switzerland for a fortnight on Tuesday 21st & returning on 5th Nov. So if you can put off your visit till after that, I should be immensely pleased & flattered. About this gliding:

I have been greatly tempted myself to try it—& probably would have found it easy. But have you ever tried drawing things seen under the microscope? It is perfectly easy *once you get into it.* But it is the mirror

287

image of ordinary drawing. And watching gliding landings made me realise that the technique was a mirror image of aeroplane landings. i.e. coming down on the glide we aeroplane pilots flatten out & hold off & finally touch ground. But the glider depends on the wind. And the wind velocity—airspeed—drops very sharply as he approaches land. Therefore to maintain gliding speed he has to INCREASE the angle. Instead of holding off he stands the glider on its head & charges the earth. So instead of a beautifully balanced slow—hold off hold off, hold off, drop dead—the glider pilot has to steepen steepen, steepen & at the very *last minute* pull up hard & drop. A new technique. DONT try it on a violently windy day: still less on a day of dead calm.

I have a book coming out on the 27th but I haven't sent you a copy. The fact is it *does* touch on the relations of the sexes!—and as I know this is painful to you, I thought better not send it. I hope to write a book one day which will keep clear of physical love & perhaps that may win your approval. My Amaryllis daughter is 15 to-day. We gave her a gramophone & shall be either cheered or maddened by it in the years to come. My daughter Nerissa (11) wrote a poem about a cat.* Did I send it to you? I think it is magnificent. But alas you dont like cats—just as you disapprove of women! My dear Tim. I really love you & value you. So please be careful of yourself.　　　　　　　Yours ever BUNNY

---

* Puss
A sleeping shape lies on the bed
A cat morose, at peace, well-fed.
Oh Puss, you sleeping mass of fur,
Give me your voice, and let me purr.
　　　　　　　Nerissa Stephen Garnett
　　　　　　　(11 years old)

1960

February 7th, 1960   3, *Connaught Square, Alderney, C.I.*

Dearest Bunny, Thanks for your letter. It looks as if I may be following your footsteps to America next September, though in a less respectable way. If you read the popular press you will have heard that some people called Lerner & Loewe, who turned B. Shaw's Pygmalion into My Fair Lady and also did Colette's Gigi, are making a 'musical' and a film out of my Arthur books. B. Shaw's estate is said to have earned £250,000 out of My Fair Lady and I have exactly the same contract as he had! They have hired the biggest theatre in New York next autumn, signed up Julie Andrews as the leading lady, and are sold out for a year ahead. I may have to fly over for the first night. You will be surprised to learn that I do not regret this! As a matter of fact I am enjoying the whole thing tremendously and have spent the last six weeks flirting with Julie—who is a *honey*—and staying with her and her husband, also a honey, in Eaton Square and going to theatres or operas or ballets every night, appearing on T.V. (which I am a wizard at) and hob-nobbing with nobody below the rank of ballerina assoluta. I am a complete *professional* myself now— as we theatricals say—and I bet I had a better Xmas morning than you did. I spent it with Julie & her husband the impresario, opening the various tiaras, cadillacs etc. which we had put in each other's stockings. Half the theatrical world is coming to stay in Alderney next Easter & Summer, and I myself am being packed off to Zurich soon, to be made into a Swiss company! Luckily I am far too old to be spoiled by all this— it is merely my latest craze—and the valuable parts of my old life still adhere to me. I dont know whether I told you that about seven years ago a living Wart discovered in me a real Merlyn, just as if we had written The Sword in the Stone about ourselves. He is now a splendid figure nearly six feet high, and we are still devoted to each other, and I share my dazzling theatrical life with him, and Julie and co. are his gods & goddesses. He is madly in love with Julie's younger sister, aged 15. When I am next in England I will come to tell you all about it, but it is a racketty life and it is difficult to find fixed dates. I have to fit my own dates with those of other people who are earning big money through their appointment books. Lovely to hear from you. This is just an interim report.

love from TIM

February 8th, 1960   *Hilton Hall, Hilton, Huntingdon*

Dearest Tim, I was delighted by your letter and by your news. I am very glad that you are not alone. With advancing age one needs someone to care for, and what would Merlyn be without a pupil?

I am also delighted that you should turn into a company & become a rich man. It will suit you just as well as being penniless: probably make very little difference except to those who sponge on you—among whom I hastily subscribe myself—not as a permanency—but as an irregular lapper up of champagne, drunk to Your Honour's health.

Talking of champagne—I am giving a party on Midsummer Night—or possibly the night after—24th Friday or 25th Saturday of June. I shall have Professor Harry Moore* and his wife staying here. Will you come & bring the Wart—or perhaps I should call him Arthur as he is now grown up. If you can come I will ask my oldest friend Harold Hobson (NOT the theatrical critic but the engineer) to put you up. He lives in the village about 250 yards away. I do hope you'll come & if you can bring some of your most lovely theatrical beauties, I will get some actors & actresses also. Actually Prof. Moore started life by being a ham actor which is why he is such a good English lecturer—able to roll his eyes finely at his students. Also I am fairly strong now in the aristocracy & can guarantee at least a Viscountess with a ravishingly lovely daughter of about 20. I expect strawberries in Alderney will be over by then—but you will find masses here.

Then another attraction for you is that you will be the lion of the occasion —a great maned & bearded lion. I shall invite E. M. Forster, but there's no possibility of his coming—he's 81—so you will be in solitary glory.

Please come. My twin daughters are real charmers—Fan is building a canoe which will soon be finished. Nerissa occasionally says or writes good things. I told her the Tomcat had fleas. She replied that she knew it & had been bitten. I said: 'You shouldnt fondle him so much.' 'Fondling is worth a flea,' she replied. This place is far more civilised & improved since you last saw it, which was just after the war. We have actually laid paving stones in the sort of sunk bit outside the door into the garden, and I am making a bower under the mulberry.

By the way, put me & my family down for free seats when the Once & Future King opens in London. Regards to Arthur.

Very much love BUNNY

* Of Southern Illinois University.

290

P.S. I am full of essential information about New York & can give you an introduction to Leo Lerman who writes the theatre programmes & is the most useful man in the city & to Henry Poor who leads an Un-American way of life in a house he built himself of stone in the woods at Haverstraw. I mean built with his own hands.

February 12th, 1960   *Alderney*

Dearest Bunny, I will try very hard to come to your party on Mid-summer Night, but there are certain practical snags which I shall have to fit in with. For the last 5 years or so I have been meddling with deaf-and-blind people. There are four of them, with their guides. Every summer I pay their fares over by air and entertain them for a week each. (It is exhausting. You have to become their eyes & ears, and talking on fingers all day is much more tiring than talking through your mouth.) They generally come in June and July, with intervals of a week between them so that I can recuperate. It is practically the main feature of their year, so I couldn't possibly let them down. On top of this, I have an arrangement to make a film of Julie Andrews & Svetlana the prima ballerina *when their engagements permit them to come over*. At present we are not sure when this will be. So you see I can't promise to come for certain. Also I couldnt bring the Wart, who would instantly lie down and kiss the feet of *all* your daughters, because unfortunately he will be at school.

The deaf-and-blind. I have just had a letter today, at the same time as yours, to say that my most enchanting one has been knocked down by a lorry & is recovering in hospital. I shall have to spend the rest of the afternoon writing to her in Braille, which I write very slowly, but she will be in total silence & darkness with (probably) nobody in the hospital able to read a longhand letter to her on her fingers. She is about 60 years old, quite penniless, and a *lioness*. Her nickname is Puck, and she knows all about you, having read your autobiography and listened to endless stories about you from me. She is the most dauntless spinster I have ever met. Do you know, I have actually *taught her to swim*. How would you like to face the waves which you can't see or hear and conquer them? If anybody offered her a parachute jump, she would accept it at once. We adore each other. The others give me the warmest love too, but she is my secret favourite. She is very intelligent, but has not heard her own voice for 50 years, with the result that she bleats and is consequently treated as an idiot. I won her heart the very first day we met by simply handing her a cigarette and a match box, and NOT offering to light it for her. She has made friends with my very ancient friend Sir Sydney Cockerell and also with a protegée of his called Lady Cholmondely, who send her magnificent presents which she instantly gives to somebody else. She lives on about £4 a week. If you would care to write her a brief encouraging note, *perhaps* there would be somebody at the hospital to read it to her and it would be a blessing in her loneliness and I know she would value it very much. She can't quite make you out—the confessions of your amours are a bit frightening for an old, blind, Edwardian virgin—but she loyally accepts you as a friend of mine, and of course, when you are in the black silence, any message from outside is a boon. Why not tap out a short message on the wall of her cell?

Thank you for all your news. The party sounds very exciting. If I can fit it in with the deaf/blind visits, I will try to come & bring Julie and her husband & perhaps Svetlana and hers. Might be possible between the d/b.

Now I must stop and set about that bloody braille. It is an exasperating script.   Best love from TIM

Just remembered that Puck can actually read ordinary longhand scribbled on the palm of her hand—so, if you did send a note, the hospital could communicate it to her. She has a fractured skull. Have sent her a telegram & flowers by INTERFLORA, which at least she can smell.

June 1st, 1960   *Alderney, Channel Isles*

My very dearest Bunny, Truly I will try to get to your midsummer party, but may I leave it up in the air for the time being? I am frightfully busy with a series of little local chores from which it is difficult to get disentangled. For instance, Puck is not my only deaf/blind dependent—I have two others, whose visits here I must fit in before my Wart and his family come for their summer holidays. 'Jersey Airlines' have become the most inefficient line in the universe, bar none, and you have to wangle for tickets months ahead, being told that there are no seats and then seeing the aeroplanes arrive empty. On top of this, my present red setter bitch, whose name is Jennie (Guinever), has just presented me with 10 grandchildren who can't even see yet. If they were movable before Midsummer and IF I could get a coinciding ticket and IF the deaf/blind friends—who never come for less than a week—can be fitted at different dates, I will be there. But it needs such a lot of shuffling. Surely puppies can't be moved under six weeks?

Julie Andrews and her delightful husband were here last month and return here on Monday. They are both absolute darlings. I approached them about coming to your party, but they seemed vague. Dont forget, they have hardly been married a year, are still starry-eyed with each other, are young and impolite, and are daily and ten times daily being bidden to parties & functions when they long to be with each other. (They like staying here because I have learnt to invite no guests & bring them breakfast in bed!) Svetlana Beriosova is dancing abroad at the moment—I think it is S. Africa, but she buzzes round the world very fast.

You gave such pleasure by writing to Puck. How did he find out how to get it done in braille, she asked me in a flutter! It was a brilliant piece of consideration. I really do feel I have done a little to lighten her darkness —through me, she is in constant correspondence with Sydney Cockerell, Lady Cholmondley, David Garnett (constant?) and Julie Andrews! Julie actually drove me all the way down to Eastbourne to see her after her accident, and did NOT arrange to be met by press photographers as Lady Bountiful! They fell into each others arms. I feel proud and happy and surprised to have, though few, such *good* friends—I mean good like bread. The result of Puck's accident is that now she can't smell or taste either, and is growing a bit forgetful. For the first time in her life, she has begun to tell me the same story twice. I am hoping and believing it is only the result of the concussion and that it will wear off in time, but she is no longer young. I generally have her here in summer, but this year we will wait till the autumn, to give her brains more time to heal. If I thought you would swear by the holy ghost to return it, I would lend you a photograph album with pictures of her and my life here.

An acquaintance of yours called Thomas Cranfill has asked me to write for the Texas Journal at practically no remuneration. Must I? I have 3 or 4 poems I want to publish, but I thought of the Times Lit. I am supposed to be persona grata there (T.L.S.) but as usual have forgotten the name of the editor with whom I usually correspond. Is it *Alistair Crooke*? *Do* answer! Or shall I send them to the New Yorker, where I am also persona grata—they keep asking me for things. Again, I have forgotten the editor's name! Chiz, chiz, chiz, as Molesworth mi. says. PLEASE tell me the name of the editor of New Yorker, write to me saying you understand about the midsummer party, give me your news and forgive my inefficiency. I thought they were rather good poems. Shall I send them to you with the album? best love from TIM

P.S. Tony Walton, which is the name of Julie's husband, read your Aspects of Love and the cross letter you wrote to me about it. He agrees with you, not me.

1961

November 17th, 1961   *at/ Nethercliffe*
                                                    10 *Ashley Road*
                                           Walton-on-Thames, Surrey

Dearest Bunny, Your letter has been following me around on my travels
and only caught up with me today. I have some mysterious disease of my
right leg which nobody seems to know much about. At one time it was
rumoured to be what George 6 died of. It has also been terminal arthritis,
and is at present being called intermittent claudication. Anyway, I am
staying with the family of an enchanting physiotherapist (who is Julie
Andrews' father-in-law) for a second dose of massage etc. I will be here
till December 3rd. Naturally I have to fit in with the arrangements of my
hosts, but if they have not arranged something else I could probably
meet you for lunch or dinner in London any day between now and then.
I have oceans of things to tell you about. I will try to ring you on Monday
evening, when you have had time to digest this.

I *must* go back to Alderney on Dec 3rd—when you could fly there if
you wanted to, as I shall be alone till about the 18th.

Then I have to go for Xmas to some charming first-cousins I have
discovered in Derbyshire.

From Jan 1st to Jan 6th I am taking two of their sons to London
theatres, already booked.

Do lets try to fit something in.

I have to go to America later, to stay with my beloved Julie.

love from TIM

December 14th, 1961   3, *Connaught Square, Alderney, C.I.*

Dearest Bunny, The specialist said that I ought to have an operation on
my back because there was a bottle-neck or blockage in one of the
arteries, which prevented the blood from reaching my leg. It is more or
less the same thing that George the Sixth had, so at least its royal! I am
going to have my Christmas holiday first, stay with my cousins in Derbyshire and take their two boys to London for a round of theatres. Then I
shall probably go into St. Thomas' hospital as a public patient on National

Health, as I see no point in paying £100 a week for a nursing home and may as well get something free for all the taxes I have paid. One in a hundred are said to die of this operation, so its about the same gamble as the outsider in a steeplechase.

I dont know when I shall be able to fit in a visit to you, owing to this nuisance. Its rather a new sort of operation, not very established yet, which is a bore. I rather regret being chopped up by surgeons who are still a bit experimental. They always remind me of little boys with a new bicycle, who want to take the wheel off to count the ball bearings and generally lose a few when it comes to putting them back.

I am being approached by the leading lecture agent in America, who wants to send me on a three month tour. (Oh, hang, I told you this before. I am getting gaga.) I thought I would lecture on the *poets of my youth* (Rupert Brooke, J. E. Flecker etc. any information or tips about from you thankfully received) also *Shakespeare as a Ham, Luck in Literature* (i.e. my own pure luck, like winning the pools, when Sylvia Warner and The Midnight Folk and The Box of Delights are practically unknown, and Hopkins had to die before publication) and *Writers Must Live First*, which is, e.g., about how I go down in a diving suit with Commander Crabbe before saying that knights in armour are like Deep-sea divers.

Do tell me a lot about Georgian poets, and suggest some or many.

Best love from TIM

1962

Dearest Bunny, Thank you for your generous and reviving letter. It has cheered me up a great deal.

I spent some time rushing round other specialists last month and they now want me to go into St. Thomas's hospital, at least for an arteriogram, which will be followed if necessary by what they call lumbar sympathectomy. They ask me to go in the second or third week of this month. Unfortunately, if I spend more than 3 months per annum in England I get liable to English Income Tax, and I have spent more than two. It is a one-month-in-bed operation. At present I am trying to find out from the authorities in Guernsey whether I am allowed extra time in Britain if it is on medical grounds.

I have made a new will and all that lark, depositing £20,000 for the bank to gamble with on the stock exchange in my absence, if I go.

Until things are settled I am indulging myself in my favourite vice—painting. It is a self-portrait at the moment, and it ebbs and flows. As soon as it is more or less right I get excited and overdo it and have to start again.

Forgive me for not writing a proper letter. I think I feel upset or something. It is hateful to be cut up, however unhappy one's life may be.

Best love from TIM

May 11th, 1962   3, *Connaught Square, Alderney, C.I.*
Dearest Bunny, I go into St. Thomas's Hospital on the 20th, but they may decide not to operate. My cousins took me to Chatsworth a week ago and I walked all over the house and gardens, only packing up towards the end. Dont trouble to visit me unless you happen to be in London anyway, but certainly I would value a letter or two.

My latest news is a bit insane. I had bought by telephone an ex-naval destroyer's launch from the Belsize Boatyard in Southampton, but when I went to see her I found in the same yard the lifeboat of Lady Docker's yacht Shamara. The only reason why she was on the market was that Lady D. had sold Shamara and given the lifeboat to the captain, who preferred the money. I couldn't resist her. She is fully up to the standard of the gold-studded Daimler—solid mahogany, all varnish, no paint, caravel built, 26 ft long, 8 ft beam, 20 ft mast with new sail, nylon bottom, and I am putting in 2 diesel engines. I hope to sail her across here round about July the 1st. She is unsinkable, with built in buoyancy tanks and so massive that she will stand the two engines. She is an open boat, but I am having a dodger. It will be something to survive the operation for.

At present I am fearfully busy winding up my affairs with builders, bills, boatyards etc. so forgive me for not writing a longer letter.

I have bought about £100 worth of plaster statues, busts etc. from the B. Museum, with which to beautify the garden!

A regular Heliogabalus.   Best love from TIM

On May 22nd, 1962, Tim rang me up at Hilton Hall in the evening and told me that he had just come to from the anaesthetic after an operation on his heart at St Thomas's Hospital where he was in a private room, and that he was longing to see me. I told him that I would visit him at 2.30 on the twenty-fourth. At the end of our talk Tim's voice got blurred and faded away.

I found Tim alone in his room in the hospital at the appointed time and he stared at me with astonishment. 'How on earth could you possibly know that I was here?' he asked me. He had entirely forgotten ringing me up just after coming to, and though I told him what he had said and what we had arranged, he still could remember nothing about it.

May 25th, 1962   *3, Connaught Square, Alderney, C.I.*

Dearest Bunny, It was wonderfully kind of you to come all that way to see me and it cheered me up a great deal. The professor is quite happy about letting me enjoy the summer months and has booked me in again on September the 30th. I leave here tomorrow for 'Nethercliffe, 10 Ashley Road, Walton-on-Thames' where I am to have a week of physiotherapy. The professor says there is no immediate hurry about the operation and that in any case it will be slightly less dangerous than the X-ray was! He now confesses that when the enormous great syringe thing was withdrawn from the aorta, the hole at the point had to be self-sealing like an aeroplane tank, and if it hadn't been there was nothing to do about it! I have seen the X-rays in which the weapon looks prodigious, and I dont wonder I was under for four hours.

Anyway, this means I shall be in Alderney for your visit on Friday July the 20th. The only thing that might prevent or interfere with this, is if the boatyard doesn't deliver Lady Docker's boat on July 1st as promised. I will write again before then.

During the week's physiotherapy I am also going to try to learn to hypnotise myself! At a doctor's in Wilton Crescent.

love to all from TIM

On June 22nd, 1962, I flew to Alderney and stayed with Tim at 3 Connaught Square until Monday 25th when I returned to Hilton. During my visit I met Tony Walton and his wife Julie Andrews with whom I lunched on Saturday and Sunday, and who came to dinner with Tim on each of those days. Dr Stephen Black and his family were fellow guests at Connaught Square.

I had an intimate talk alone with Tim on Sunday: a talk which arose from my letter of January 10th, 1956, about our views on women and sexual morals. This had been in his mind, I believe, for several years. I discuss this in my preface.

But the question remains: Had he realized that he was a sadist at an earlier period—when for example we were at Sheskin? Or had he only become aware of the sadistic streak in his nature in later years?

He was a warm and considerate host and obviously devoted to Julie and Tony. But I was shocked at his physical condition. It was warm weather and when he stripped to the waist, Tim was the image of Falstaff. And to sustain the part we banqueted royally and caroused into the night while Tim called for song after song from *Camelot* and Julie good-naturedly obliged, though she would have rather been talking or listening to our conversation.

June 29th, 1962   3, *Connaught Square, Alderney, C.I.*

Dearest Bunny, Your book[1] arrived after breakfast this morning and I have sent the Blacks away in the car with themselves so that I can read it. Now, although I have hardly got beyond the arrival at San Freddy, I feel it is irresistable to stop and tell you at once that it is going to be a *very* good book. Certainly I will lend it to Julie & Tony when I have

[1 *A Shot in the Dark.*—D.G.]

finished, but its only fair to let me have first go. In fact, I wish I hadnt stopped now, to write this letter.

The elder Black baby has got some spots, so in case it may be a virus disease we have banished the pregnant Julie. The Blacks go tomorrow, when I will resume relations.

Sir Ambrose took Black and me round the island in his boat two days ago, and Nicky Allen took Black and Jackie round yesterday. They are enjoying themselves and are happy and I have learned to hypnotise myself to sleep—a great blessing.

David Hammond has managed to hit eight clay pigeons in a row.

I think I am very lucky to have such friends as I have, but now dearest Bunny kindly sit down and shut up as I am *busy*. I have a *book* I want to get on with reading.   love from TIM

I hope you will come here again soon. You are much younger and more vigorous than I am.

July 26th, 1962   3, *Connaught Square, Alderney, C.I.*

Dearest Bunny, Before I get involved with my next lot of guests I must just find time to write you a brief note of congratulation about your book. It is very craftily constructed and began in an imperceptible sort of way to draw me into its strange triangle until I was deeply concerned for the welfare of everybody—even the villain and villainess if they can so be described. This time I have no criticism to make, dont want to smack *any* of the characters, and I was really amazed and convinced and overwhelmed by the hero's decency and rightness in meeting the lesbian in the heroine's bed without reproaches or ignobility. He is very obviously you—though you will probably deny or be ignorant of the fact. It seems to me a *satisfying* book, and in some ways rather a twin to No Love.

At present the Waltons have got it, but only Julie has read it so far, as Tony has been working. She agrees with me about the way it gathers momentum.

I have had a minor row with Tony, who can be exasperating when he feels like it, and, being wildly busy with my own concerns, have not seen them for about a week.

We collected Lady Docker's boat from Southampton and had a re-markable passage. We found the Cherbourg light, also the terrifying one at Cap La Hogue which invites you to the death trap of the Race, but

Alderney and the Casquets were lost in local fog. So we had to motor due north again, with fuel running out, and hang about in the hope of the fog lifting. We had left S'hampton at 9.10 a.m. and did not make Alderney —fog rising suddenly over the great full moon cross swell which had drowned six people in Jersey that day—until 2.45 a.m., by which time the Inner Harbour was too dry for entry. So we slept on thwarts or bulwarks until dawn and did not reach our own beds till almost 24 hours after we left England. We feel she has earned her red ensign.

Eleven people are coming to stay four days hence and the builders have not even started the plumbing of the new bedroom. It is for three boys to sleep in, in bunks, unless they prefer my tent or hammocks in the Temple.

I have bought me three lobster pots for household use and been once to Cherbourg already.

Every fisherman in Alderney says, apparently with sincerity, that Popsie 2 is the most splendid boat that has ever lived in the Inner Harbour. She has not got one inch of paint on her (even underwater it is a nylon sheeth which cost Lady D. £430) nor one inch of metal which is not brass or copper. Harry and I, who have risked our lives in her, worship every flash of her varnish. Incidentally, she sails like a dream.

Love from TIM

September 24th, 1962   *Alderney*

Dearest Bunny, You sound as if you had a marvellous time in France. I didn't know you had been there and Julie and Tony didn't tell me, after having lunch with you.

The calamity to my house-painting has proved to be a blessing. Stuck with this ghastly terra cotta colour, it suddenly dawned on me that Tony had just done some remarkable stage sets for the American musical called 'A Funny Thing Happened on the Way to the Forum', so I decided to take the whole thing as a sort of theatrical joke and handed over the direction of operations to him. The result is the admiration and talk of all Alderney. We have blue surrounds to half the windows, yellow ones to the others, an ice blue wall between mansion and cottage, three different coloured doors ranging from a rich plum to orange, white pillars and pediments and, believe it or not, a certain amount of gold leaf on door knockers and other architectural ornaments! The remarkable

301

result is smart and elegant in a Pompeian sort of way and hardly anybody disapproves of it. I am thinking of having a gilded bust of Hadrian over the back door and CAVE CANEM on the mat. Incidentally, they have finished the triumphal arch in the garden, which will have an inscription DIVA IVLIA. Only half the statues have arrived from the British Museum. If you should happen to be calling there, I do wish you could find time to give them a cursing. It helps to do it personally. Especially from somebody of your lineage.

I have spent a lot of the summer making darts to France in my new boat, often quite exciting in bad weather, lighthouses lost etc. She is coming out of the water for the winter next week, bless her stout heart. I have hitherto wasted my life in Normandy by not realising that the only thing to drink there is home-made cider and home made calvados. We had one of the great meals of my life at Omonville—*everything* home made or home grown or home caught, from the lobster through the chicken to the cheese. Even the bread and butter and salad and peaches and of course the cider and calvados. It was out of doors at a one-roomed estaminet on a sunny day with my boat on the sparkling harbour in front of us and not a single shop in the village. The local maidens were diving from the high jetty. I find that French girls swim if possible better than French boys.

Thank you for the kindness in your letter, it has made my day for me.

I am thinking of taking a brief sea trip to India, instead of having that operation. If I favour my leg it doesn't seem to get any worse and there are so many contrary medical opinions.

Julie & Tony, who have now gone back to England to have the baby, gave me a lot of news of you. Best love from TIM

These amateur photographs were taken by Tony.

October 12th, 1962, etc. *Alderney*

Dearest Bunny, I fancy this is not going to be a post card.

First of all, may I say how delighted I was with the Familiar Faces[1] and that I started it again as soon as I had finished it, then going on to The Golden Echo and am now madly searching for the second volume, which my char has tidied away somewhere. There is a menacing sentence at the bottom of p. 167 (F.F) in which you hint that the fourth volume

[1 The third volume of my autobiography.—D.G.]

may never be completed. This would be UNPARDONABLE. Just as I have nothing to live for, you have nothing to die for, and in the same proportions. I *refuse* to do without the fourth volume.

Now some detailed remarks.

On *page 112*, top paragraph, your description of Lawrence's personal ethic[1] is an exact description of mine. People who are not hoodwinked by the sexual attraction of women do find it difficult to forgive their ulterior motives, their mendacity and their utter selfishness. On the rare occasions when you are not sexually attracted by a woman (e.g. Dorothy on p. 92) you yourself perceive (p. 90) that an aeroplane flight might just as well be an underground journey—their impressions are 'entirely internal and subjective'.

This is not a criticism of you, it is a confession about Lawrence and me. We are both about 12 years of age and when we go out with our catapults it is birds we are after, for their own sake. 'He approved of all first-hand people who did things for their own sake.'

No need to labour this, or I shall make you cross, but I can't help just one more sentence. (or two!) For me (and for Lawrence) people can't do one thing for the purpose of another. You can't marry for money, talk for victory, paint for fame, be a poet to shew off. You must marry for marriage, talk for the truth, paint for the painting, be a poet for the poem itself. This is incidentally why I have always loathed Edith Sitwell. She tried to be a poet to make up for being ugly, not for the sake of being a poet. I loathe her ethically. As a person I should probably pity and like her.

Let's take the book in due order.

page 2. I have always read the Blake poem myself in the sense that it was the lady who lay as still as a maid for the angel.

page 5. Your guess at the Scotties of Theodore Powys is not the most amazing of your pieces of insight. You always do take my breath away, but I have never been so astonished as when I wrote an unsigned article for the T.L.S., and you, without even knowing that I ever wrote for that paper, instantly wrote to accuse me of it!

page 7. Thirty years ago, Ian Parsons told me a wonderful story about you and Sylvia Warner.

[1] T. E. Lawrence, not D. H.—D.G.]

303

Bunny reads latest passage from No Love, on which he is then engaged, and ends with the Admiral entering the hall with his umbrella.

Bunny: 'Then he puts his umbrella into something or other, I dont know what ...'

S.T.W.: 'I know! I know exactly! He puts it into one of those drain pipes with ...'

Bunny (enraged): 'Certainly not! He puts it in an *elephant's foot*!'

page 27. I did not realise that Lady into Fox was 'a reductio ad absurdum of the problem of fidelity in love', so I now withdraw my long standing objection to that book. However (dont be cross) Lawrence and I still believe in fidelity, just as many animals like ravens do, who mate for life. It is a romantic, useless and painful belief.

page 31. The poem at the bottom of the page is also an exact description of me, or it has been for two years now.

page 32. Is *Jack Robinson* still in print? I never heard of it.

facing p. 32. What the hell are you doing in the window and why can I find nothing about La Bergère in the book?

page 35. How *did* Gerald Brenan solve the problem of rent for two flats, or is it too secret to tell me?

page 41. This connects up also with p. 105, on which you either insanely or maliciously claim to be 'ignorant'! Now it is a fact that for the last quarter century you have been the only man I knew who *always* knew more about *everything* than I did. (I can remember a tomb at Trim where you read the Talbot blazon ... However.) The present example is as follows. Two weeks ago I was asked to write the preface to a volume of Fairy Stories and in them I came across the Cauld Lad of Hilton. My immediate reaction was to write and tell you about it. My second thoughts were, Well, Bunny always knows everything before I do, so why bother him? How right I was.

page 51. And how right you are about King Lear. I have been feeling like him for two years, having lost my Cordelia, and it is much too deep a feeling for screams. He never (the actor never) should raise his voice at all. Oh, let me not be mad, not mad, sweet heaven, is a plain matter of fact remark like, I hope the Joneses wont come to tea on friday.

page 53. I am very interested to wonder why you, a precise joiner of words, used the adjective 'obscene' for totality of eclipse. I know it was the right word, but can you explain why?

page 59. I spent many hours trying to teach arithmetic to one of the Appleton boys, so that he could pass an examination to become a policeman. Do you know if he ever passed?

page 63. Nothing maddens me more than niggling criticism, but if your fourth volume also contains pages of errata, do put a comma after 'grouse' in line one? For a few seconds I paused amazed, picturing the grouse and fireworks whizzing about the sky. I am sure only Lord Berners would have been eccentric enough to discharge such a feu de joie.

page 76. Your compliance with Moore's criticism. Do you remember that I rewrote almost half of Mistress Masham's Repose because you told me to? I am sure I am much fonder of you and admire you much more than you ever admired him.

page 81. I dont agree with you about Go She Must. It is a satisfactory book.

page 101. Also I dont agree with you about The Purple Plain. I think it is magnificent and obscurely owes something to The Grasshoppers Come. Both are tales of endurance.

page 105. Any other editor but you (or perhaps I?) would have suppressed Lawrence's ill-natured reference which you quote again in full on this page i.e. would have suppressed it in the edition of the letters, would have left that letter out. All it means is that you were better educated and a better craftsman than he was, and this is true. Anyway, it has always constituted one of my better anecdotes about you—to illustrate your adamant integrity.

page 112. If Lawrence was a homosexual as people say, surely he was under the strain of 'living among an alien people' wherever he was? In fact, probably they were less alien among Arabs and in barracks?

page 151. I *long* to read The Lobster Quadrille by Tomlin, which I have never heard of. Can you tell me where I can get it from?

page 153. Financial help from Keynes. The only people who have tried to give me money when I was on my uppers were you and my old tutor

305

L. J. Potts of Queens'. At least, I *suspect* it came from Potts. He would never admit it. It came anonymously. When he died, I repaid £400 to his widow in case my guess was right.

page 156. Unconscious control of legs. I was flying one evening, after watching a man fly in the afternoon at the Hendon air display. I was Tommy Rose's best pupil, had won a prize from the Daily Express, and my first solo had been under six hours, but I *could* not land the aeroplane. I felt no fear whatever, but had to go round and round and round and round, attempting impossible landings about 20 ft up. There was a little man inside me like this

who *would not* let me land. I swear he actually wrestled with me for the stick! I felt nothing but *exasperation.* Eventually I positively dragged it out of his hands and did land 20 ft. up, with the highest bounce ever known at Sywell. I repeat that I did not at any time feel any conscious fear at all.

page 158. Yes, when you come to think of it, Constance did more for English literature than the whole of the rest of your family put together. Only, somebody was bound to translate the Russians sooner or later, but nobody was bound to write the Twilight of the Gods, discover D. H. Lawrence or write Pocohontas etc.

page 167. What was 'Mr. Mumford's'?

page 173. William's description was coldly logical. He was the *little* piggy wig and Richard, as his elder brother, was the pig's better. It shews full understanding of the rhyme.

page 189. Yes, but *when* had Ray been staying with your boys at Vanessa Bell's little house, La Bergère, at Cassis?

page 200. Another niggling criticism for your future list of errata. By a slip of the pen you have got the falcon on my wrong hand. As you know, all right handed people carry their hawks on the left hand and the slip is like making somebody mount a horse from the wrong side.

page 214. I was in a difficult position about Ray's 'fit'. I knew and had been told to tell the boys that she had cancer. She had her dreadful attack in front of them. The doctor was one of those drunk Irish ones in the remotest country practice.

page 218. Ray was one of the *best* women I have ever met.

page 219. I *refuse* to cancel out 'Karl and I fear that Egon is pleasure loving.'

hark back to page 196. Strange how selective the memories of different people are. 'Just as I grassed the 14 pounder' etc. This was one of the actual days on which you altered the whole course of my life. Ten minutes later we put the fish in the car, which stood on the road between Doolistown and the local Chapel of Ease, and got in the car, and began eating our sandwiches. I was in the front seat, Ray was in the back. At the time, I was trying to be a rigidly logical dogmatic Christian—which, like being a Roman Catholic, is the only possible kind to be, if you have got to be one at all. I was holding forth about death and damnation and immortal souls (it was before I knew that Ray had cancer) and laying down the law about people's free choice between going to heaven or hell and saying you had to take the consequences of your actions and all that tragic rigmarole. Very quietly, you said, 'I think (pause) the enormous facts of birth and death (pause) are so *tremendous* (long pause) that all these fairy stories or fables about them are (struggle for the right words) are (long struggle) that they *degrade* them.'

I am now an agnostic.   your loving TIM

October 16th, 1962   *Hilton Hall, Huntingdon*

Dearest Tim, Thank you a thousand times for the most wonderful letter I have ever received. It would have been well worth writing *Familiar Faces* even if you had been the only reader.

I will deal with some of your points *seriatim* ...

p. 32. Jack Robinson by George Beaton (a pseudonym) was published by Chatto. They may have a few copies left. Do read it.

p. 32. La Bergère was a cottage on Col. Teed's wine-growing farm at Cassis. Vanessa paid for its rebuilding & had a lease of it until the 2nd war 1939. She lent it to Ray & me & Ray took a photograph of me climbing into the window naked.

I can't remember why I was naked.

p. 35. Gerald said he would settle the rent of the 2nd flat for her & appropriated the money once a month. She never had to worry about it again.

She used to go out for a walk take a taxi & drive to her 'other' flat which was the one & only one. She persisted that there were two.

p. 51. Total Eclipse. *obscene*. It is the only word which describes my feeling of horror & repulsion. It was a reversal of the natural and also a threat.

p. 59. Tommy Appleton became a policeman in, I think, Bishop Auckland. After the failure of his parents' health, they went & lived near him. Hollin House stands empty.

p. 63. Will attend to it (a comma).

p. 112. But T. E. Lawrence wasn't homosexual. I know that for a fact as I have read a correspondence which I could not publish between him & a friend who was a homosexual. Lawrence may even have wished he were one. He was a masochist, in the strict sense of the word.

p. 151. I enclose The Sluggard's Quadrille. Did I give it the wrong title? Send it back to me. I have written a lot of notes, identifying the quotations of as many as I could. I should be awfully grateful if you could help me identify those I have missed. I want to publish Tommy's few poems before I die. But Leonard Woolf wont do it in The Hogarth Press & I dont know who will do it.

p. 167. I discovered when the book was in proof that I had left out a whole chunk about H. G. Wells—I had also lost it. Now I have found it & if I ever write a 4th volume I will put him in that. H.G. lived in Hanover Terrace Regents' Park. His house had a garden & at the back a little mews house which he had furnished. He told me & Siegfried Sassoon that we could stay in it whenever we wanted a bed in London. There was no sort of obligation even to see H.G. though I usually had tea with him or drinks after dinner. I was very fond of him & I cheered him up when he was feeling depressed. This mews house H.G. called 'Mr Mumford's,' after some imaginary figure.

p. 189. I think about 1929, Ray stayed at La Bergère. I joined her there later.

Well thank you very much dear Tim. Please let me know if & when you go to India. Also tell me Tony Walton's address in England.

I am much more excited about writing than I have been for some years. This last book of mine about my twin daughters is something new & I shall be fascinated to hear what you feel about it. At present only Angelica & Amaryllis & the twins have read it. I'm waiting to hear what Peter Watt & Richard think of it. I'll send it you as soon as I've a proof or something—   Your loving BUNNY

The imagery of The Sluggard's Quadrille is all taken from Alice in Wonderland. "'Tis the voice of the Sluggard, I heard him declare ...' etc. You must refer to that. But I think no one, not even City of Dreadful Night Thompson has expressed such depression & horror.

November 5th, 1962   *3, Connaught Square, Alderney, C.I.*

Dearest Bunny, This is only a scribble to return The Sluggard's Quadrille, to tell you that Julie's address is 70 Eaton Square and to wonder where I misquoted Peacock?

I agree that the Quadrille is good—its the right poem for people of my age! Does life get better after sixty?

On thursday I am off to Italy—God knows why. I am to fly to Milan, thence to Pisa next day, after which I struggle on by road or rail to Florence. There are two people there I slightly want to visit—Sir John Verney, a descendant of Florence Nightingale's suitor, who is a really enchanting person and author of one of the best war books called Going to the Wars, and the ex-President of Harvard called Professor Murdock, now occupying Berenstein's Villa I Tatti.[1]

After that I may wander off to Venice or Rome or come back to Paris and do some theatres. Travelling alone is not much fun, but Harry Griffiths seems to think a change would do me good.

I have just refused to have that second operation.   love from TIM

November 14th, 1962   [*Firenze*]

So far as I can see I am having a wonderful time here and getting over the sorrows of middle age. My hosts the Verneys are enchanters and you

[1 Bernard Berenson left his villa and library to Harvard University.—D.G.]

must read his book called Going to the Wars. I think I will go on to Venice and Naples and perhaps do a Byron and never come back any more.   love from TIM

December 1962   *Pensione Bandini, Piazza Santo Spirito 9, Firenze*
Dearest Bunny, I seem to have got stuck here and this evening had a most interesting dinner with about seven present, one of whom was again Harold Acton. He greeted me with warmth, saying, 'I have just been reading about you and your whiskers in David Garnett's book.' I said, 'Have you read the other two?' He said, 'Yes'. Whereupon we fell into a great discussion of all mutual friends ...

I have had plenty of other people to meet since I came here, quite apart from my adored Sir John Verney, who has had (I think) 8 children. One of them (not the children) was the Countess of Onslow and by the grace of God I happened not to mention to her various names. Reginald Ross Williamson and his wife have also been here, as also is *Wilfrid* Thesiger. The latter is a sort of mad, piratical, resentful version of the great actor. He was practically beaten to death at his various schools and consequently has to be an explorer and superman, but is a dear, scared fellow at heart, who looks like an 18th century highwayman who has just broken his nose three times and been hanged. (Beggar's Opera.) (Or Pistol, Nym or Bardolph.)

In this very pensione here there is an old, plump, tired spinster who always has the best chair after meals in the sitting room. There she sits, holding a magnifying glass to her tired eyes and examining the local paper or some Penguin or Tauchnitz. Gradually she nods off to sleep in the mild Tuscan afternoon sunlight which streams in through the window (which she is depriving me of, at opposite side of room) and then her dear old snoozing face takes on all the gentleness and magnanimity of the dead. I enquired about her. Lo and behold, I was dead right. This ancient, serene, having-suffered, old profile was that of an *ex-mistress of Gordon Craig*! She has had one illegitimate son by him ... Her bedroom is next to mine and I often hear the typewriter, no doubt writing to him. (Also she snores.) Nobody ever speaks to her, except to say Buon Giorno. You know: the pensione thing for English spinsters.

Needless to say, dear Bunny, I am laying on a party for her next week in a private room (private because Acton is in mourning) in which she will get homage from Thesiger, Verney, Acton, English Consul & me, with wives if any. She doesn't know this yet, and may well refuse. I dont think she is a condescendable-to sort of person. She is just old and wise and tired and once brave.

I am getting so very old myself that I can't remember what I told you in my last letter? Did I tell about the Medici villa at Artimino, called La Ferdinanda? This I have *got* to rent for two months next summer, if possible. The whole of Hilton Hall would fit twice into the Dining room. (I only mean the main dining room.) It belongs to a very rich Swiss lady called *la Contessa di Sommaruga* (address: Castello la Ferdinanda, Artimino, Sigra.) It is quite desolate and she obviously seldom goes there, but its view covers half Italy, its approach through a forest, and it was built as a hunting lodge for Ferdinand the Second (?) Medici. All the beds are canopied, all the out-of-tune pianos or harpsichords have faded silver-framed photographs of the King of Spain, all the vast interior walls (larger than the largest squash-court multiplied by two) are hung with simply *terrible* portraits of Medicis or Hapsburgs or mythological scenes of the greatest complexity. We spent two hours going over it, and never reached the top and best floor. In the gardens there are loose wild dogs at night for biting trespassers. There is an interior well for disposing of the bodies of unwelcome guests. (Incidentally, you had better tell Angelica that it *does* have water and electric light and there are several toilets and *one* bath.) In the gun room there are two stuffed eagles. It has countless vineyards and a Chianti (not sophisticated) named after itself. It feels as if it was—I have not measured it—about 20 miles from Florence. The chimneys of its roof look like a sort of mad dovecote. Damn, I will have to send you my *only* photograph of it—it is quite lost and not tripperish—and the photograph was taken by an idiot. Please, *Please*, PLEASE will you return it? (Best to Alderney.) If your family and Michael Howard's family and Verney's family and I were to dwell there for two summer months, it would be difficult to meet indoors except by appointment and map. Then we should have to thread our way between inferior portraits of Medici cardinals smelling of garlic. (Of course there is a private chapel and we would have to invite the local p.p. there.)

Well?   love from TIM

In this Pensione there is a Tauchnitz copy of No Love. I read it again and it has not aged by one day.

That was Tim's last letter to me.

He was to live for just over another year, during which he went on a whistle-stop tour of the United States, lecturing on the poets he had liked when he was a young man, 'The Pleasures of Learning' (largely autobiographical), 'Luck in Literature', and 'In Search of an Emperor' (Hadrian). Tony Walton's sister Carol went with him as his secretary and manager. For her sake he refrained from drinking and as a result the tour was a success. His diary of it has been published in the United States under the title of *America At Last*.

Late in January 1963 he sailed from New York on a cruise for Greece, drank heavily and was found dead in his cabin from coronary heart disease on the arrival of the ship at the Piraeus.

A full understanding of Tim's character can be gained only from the biography by Sylvia Townsend Warner, for which no praise can be too high.

INDEX

315

Disney, Walt, 39, 92
Docker, Lady, 297, 299, 300–301
Dunsany, Lord, 45, 70, 76

EDWARDS, GEORGE, 121
Elizabeth, H.R.H. Princess, later Queen Elizabeth II, 241

FARSON, NEGLEY, 122
Fay, John, 78
Figgis, William, 99, 163
Forester, C. S., 175
Forster, E. M., 234, 290
Frazer, Sir James, 80
Fry, Roger, 178, 272

GALWAY, BISHOP OF, 74, 93, 264
Gardner, Professor Percy, 261
Garnett, Amaryllis Virginia, 135, 137, 140–41, 147, 150, 174, 176–7, 184, 198, 203, 222, 255–6, 281, 288, 309
Garnett, Angelica, 71–2, 77–8, 79, 81–3, 89, 92, 94–5, 101–2, 114, 115, 120, 122, 124–5, 126, 128, 136–7, 141–3, 147, 149–50, 152, 154–6, 158–60, 161, 165, 169, 176, 179, 191, 196, 198, 205, 213, 216, 218–19, 220, 256, 281, 282, 285, 309
Garnett, Constance, 226, 306
Garnett, Frances Olivia, 290, 309
Garnett, Henrietta Catherine Vanessa, 196, 198, 203
Garnett, Nerissa Stephen, 271, 288, 290
Garnett, Oliver Grierson, 284
Garnett, Ray, 15, 20, 24, 33, 35, 39, 40, 41–2, 43, 44–5, 47–50, 51–2, 53–5, 57, 58–63, 69, 71, 86, 95, 114, 174, 180, 185, 192, 306–7, 308
Garnett, Richard, 35, 55, 62, 64, 71, 77–8, 81, 84, 88–92, 94–5, 96–7, 98, 100, 101, 113, 114, 120–22, 124–5,

135, 143, 149, 154–5, 158–9, 176, 183–4, 191, 198, 200, 203, 206, 218–19, 225, 229, 268, 270, 271, 306, 309
Garnett, Richard (cousin), 35, 125
Garnett, William, 47, 53–5, 57, 62, 64, 71, 77, 79, 81, 82, 89, 90, 94–5, 97, 114, 120–22, 124–5, 127–8, 135, 137, 143, 147, 149, 155, 169, 177, 185, 198, 203, 210–11, 218–19, 281, 286, 306
George VI, King, 295
Gloucester, H.R.H. Duke of, 256–7
Grant, Duncan, 150–51, 160, 176–7
Grierson, Sir Herbert, 268, 270

HAKE, HENRY, 205–6, 207
Hamilton, Hamish, 72
Hamilton, Mrs Hamish, 72
Hammond, David, 300
Hayward, John, 72
Hedley, Mr and Mrs Robert, 113–14, 127–8, 154, 185, 201, 210–11
Henderson, Nigel, 9
Herlitschka, Mr and Mrs Herbert, 42
Hitler, Adolf, 42, 50, 68, 73, 86, 90, 98, 103, 123
Hoare, Major, 24
Hoare, Mrs Michael, 24
Hobson, Harold, 290
Hodgson, Ralph, 31, 32
Horder, Lord, 94
Howard, G. Wren, 281
Howard, Michael, 286, 287, 311
Huxley, Julian, 115, 117–19, 283

JACKSON, HARVEY, 169–70
James, Henry, 164
Jefferies, Richard, 80
Johnson, Samuel, 194, 237
Joyce, Peter, 59, 60